# THE VALLEY
OF THE KINGS

A publication of the Theban Mapping Project

Theban Mapping Project

WORLD MONUMENTS FUND

# THE VALLEY OF THE KINGS
## A Site Management Handbook

Kent Weeks
Nigel Hetherington

With a Kings Valley Condition Survey
by Dina Bakhoum

The American University in Cairo Press
Cairo  New York

First published in 2014 by
The American University in Cairo Press
113 Sharia Kasr el Aini, Cairo, Egypt
420 Fifth Avenue, New York, NY 10018
www.aucpress.com

Copyright © 2014 by The Theban Mapping Project

All rights reserved. No part of this publication may be reproduced, stored in a retrieval system, or transmitted in any form or by any means, electronic, mechanical, photocopying, recording, or otherwise, without the prior written permission of the publisher.

Exclusive distribution outside Egypt and North America by I.B.Tauris & Co Ltd., 6 Salem Road, London, W2 4BU

Dar el Kutub No. 22048/12
ISBN 978 977 416 608 2

Dar el Kutub Cataloging-in-Publication Data

Weeks, Kent R.
    The Valley of the Kings: A Site Management Handbook / Kent R. Weeks and Nigel J. Hetherington.—Cairo: The American University in Cairo Press, 2014.
        p.     cm.
        ISBN 978 977 416 608 2
        1. Egypt—Antiquities
        2. Valley of the Kings—Egypt
        I. Hetherington, Nigel J. (jt. auth.)
        932

1 2 3 4 5    18 17 16 15 14

Designed by Jon W. Stoy
Printed in Egypt

# Contents

| | |
|---|---|
| Preface | vii |
| **1. Introduction to the Site** | 1 |
| Site Definition | 1 |
| Historical Development of the Valley of the Kings | 12 |
| **2. Current Risk Factors** | 35 |
| The Natural Environment | 35 |
| Human Activity | 48 |
| Summary of Risk Factors in the Valley of the Kings | 56 |
| **3. Tourism and the Valley of the Kings** | 57 |
| Tourism in Egypt | 57 |
| Tourism in Luxor | 61 |
| Tourism in the Valley of the Kings | 64 |
| **4. Stakeholder Surveys** | 68 |
| Stakeholder Survey Stage One: Valley of the Kings Site Survey | 68 |
| Stakeholder Survey Stage Two: Online Survey | 103 |
| **5. Valley of the Kings Condition Survey** | 124 |
| Current and Recent Archaeological Intervention in the Valley of the Kings | 124 |
| Previous Work by the Theban Mapping Project | 125 |

| | |
|---|---|
| Current Tomb Condition Reports | 128 |
| Tomb Environmental Monitoring | 137 |

## 6. Valley of the Kings Infrastructure — 147

| | |
|---|---|
| The Visitor Experience and the Valley of the Kings | 148 |
| Roads and Pathways to the Valley of the Kings | 149 |
| Types of Transport | 154 |
| Vehicle Parking | 157 |
| Vendors' Area | 159 |
| Visitors Center | 162 |
| Tramline and Road from Visitors Center to Valley of the Kings | 171 |
| Security Entrance and Camera Rules | 175 |
| Toilets | 179 |
| Shelters and Rest Stops | 181 |
| Tomb Interiors | 183 |
| Site Utilities | 190 |
| Site Fabric | 192 |
| Summary of Proposals and Status as of 2012 | 193 |

## 7. Visitor Management in the Valley of the Kings — 195

| | |
|---|---|
| Carrying Capacity | 195 |
| Carrying Capacity of Tombs in the Valley of the Kings | 216 |
| Ticketing Procedures | 232 |
| Visitor Experience in the Valley of the Kings | 237 |
| Summary of Proposals | 240 |

## 8. Site Management at the Valley of the Kings — 241

| | |
|---|---|
| The Supreme Council of Antiquities (SCA) | 242 |
| Site Management and Cultural Resource Management Training | 249 |
| Emergency and Disaster Planning | 253 |
| Site Maintenance | 255 |
| Site Management Information Systems | 260 |
| Summary of Proposals | 260 |

| | |
|---|---|
| Notes | 261 |
| References | 263 |

# Preface

The Theban Mapping Project (TMP) began work in the Theban Necropolis in 1979. Since then, it has devoted much of its time to the preparation of an archaeological map of the Valley of the Kings (KV), to conducting existing-condition surveys of all its accessible tombs, and to developing a comprehensive site management plan, the first ever undertaken in Egypt. KV has come to be recognized as a fragile part of humankind's cultural heritage that is in need of monitoring and constant care. Its irreplaceable contents must be carefully managed and protected, and the delicate and precarious balance between environmental pressures and economic demands must be controlled if it is to survive for future generations.

The following management plan for KV is the result of nearly a decade of work. It is far from the last word on the subject of site protection, and it does not pretend to offer answers to all the many questions of archaeological conservation and tourist control posed by the site. But it is a start, and we hope it will stimulate discussion and action among the many stakeholders who are responsible for determining KV's future.

The preparation of a KV management plan has always been a part of the TMP's work, but it became a principal concern of the project in 2004. A first edition of the plan appeared in 2007. Additional work has been conducted since then, including continued condition surveys, photographic recording, and updated stakeholder surveys. This book includes this updated material, but it has not been possible to obtain more up-to-date tourism figures for Luxor and KV than those included in this report. Tourism dropped markedly after the Arab Spring, and we are told that Luxor hotel occupancy in winter 2012 was at 20 percent of pre-2010 levels. This does not bode well for the economy of Egypt, but one hopes that the government can take advantage of the less crowded conditions in KV to reexamine its cultural resource management procedures and implement some of the changes proposed here.

A question that has been frequently asked—we ask it ourselves—is whether this plan will be implemented or simply shelved, as so many proposals for archaeological conservation have been in the past. We are optimistic. Indeed, several parts of the plan—on-site signage, the new Visitors Center, and new parking areas, to name a few—have already been completed, and others—better tomb lighting and traffic management, for example—are ready to implement.

There is a bit of anecdotal evidence that further supports our optimism. In 2011, the TMP opened a library as part of its Luxor West Bank office. It includes a large collection of books in English and Arabic on Egyptology, archaeological methodology, site conservation practices, and management plans around the world. The library is the first such facility in Egypt that makes available works essential to the proper training of archaeological site managers and conservators. In just six months, the library, which is open to all at no charge from 3 to 9 pm, seven days a week, was being used by over two dozen adults daily. These include tour guides, inspectors of antiquities, members of the government's conservation staff, and students—all persons working with Theban monuments, all voluntarily making extensive and enthusiastic use of the library's resources. When asked why they come, the answer most of them give is this: "We know the monuments of Thebes must be protected, and we want to help. We want to learn to do our jobs better." Our library also contains a children's section, with Arabic-language books on Egypt's history and its monuments. Here, too, the collection is being used heavily by primary and secondary school teachers and students, who come voluntarily, individually and in small groups, to learn more about their country's history. That so many Supreme Council of Antiquities (SCA) staff members are using the library bodes well for the future of the Theban monuments; that so many enthusiastic youth are also coming offers great hope for the long-term survival of one of Egypt's greatest assets.

Chapter 4 ("Stakeholder Surveys") was prepared by Nigel Hetherington and is based upon surveys undertaken by the Social Research Center of the American University in Cairo. Chapter 5 ("KV Condition Surveys") is a summary of reports prepared for the TMP by Dina Bakhoum. Editorial assistance was provided by Lori Lawson and Magdy Abu Hamad Ali. On-site work was supervised by Ahmed Mahmoud Hassan. Many individuals supported the work of the TMP summarized here, but we must give special thanks to Dr. Gaetano Palumno and Ms. Bonnie Burnham of the World Monuments Fund; Mr. Neville Agnew of the Getty Conservation Institute; Mr. Bernard Selz, Ms. Deborah Lehr, Mr. Bruce Ludwig, Mr. and Mrs. Howard Zumstag, Ms. Mary Arce, Janice Jakeway, Richard Flanagan, Bob and Carole Braxton, Ms. Eileen Gutierrez, and Wilderness Travel. The staff of the Supreme Council of Antiquities, now the Ministry, have been very helpful, and we must offer particular thanks to Mr. Mansour Boraik for providing much of the statistical data in chapter 4. Thanks also to Ali Ibrahim Youssef for his help with contemporary data collection.

# 1 Introduction to the Site

## Site Definition
### Thebes and Modern Luxor
Thebes is one of the largest, richest, and best-known archaeological sites in the world. It lies about 900 km (560 miles) south of Cairo on the banks of the River Nile. On the East Bank, beneath the modern city of Luxor (fig. 1), lie the remains of an ancient town that from about 1500 to 1000 BC was one of the most spectacular in Egypt, with a population of perhaps fifty thousand. Even in the Middle Kingdom, four centuries earlier, Thebes had earned a reputation as one of the ancient world's greatest cities. Within it, the Egyptians had built huge temple complexes at Karnak and Luxor. These are two of the largest religious structures ever constructed, the homes of priesthoods of great wealth and power. On the West Bank lies the Theban Necropolis—covering about 10 km$^2$—in which archaeologists have found thousands of tombs, scores of temples, and a multitude of houses, villages, shrines, monasteries, and work stations.

Thebes has been inhabited continuously for the last 250,000 years. The first evidence of the Paleolithic in Africa was found there. However, the most important period in its history was the five-century-long New Kingdom, when what the ancient Egyptians called this 'model for every city' achieved unrivaled religious, political, and architectural stature. Every New Kingdom pharaoh—there were thirty-two of them—and

Fig. 1. West Bank Luxor. © Theban Mapping Project

many before and after that date added to the site's huge architectural inventory. The monuments erected during Dynasties 18, 19, and 20 have ensured that even today, thirty centuries later, Thebes is one of the world's foremost archaeological sites. Not surprisingly, it was one of the first sites listed by UNESCO as a World Heritage Site (in 1979).

The name 'Thebes' was given to the town by early Greek travelers. Some historians believe the Greeks misheard the local name for an area around Medinet Habu, 'Jeme'; others think that it came from 'Tapé,' or *tp*, meaning 'head' in ancient Egyptian. In the Bible, Thebes was called No, from the ancient Egyptian word *niw*, meaning 'city.' The Egyptians also called it Waset, the name of the nome (administrative district) in which it lay, or *niwt 'Imn*, 'city of Amun,' which the Greeks rendered as 'Diospolis,' 'city of Zeus' (the god with whom the Greeks equated Amun). The Egyptians had many epithets for Thebes: "City Victorious," "The Mysterious City," "City of the Lord of Eternity," "Mistress of Temples," "Mistress of Might," and others. The more recent name for Thebes, Luxor, derives from the Arabic 'al-Uqsur,' meaning 'the castles,' which in turn may derive from the Latin word *castrum*, meaning a military garrison.

Between the river and the desert edge, the Nile Valley floodplain consists of a thick layer of nutrient-rich silt deposited by millennia of annual Nile floods. Today, perennial irrigation waters fields of sugar cane, clover, wheat, and vegetables, and makes possible two crops annually. Before the completion of the Aswan High Dam in the 1960s, which ended the annual Nile flood in Egypt, the river rose every year in June, and for the following four months covered the floodplain with 30–50 cm of water. It filled shallow, natural 'basins' that were a product of uneven silt deposition across the floodplain. About six such basins lay on the Theban West Bank, each covering several square kilometers. After the floodwaters receded, these now water-saturated basins were planted and their crops harvested in late autumn and winter. In dynastic times, farmers grew wheat, barley, sorghum, pulses, onions, garlic, and melons. These were vegetables of such quantity and quality, grown with such ease, that European visitors constantly remarked about the wondrous Egyptian soil. Some believed that life generated spontaneously in this rich Nile mud and that simply drinking Nile water could cause a woman to become pregnant. The valley's fabled richness became for Europeans proof of the special place Egypt occupied in the hearts of the gods. Nowhere but in

| New Kingdom Pharaohs |
|---|
| **Eighteenth Dynasty** |
| Ahmose I 1539 BC–1514 BC |
| Amenhotep I 1514 BC–1493 BC |
| Thutmose I 1493 BC–1482 BC |
| Thutmose II 1482 BC–1479 BC |
| Thutmose III 1479 BC–1426 BC |
| Hatshepsut 1479 BC–1458 BC |
| Amenhotep II 1426 BC–1400 BC |
| Thutmose IV 1400 BC–1390 BC |
| Amenhotep III 1390 BC–1353 BC |
| Akhenaten 1353 BC–1336 BC |
| Smenkhkare 1336 BC–1333 BC |
| Tutankhamun 1333 BC–1323 BC |
| Ay 1323 BC–1319 BC |
| Horemheb 1319 BC–1292 BC |
| |
| **Nineteenth Dynasty** |
| Ramesses I 1292 BC–1290 BC |
| Seti I 1290 BC–1279 BC |
| Ramesses II 1279 BC–1213 BC |
| Merenptah 1213 BC–1203 BC |
| Seti II 1203 BC–1196 BC |
| Amenmesse 1196 BC–1190 BC |
| Siptah 1196 BC–1190 BC |
| Tawosret 1190 BC–1188 BC |
| |
| **Twentieth Dynasty** |
| Setnakht 1188 BC–1186 BC |
| Ramesses III 1186 BC–1155 BC |
| Ramesses IV 1155 BC–1148 BC |
| Ramesses V 1148 BC–1143 BC |
| Ramesses VI 1143 BC–1135 BC |
| Ramesses VII 1135 BC–1129 BC |
| Ramesses VIII 1129 BC–1127 BC |
| Ramesses IX 1127 BC–1108 BC |
| Ramesses X 1108 BC–1104 BC |
| Ramesses XI 1104 BC–1075 BC |

Table 1. Kings of the New Kingdom

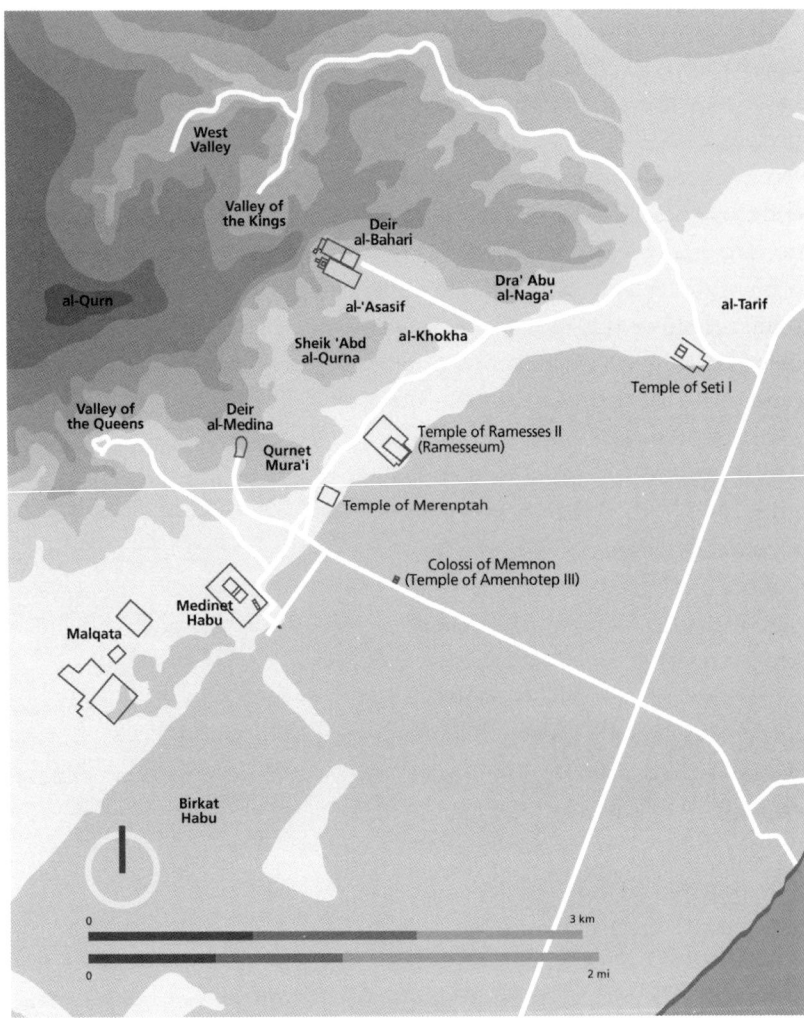

Fig. 2. Location map, Luxor. © Theban Mapping Project

Egypt were the silts so rich, crops so plentiful, fields so easily tended. Even today, the Theban area has a great reputation for agricultural excellence, and tourists who come to admire its monuments often leave equally impressed by its landscape. Azure skies, green fields, blue river, golden hills, crimson sunsets, and fluorescent afterglow give Thebes the appearance of an over-imagined painting. Europeans were certain that here lay the landscape in which God had created the Garden of Eden.

Introduction to the Site

The close proximity of limestone for building and plentiful agricultural land helped maintain the wealth and prestige of ancient Thebes. But the reasons that it grew from a sleepy Old Kingdom hamlet to a substantial Middle Kingdom town and a formidable New Kingdom city were political and religious. The reunification of Egypt after the defeat of the Herakleopolitans at the end of the First Intermediate Period was largely the work of Theban rulers, who appointed Theban officials to high government positions, thereby assuming control of the entire country. During the Second Intermediate Period, Theban rulers again achieved prominence. With the expulsion of the Hyksos in the Seventeenth Dynasty, they again governed Egypt.

But Thebes was inconveniently located too far south to rule a country becoming, in the New Kingdom, increasingly tied economically and politically to western Asia. The town of Pi-Ramese was built in the Nile Delta to ease problems of international communications, and it assumed importance as Egypt's diplomatic and military center. Memphis, at the apex of the Nile Delta, served as the headquarters of Egypt's internal bureaucracy. Inconvenient location notwithstanding, Thebes prospered and was revered. In part, this was due to the religious, political, and economic power wielded by Amun, the principal god of Thebes. Credited with having freed Egypt from its enemies, making it the wealthiest and most powerful country in the ancient world, establishing Thebes as "the queen of cities," Amun, joined with the Heliopolitan solar deity as Amun-Ra, became the "king of the gods," the leader of the Egyptian pantheon. The Theban temples of Amun, with their huge landholdings and large cadres of priests that managed them, ensured that Thebes was Egypt's preeminent religious center. It remained the perceived capital city of Egypt long after actual bureaucratic authority had moved away. This state of affairs continued into the Late Period. Eventually, however, as Egypt's wealth and power declined, so invariably did that of Thebes. There are Late Period, Greek, and Roman references to Thebes, and a large number of Christian monasteries, churches, and hermitages on the West Bank. But from about the eleventh century AD, Thebes virtually disappeared from history. It was not until the coming of European visitors in the eighteenth century that Thebes, by now called Luxor, resumed its place as one of the most famous cities in the world.

## The West Bank

The boundaries of the Theban West Bank have changed significantly during the last century. In common local usage, "the West Bank" has referred to the west bank of the Nile directly across from the city of Luxor, and the term implied no specific boundaries (fig. 3). The term 'Theban Necropolis' could also refer to this area, but it was usually limited to the desert lands west of the cultivation into parts of a complex wadi system that contains archaeological remains. Its northern and southern boundaries were not clearly defined.

In ancient times, designations of the West Bank were vague. The area was called "West of Thebes," "the Great West," or "the Beautiful West," but its boundaries were never mentioned. Today, somewhat more precisely, "the West Bank" is defined administratively as the west bank of the Nile lying within the modern boundaries of Luxor City. The northern boundary lies beyond the modern villages of al-Tarif and the complex called New Thebes. The southern boundary is near Armant. The western boundary is not specified, but is meant to extend far enough into the desert to include any archaeological sites. The eastern boundary is the River Nile.

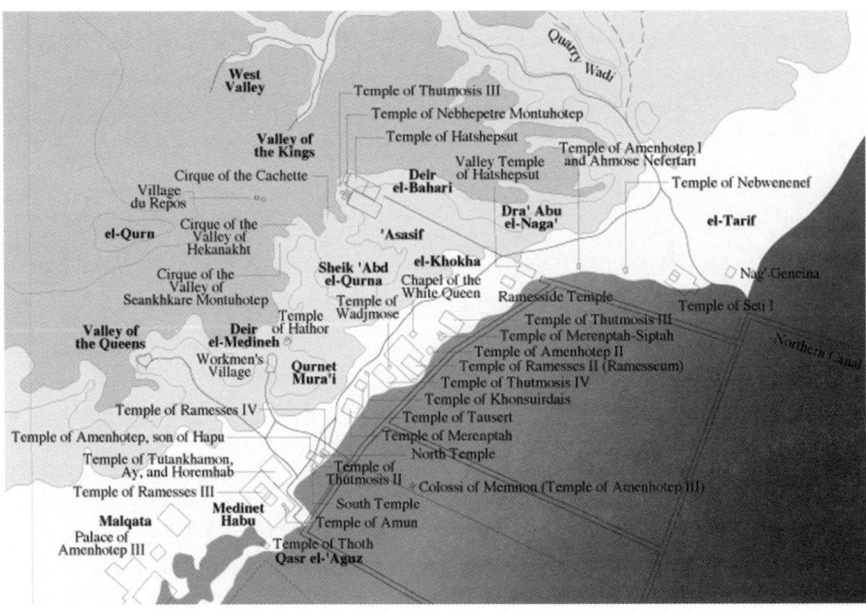

Fig. 3. Location map, KV in West Bank. © Theban Mapping Project

Introduction to the Site

The West Bank area known as "antiquities land," that is, land controlled by the Supreme Council of Antiquities (SCA), was broadly defined and enlarged in a law passed in 1956. Prior to that date, the Colossi of Memnon (but not the mortuary temple of Amenhotep III, of which they are a part) lay on a small 'island' of government-owned land surrounded by private fields. In 1956, several hundred square meters of the temple in private hands were incorporated into antiquities land, creating a single, contiguous archaeological zone. (A very substantial part of the temple compound surrounding the central core, however, still lies beneath privately owned sugar cane fields.)

There are still many irregularities in the "antiquities land" boundaries. Some date back to a decision made in 1926, when the Egyptian government issued a decree declaring the West Bank to be a protected area. The 1926 Survey of Egypt graphically showed the area's eastern boundary on its 1:500 "Theban Necropolis" map sheets. Generally, that boundary was drawn along the edge of the cultivation, regardless of whether antiquities lay east of it or not. This arbitrary (and, frankly, inexplicable) line resulted in some temples lying partly in the protected antiquities zone and partly in unprotected private lands. The memorial temple of Thutmose III is an example: its First Pylon and courtyard lie in private agricultural land (now rented out as a launching point for hot-air balloons) outside the antiquities zone; the part from the Second Pylon westward lies within it. Recent attempts have been made by the SCA to rationalize such boundaries, but this is still very much a work in progress.

Thebes was designated a World Heritage Site by the United Nations Educational, Scientific, and Cultural Organization (UNESCO) in 1979, but none of UNESCO's documents correctly define its boundaries either. They were said to include the East Bank temples of Karnak and Luxor and the West Bank "necropolis, funerary temples, royal palaces, and a village of craftsmen and artists." SCA officials have been no more precise about its East Bank borders, but they are trying to be more precise about its limits on the West Bank. They argue that the World Heritage Site begins at the Nile, then extends west through agricultural land into the desert beyond the Valley of the Kings. The northern boundary includes the archaeological zone of al-Tarif; the southern includes Malqata and Deir al-Shalwit.

For inexplicable reasons, the coordinates given by the World Heritage Convention for the boundaries of "Ancient Thebes with its Necropolis"—Long 32° 35–40' E, Lat 25° 42–45' N—do not include some of the pertinent monuments, most notably Luxor Temple. In the map below (fig. 4), the coordinates have been corrected by the TMP and the entire protected area is shown within the rectangle, the two longitudinal lines representing 32° 30' E and 32° 40' E and the two latitudinal lines showing 25° 41' N and 25° 45' N. The 2 km buffer zone (see below) would add another two minutes to each boundary.

For economic reasons, some officials and entrepreneurs maintained that the eastern boundary of the archaeological zone is not the Nile but the main Cairo–Aswan highway that runs north to south several kilometers to the river's west. This definition, they believed, could allow new hotels and cruise ship moorages to be built along the river. The SCA,

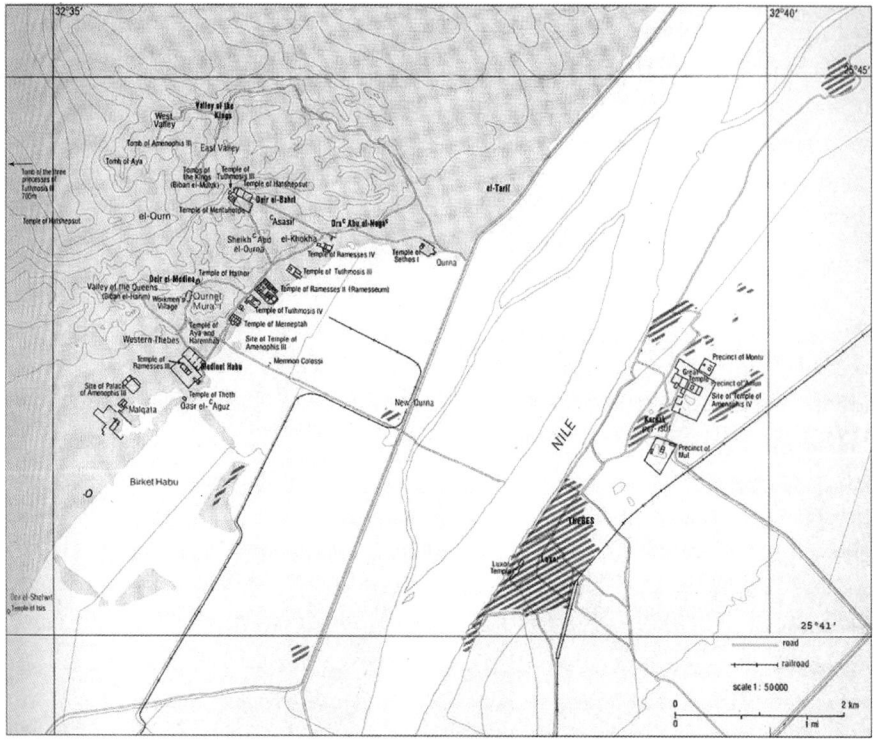

Fig. 4. WHC zone. © Theban Mapping Project based upon various historical sources

8 | Introduction to the Site

however, argues that the World Heritage Site does extend to the Nile, and that the area to be protected must include the cultivated floodplain and the Nile riverbank. Justification of this view is that the panoramic view of the West Bank from Luxor is as much a part of the area's heritage as its individual monuments, and it is clear that UNESCO's intention was to protect that view. Indeed, a law defining the River Nile as the eastern boundary of the site was passed by Egypt's National Assembly in 1983. It was based upon official *amlak* (cadastral) surveys of the area. This was reaffirmed in 2005 by the Luxor City Council when it gave orders to demolish new construction along the banks of the Nile. The reasons cited were that such construction was unsightly, detrimental to the landscape, illegally built on government land, and in violation of antiquities laws.

In 1980, President Sadat decreed the West Bank to be a Cultural Heritage Site, and prohibited any building activity that encroached upon it or altered its character. In 2004, President Mubarak reaffirmed the 1980 decree, and further declared that SCA-owned lands should be surrounded by a 2-km-wide 'buffer zone' in which only limited building activity would be permitted.

**The Valley of the Kings**
Known today in Arabic as Wadi Biban al-Muluk (the Valley of the Gates of the Kings) and in antiquity as "The Hidden," the Valley of the Kings (KV, for "Kings' Valley") consists of two branches of a complex West Bank wadi system in the desert west of the temples at Deir al-Bahari. It is called in Arabic *wadiayn*, "the Two Valleys," further identified as the East Valley and West Valley (figs. 5 and 6). For purposes of this masterplan, we consider the term 'Valley of the Kings' to include both the East and West Valleys, the entire watershed defined by the hills surrounding them (fig. 7), and the roads and paths that connect them to the Nile Valley.

The East Valley is the better known and the most visited by tourists because of the many royal tombs found there. There are two royal tombs in the West Valley, plus a few small, undecorated tombs of unidentified royal family members. The Valley of the Kings is less than a kilometer as the crow flies from the Nile floodplain, but the modern road leading to it describes a great arc over five kilometers long (fig. 5).

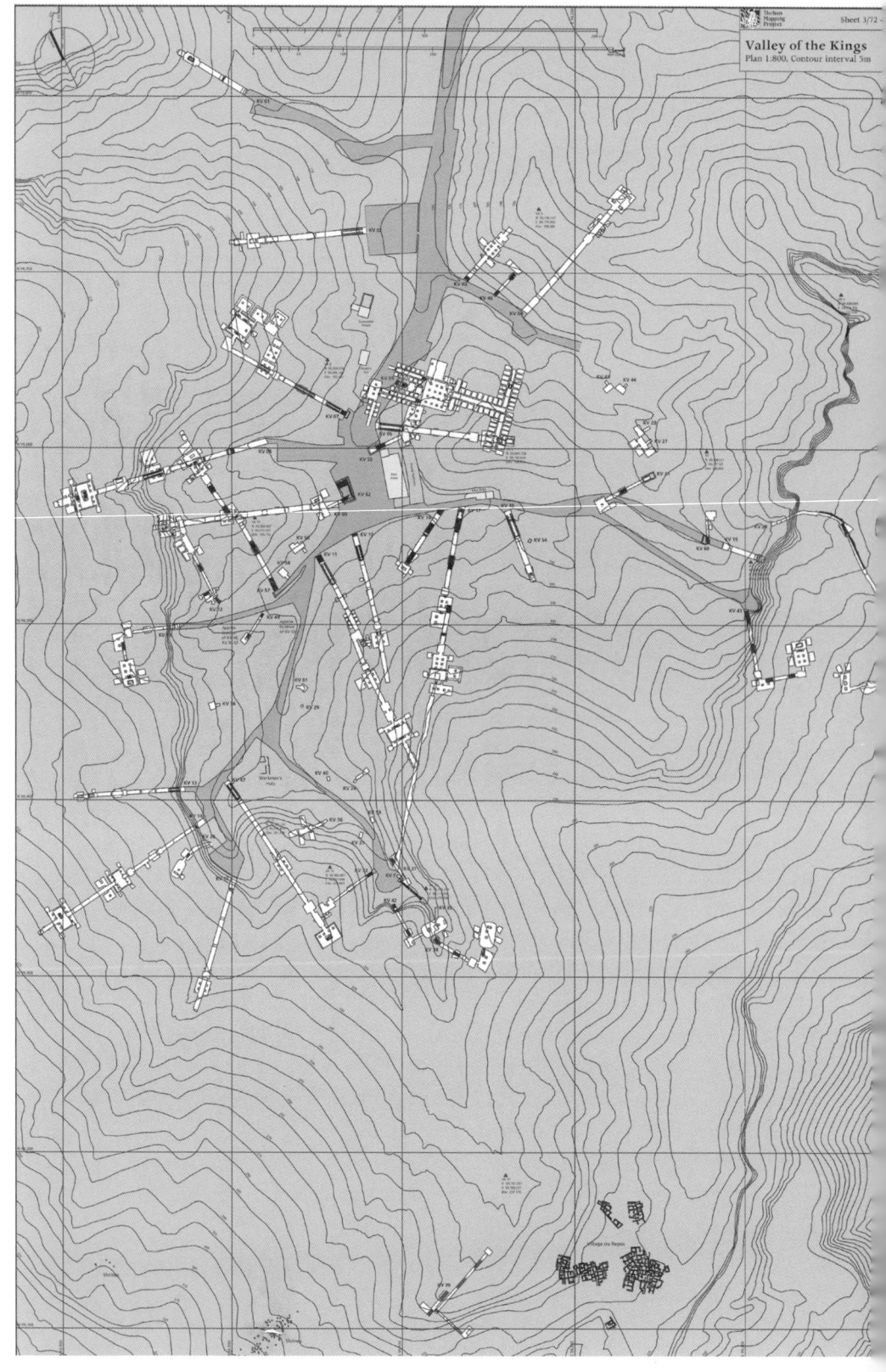

Fig. 5. Map of East Valley. © Theban Mapping Project

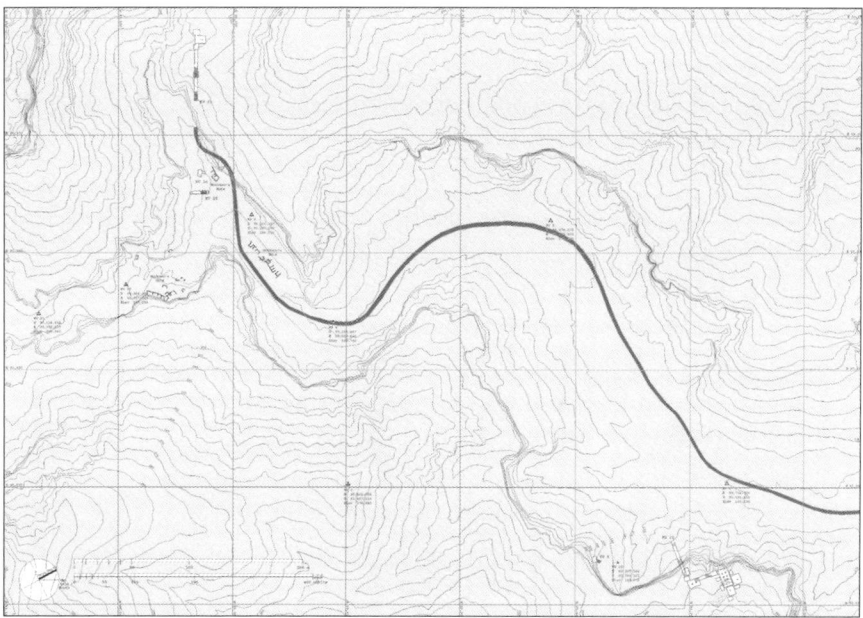

Fig. 6. Map of West Valley. © Theban Mapping Project

Fig. 7. Hydrological map of the East Valley of the Kings 2000. © Theban Mapping Project

Wadis are small, steeply sided valleys, or arroyos, found throughout the limestone hills of Egypt. They were cut into bedrock millions of years ago by heavy rains that fell almost continuously over the North African landscape, eroding bedrock created millions of years earlier when it lay beneath a great sea called Tethys, the precursor of the Mediterranean. Virtually all exposed bedrock in this part of Egypt is limestone, and it contains small pieces of chert embedded in its several strata (making the bedrock look rather like a bowl of cream and raisins). These chert nodules were used from the Paleolithic through dynastic times as the material of choice for making tools. There is also an underlying, discontinuous strata of montmorillonite, a dangerously unstable stone also called Esna shale (in Arabic *tafla*). Esna shale is known in the Valley of the Kings, and can be seen exposed in several KV hillsides and tombs. When this shale is exposed to water or even high humidity, it expands and can exert tremendous pressure on the limestone strata above it. As it expands, it can seriously damage the tombs that are cut there.

## Historical Development of the Valley of the Kings
### Introduction
The Valley of the Kings served as the burial place of Egypt's pharaohs during the New Kingdom, from 1550 to 1070 BC. For the first time, Egyptians located royal tombs away from the other component parts of the royal memorial temple. They built the temples along the edge of the West Bank cultivation, where they could be reached by religious processions that traveled from Karnak Temple by boat along canals cut through the fields. The tombs were dug several kilometers away, in the solid, dry bedrock of the isolated and easily guarded Valley of the Kings, called Wadi al-Muluk.

The first ruler to be buried here may have been Thutmose I, the third king of the Eighteenth Dynasty; the last was Ramesses XI, last ruler of the Twentieth Dynasty.

During its five centuries of use, at least sixty-four tombs were dug in KV. Each was assigned a number, 1–22, by John Gardner Wilkinson (1797–1875, early British traveler), who worked in the mid-1800s (fig. 8).

Wilkinson's scheme assigned numbers geographically from the entrance of the Valley southward, and from west to east. Since then, tombs have been numbered in order of their discovery, the most recent being KV 62 (King's Valley tomb 62, the tomb of Tutankhamun, found by Howard

Fig. 8. An example of Wilkinson's KV numbering. © Theban Mapping Project

| KV1 | The tomb of Ramesses VII | KV33 | Unknown |
| KV2 | The tomb of Ramesses IV | KV34 | The tomb of Thutmose III |
| KV3 | The tomb of an unnamed son of Ramesses III | KV35 | Originally the tomb of Amenhotep II, Cache |
| KV4 | The tomb of Ramesses XI | KV36 | The tomb of the noble Maiherperi |
| KV5 | The tomb of some of the sons of Ramesses II | KV37 | Unknown |
| KV6 | The tomb of Ramesses IX | KV38 | The tomb of Thutmose I |
| KV7 | The tomb of Ramesses II aka Ramesses the Great | KV39 | Possibly the tomb of Amenhotep I |
| KV8 | The tomb of Merenptah | KV40 | Unknown |
| KV9 | The tomb of Ramesses V and Ramesses VI | KV41 | Unknown |
| KV10 | The tomb of Amenmesse | KV42 | The tomb of Hatshepsut-Meryet-Ra |
| KV11 | The tomb of Ramesses III | KV43 | The tomb of Thutmose IV |
| KV12 | Unknown | KV44 | Unknown |
| KV13 | The tomb of Bay | KV45 | The tomb of the noble Userhat |
| KV14 | The tomb of Tawosret later reused by Setnakht | KV46 | The tomb of the nobles Yuya and Thuyu |
| KV15 | The tomb of Seti II | KV47 | The tomb of Siptah |
| KV16 | The tomb of Ramesses I | KV48 | The tomb of the noble Amenemipet |
| KV17 | The tomb of Seti I | KV49 | Unknown |
| KV18 | The tomb of Ramesses X | KV50 | Unknown |
| KV19 | The tomb of Mentuherkhepshef | KV51 | Unknown |
| KV20 | The tomb of Hatshepsut and Thutmose I | KV52 | Unknown |
| KV21 | Unknown | KV53 | Unknown |
| KV22 | The tomb of Amenhotep III | KV54 | Tutankhamun Cache |
| KV23 | The tomb of Ay | KV55 | The tomb of Tiye (?) or Akhenaten (?) |
| KV24 | Unknown | KV56 | Unknown |
| KV25 | Unknown | KV57 | The tomb of Horemheb |
| KV26 | Unknown | KV58 | Unknown |
| KV27 | Unknown | KV59 | Unknown |
| KV28 | Unknown | KV60 | The tomb of Sit-Ra (?) |
| KV29 | Unknown | KV61 | Unknown |
| KV30 | Unknown | KV62 | The Tomb of Tutankhamun |
| KV31 | Unknown | KV63 | Cache |
| KV32 | The tomb of Tia'a | KV64 | — |

Table 2. Tombs in the Valley of the Kings. © Theban Mapping Project

Carter in 1922); KV 63, found by Otto Schaden in 2005; and KV 64, uncovered by a Swiss mission in 2011. The tomb of the sons of Ramesses II (KV 5) was rediscovered in 1995 by the Theban Mapping Project, but its entrance had been seen by Wilkinson a century and a half earlier, and was assigned its number then. In addition, there are about two dozen 'commencements,' tomb shafts that were begun but almost immediately abandoned for unknown reasons. The non-royal tombs in KV belonged to various officials, royal family members, and priests.

The Valley of the Kings lies about one kilometer west of the Nile floodplain at Thebes (modern Luxor). It was cut by torrential rains and erosion during several pluvial periods in the Pleistocene into a thick layer of limestone that lies above a discontinuous stratum of Esna shale. The Valley lies about 70 m (230 feet) above the level of the River Nile, 140 m (460 feet) above mean sea level. The immediately surrounding hills that define the East Valley rise an average of 80 m (265 feet) above the valley floor. It was probably chosen as the burial place of royalty because of its geology, its relatively convenient access from the Nile floodplain, and the pyramid-shaped mountain, 'al-Qurn,' or 'forehead,' that rises about 300 m (985 feet) above its southern end that perhaps was seen as a symbol of solar deities.

Fig. 9. al-Qurn. © Theban Mapping Project

## Tomb Construction

Tombs in the Valley of the Kings did not follow a single plan. Their layout and decorative program were based on notions of the journey taken by the pharaoh and the sun god through the night sky and into the Afterlife, and as priests revised those notions, tomb plans changed. Royal mortuary architecture therefore had theological significance. Tombs in the Eighteenth Dynasty were relatively small, with steep corridors that sometimes curved downward or made several right-angle turns before reaching an oval or rectangular burial chamber. Tombs of the Nineteenth Dynasty had steep corridors leading along a single (or a jogged) axis to a large burial chamber and multiple side rooms. In the Twentieth Dynasty, tombs were again smaller, nearly level, with wider and higher corridors (fig. 10).

The walls of KV tombs were decorated with raised relief cut in the bedrock or, if the bedrock was unsuitable, painted on a layer of plaster applied over it. After a tomb chamber had been dug, its walls were smoothed, a thin layer of mud plaster mixed with wheat chaff was applied, then painted with a white or gray wash. Scenes and hieroglyphic texts were outlined in red ink, then amended, if necessary, by senior scribes and artisans who used black ink to correct spelling errors or the proportions of figures. Raised relief was carved, the figures modeled, and paint applied. The artist's palette consisted of only six colors, each made of natural ingredients, usually mineral: black (made from soot and charcoal), white (gypsum), red (hematite or ochre), yellow (limonite or yellow ochre), blue (ground faience), and green (made from copper, or a mix of yellow and blue pigments).

The selection of a KV site for a royal tomb was made by the vizier and the country's principal architects, and later perhaps affirmed by the pharaoh. Early in the New Kingdom, during the Eighteenth Dynasty, preference was often given to sites in the base of the sheer cliffs that surround KV, ideally below cliffs over which, in the rare event of rain, a temporary waterfall would pour and deposit debris over the tomb's entrance, burying it ever deeper over the centuries. In the late Eighteenth and Nineteenth Dynasties, the preferred location was in lower-lying talus slopes; in the Twentieth Dynasty, it was one of the small spurs of bedrock that extend from the Valley's sides into the center of KV. These changes in preferred location may indicate that Eighteenth Dynasty tombs were intended to be completely and permanently sealed after the burial, while Nineteenth and Twentieth

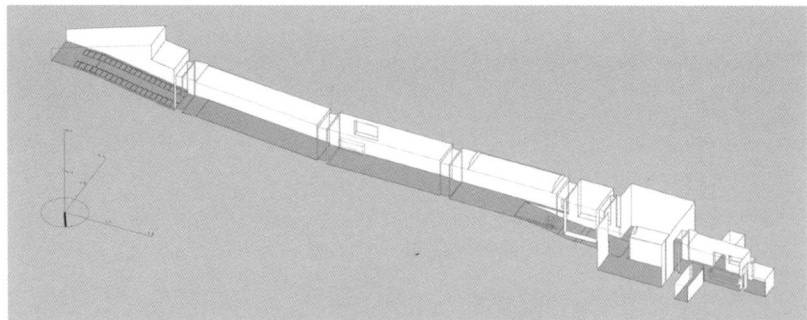

Fig. 10a. Dynasty 20 tomb style. © Theban Mapping Project

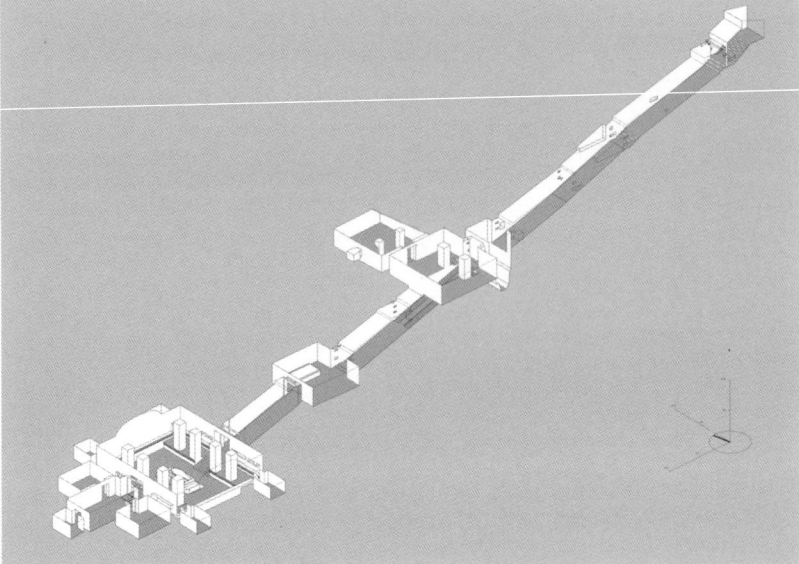

Fig. 10b. Dynasty 19 tomb style. © Theban Mapping Project

Dynasty tombs were to remain partially accessible so that ceremonies could continue to be performed in them long after the pharaoh had been interred. In this latter case, it is likely that only the burial chamber and its storerooms would have been permanently closed. The orientation of the tomb was apparently the result of geological considerations, not a desire to physically align the tomb to any particular cardinal direction: tomb axes run in compass directions ranging from 68° to 357°. In order to place decoration correctly on their walls, artists arbitrarily assumed that a tomb's principal axis ran from east to west, no matter what its actual direction.

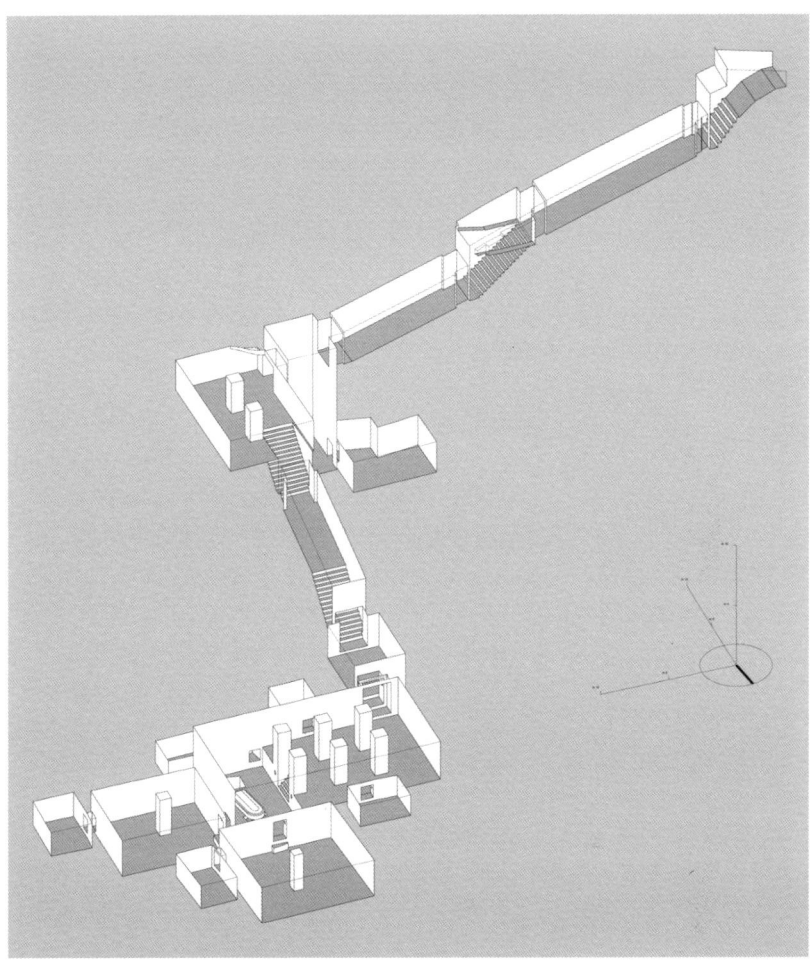

Fig. 10c. Dynasty 18 tomb style. © Theban Mapping Project

By the later New Kingdom, the Valley of the Kings was filled with tombs, and there were fewer sites available in which more could be cut. It is unlikely that ancient architects maintained a masterplan of the valley showing the location of tombs, because we know of three instances in which quarrymen dug a new tomb that collided with an earlier one. When such collisions occurred, the quarrymen presumably had three choices: immediately change the new tomb's axis and veer away from the earlier tomb; abandon the new tomb and dig elsewhere; or incorporate part of the earlier tomb into the new (fig. 11).

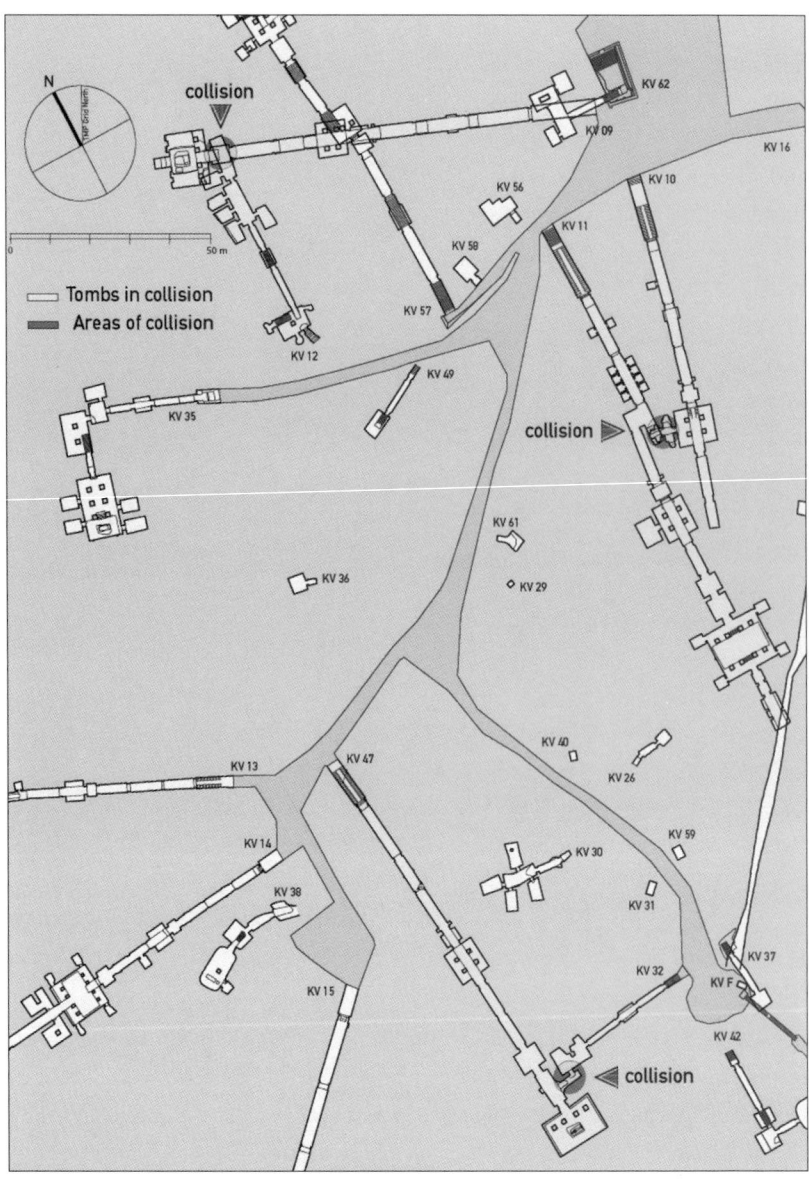

Fig. 11. KV Tombs in collision. © Theban Mapping Project

Introduction to the Site

Once a site had been chosen, rituals were performed to sanctify it. These included digging small pits near the tomb entrance, as many as four or five of them, into which were placed foundation deposits with miniature construction tools, clay and stone vessels, religious symbols, and foodstuffs. They have been found associated with nine KV tombs, though some scholars believe that all the royal tombs had them.

We know a great deal about how KV tombs were cut and decorated, in part because of thousands of objects and inscriptions found in the village of Deir al-Medina. Deir al-Medina lies about a kilometer (0.6 miles) south of KV, and during the New Kingdom it served as the home and burial place of the artisans and artists who carved and decorated KV tombs. The remains of about seventy houses can be seen in the village proper, and during the New Kingdom about four hundred people lived in these small stone dwellings built along a narrow street. Many different specialists lived at Deir al-Medina: quarrymen, plasterers, scribes, sculptors, architects, and draftsmen who possessed the skills needed to prepare the royal tombs. Their jobs were passed from father to son, and we have records of half a dozen generations of a single family employed in KV work. They were paid for their labor in kind: bread, beer, dried fish, onions, and other vegetables. Texts found in the village include journals, love letters, business documents, inventories, shopping lists, legal papers—almost every aspect of life is discussed in them—and from them we have learned a great deal about work in the Valley of the Kings.

Quarrymen worked in the tombs in a "left gang" and a "right gang" of up to several dozen men, each headed by a foreman. These gangs would begin work after a new pharaoh ascended the throne and the site for his tomb had been chosen. They dug with chert tools, one or two men in each gang cutting into the limestone bedrock, others forming basket brigades to carry away the debris. Their work was lit by oil lamps with linen wicks of carefully measured length; when a wick had burned up—they were designed to burn for four hours—it was time to stop for lunch or to leave for home. Salt was added to the oil to prevent it from smoking. The men worked eight hours a day for eight days, then took a two-day weekend. There were numerous other holidays throughout the year as well, but digging must have been hard and unpleasant. We know from our own excavations in KV 5 that work in the tombs can be miserably hot, humid, and filled with choking dust. There is an ever-present risk of being cut or bruised by sharp-edged fragments of limestone, or of having pieces of the bedrock ceiling weighing several tons collapse on one's head.

It was difficult to cut tombs with precision, and the ancient supervisors painted control marks on the walls and ceilings of tombs to help quarrymen ensure a straight axis, make a 90-degree turn, or properly position a doorway. Surveying tools were simple but effective: carpenters' squares determined right angles, plumb bobs assured vertical walls, and a piece of string measured length. With patience and care, these elementary tools permitted highly accurate tomb cutting. There is a papyrus in the Egyptian Museum in Turin, Italy, on which an ancient architect had drawn a plan of KV 2 (fig. 12), the tomb of Ramesses IV, and noted the dimensions of its chambers. We can convert these ancient measurements into modern metric units: 1 cubit = 52.3 cm (20 inches) long; 1 palm = 7.47 cm (3 inches) or 1/7 cubit; and 1 digit = 1.87 cm (0.8 inches) or 1/4 palm—and compare them with dimensions we can measure today. If we assume that the plan was drawn before the tomb was cut, not after it—and this cannot be proved—then the

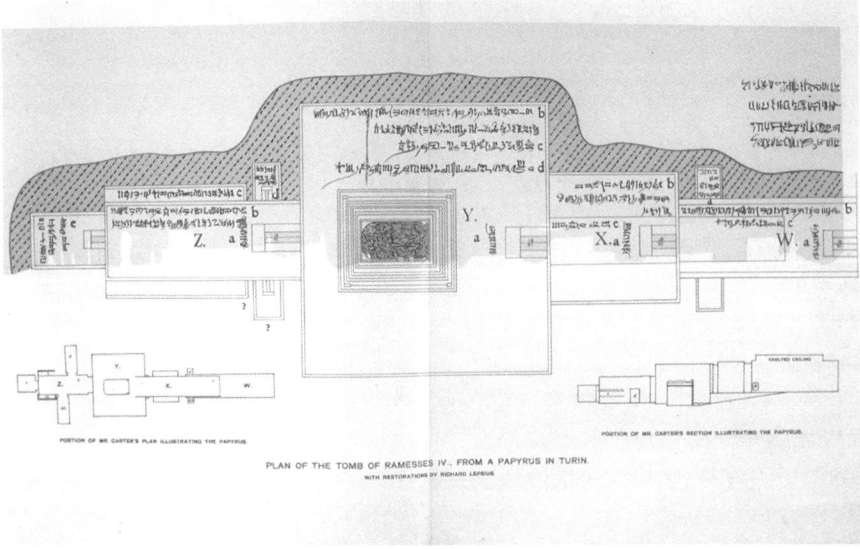

Fig. 12. Ancient tomb plan, KV 2, Ramesses IV after P. Turin, Carter and Gardiner, JEA vol. 4, 1917

quarrymen came within fractions of a centimeter of achieving what the specifications called for.

The limestone bedrock in which KV tombs were cut is a relatively soft, easily worked stone. In many parts of the Valley, the stone is structurally sound, fine-grained, and strong. However, in other places, it is heavily fissured and cracked, peppered with tennis ball–sized nodules of hard chert (often called flint) that make quarrying difficult. (Those chert nodules, by the way, were an excellent material for the manufacture of stone tools such as hand axes, chisels, and hammer stones—the very tools used by ancient workmen to quarry KV tombs. Many such chert tools have been found in KV.) Where the stone was sound, wall decoration could be cut in raised or sunken relief; where it was poor, decoration was painted on thick layers of plaster applied to the walls to provide a smooth surface.

Tomb preparation was a team effort, rather like an assembly line. While quarrymen roughly cut the tomb, other workmen followed behind, more accurately aligning and smoothing the walls and ceiling with sandstone abrasives, and making sure that corners and doorways were squared. Behind them, artisans first applied a thin plaster layer to the walls, painted lines to divide walls into scenes and registers, then drew in red-ink outline the figures and hieroglyphs to be carved there (fig. 13). Senior artists and scribes used black ink to adjust the proportions of figures or correct spelling errors. Scenes and texts were either carved in raised relief or painted on plaster.

It probably took only a few years to dig and decorate a royal tomb in the Valley of the Kings, and fifty or sixty workmen might be involved in the effort. When a pharaoh's tomb was finished, the Deir al-Medina workmen would be free to work on other royal projects—on nobles' tombs, or on their own tombs, dug adjacent to their village—until the next pharaoh was crowned and work on his tomb begun.

Royal tombs were sometimes, but by no means always, larger than nobles' tombs and they varied greatly among themselves in size. As table 3 shows, there is no correlation between the size of a royal tomb and the regnal length of the pharaoh for whom it was cut. But there is a gradual increase in tomb size from the Eighteenth Dynasty through the Nineteenth, then a reduction in the Twentieth.

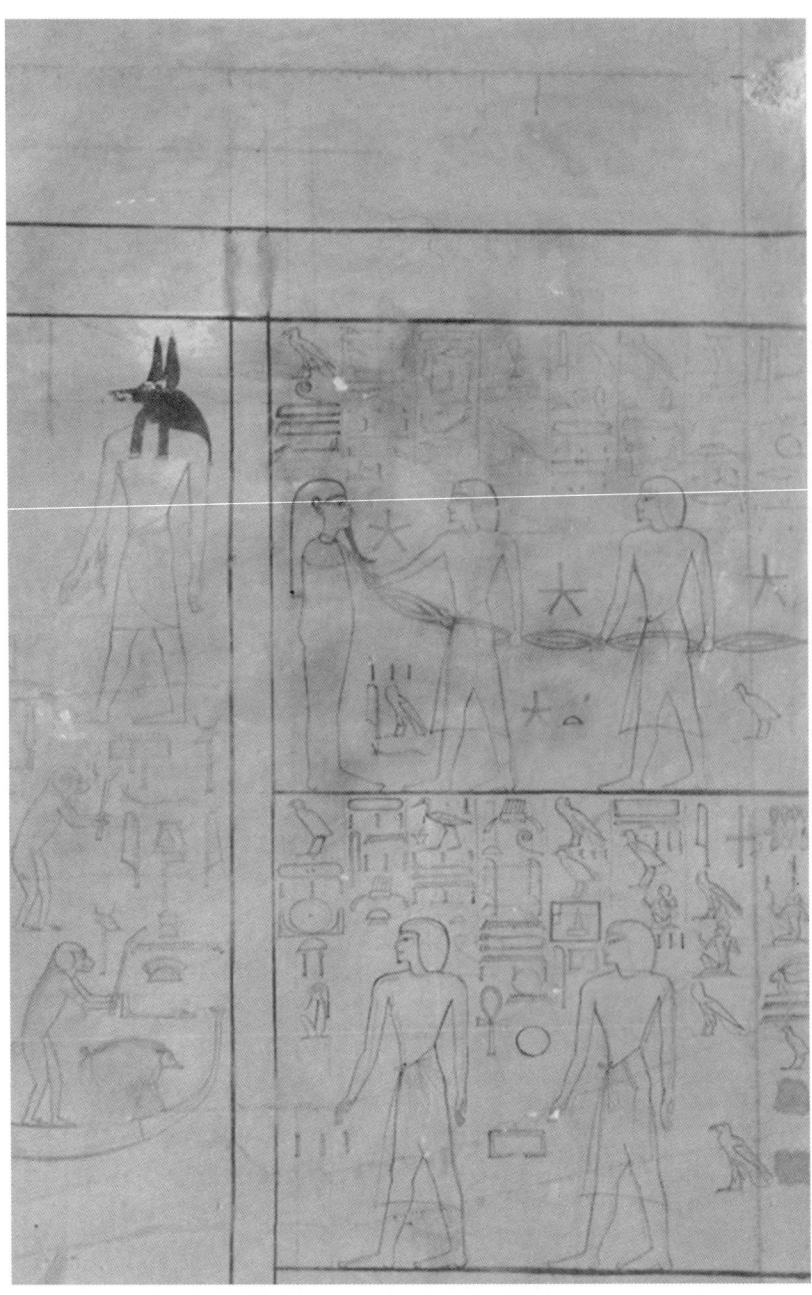

Fig. 13. KV 57, Tomb of Horemheb, showing preliminary outlines and corrections.
© Theban Mapping Project

| Tomb Number | Tomb Name | Meters$^3$ | Regnal Years |
|---|---|---|---|
| KV 8 | Merenptah | 2,622.08 | 10 |
| KV 7 | Ramesses II | 2286.43 | 67 |
| KV 11 | Ramesses III | 2174.29 | 31 |
| KV 14 | Tawosret/Setnakht | 2128.83 | 2/3 |
| KV 17 | Seti I | 1900.35 | 11 |
| KV 4 | Ramesses XI | 1,682.19 | 28 |
| KV 9 | Ramesses V/VI | 1572.26 | 5/8 |
| KV 47 | Siptah | 1,560.95 | 6 |
| KV 22 | Amenhotep III | 1,485.88 | 38 |
| KV 57 | Horemheb | 1,328.17 | 28 |
| KV 6 | Ramesses IX | 1076.35 | 18 |
| KV 43 | Thutmose IV | 1,062.36 | 11 |
| KV 2 | Ramesses IV | 1,105.25 | 6 |
| KV 35 | Amenhotep II | 852.21 | 24 |
| KV 10 | Amenmesse | 821.23 | 3 |
| KV 15 | Seti II | 816.53 | 6 |
| KV 34 | Thutmose III | 792.71 | 54 |
| KV 23 | Ay | 618.26 | 4 |
| KV 1 | Ramesses VII | 463.01 | 8 |
| KV 16 | Ramesses I | 283.83 | 1 |
| KV 62 | Tutankhamun | 277.01 | 9 |
| KV 38 | Thutmose I | 207.77 | 13 |

Table 3. Royal KV tombs by volume and regnal length. © Theban Mapping Project

## Tomb Design

The late American Egyptologist Elizabeth Thomas studied the chambers and corridors of New Kingdom royal tombs and assigned to them letter designations according to the function they were intended to serve (fig. 14). Not all royal tombs include all these chambers, and some have more than one of each.

**Chamber A:** The Tomb Entrance, called "The Passage of the Way of Shu." Shu was the god of air, and the entrance was fully open to the sky before the reign of Thutmose IV, partly open thereafter.

**Corridor B:** First corridor, called "The Second God's Passage [of Re]," referring to the fact that in some tombs, depending on their orientation,

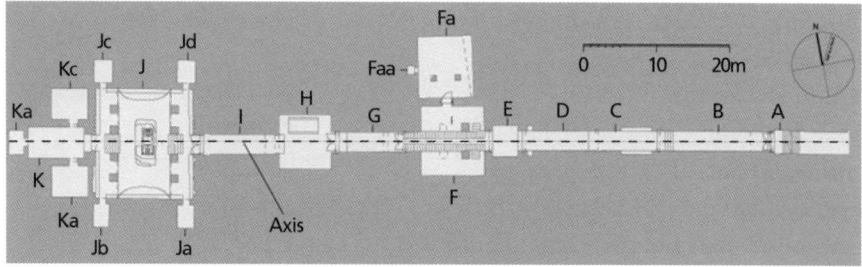

Fig. 14. KV 8 (Merenptah) with chamber designations. © Theban Mapping Project

descent, and plan, this corridor was the farthest that sunlight could penetrate. The Litany of Ra was often inscribed on its walls.

**Chamber C:** At first, a chamber with a descent, later a stairwell with recesses, then a corridor, "C" (or the niches cut into its walls) was called "The Hall Wherein They Rest." "They" referred to the statuettes of the thirty-seven gods mentioned in the Solar Litany.

**Corridor D:** A corridor whose ancient name may simply have been "The Fourth God's Passage."

**Corridor E:** "E" was a deep pit or 'well,' called "The Hall of Hindering," once thought to have been cut to prevent floodwater from entering the tomb, or to thwart tomb robbers. In 1817, Giovanni Belzoni found the corridor beyond the rear wall of "E" in KV 17, the tomb of Seti I, to be blocked and painted. He also found that ancient thieves had pierced the blocking, then continued into the tomb. If the wells were intended to be security devices, they regularly failed. Several wells have chambers cut off them, and today Egyptologists believe that they served primarily as the symbolic burial place of the god Osiris.

**Chamber F:** This pillared hall is referred to as "The Chariot Hall." (Remains of chariots have been found in several tombs, most notably the tomb of Tutankhamun.) Some Egyptologists have argued that this hall marked the transition between the upper part of the tomb, equated with the "Upper Duat" (a part of the Netherworld), and the lower part, or "Lower Duat."

**Corridors G, H, I:** Their functions were apparently simple: to offer additional wall surfaces for decoration and texts and perhaps to provide storage space for funerary goods. "G" was called "Another God's Passage." Originally a stairwell called "The Other, Second, God's Passage," "H" later became a corridor, then, at least in KV 57, 8, and 11, a chamber.

First a room, "I" became a corridor in later tombs. The Turin plan of KV 2 described it as "The Ramp."

**Chamber J:** The burial chamber, "J," was called "The Hall in Which One Rests," or "The House of Gold," clearly references to the sarcophagus and shrines that were placed in it. Another name was "The Hidden Chamber." The plan of this chamber changed through time: it could be cartouche-shaped, rectangular, pillared, vaulted, and/or with a sunken central floor level. Four small side-chambers (designated chambers Ja to Jd)—two of them intended for storing food and drink, two for statuettes and ritual equipment—were often cut through its walls. Occasionally, as in the tombs of Amenhotep III, Horemheb, and Seti I, there might be more than four side-chambers.

**Chamber K:** "The God's Passage which is in the *Shabti*-place," also called "The God's Passage which is on the Inner Side of the House of Gold," is found in a few tombs. Of unknown designation, it was originally a corridor, later a chamber.

**Chamber L:** This room of unknown purpose was originally a corridor, later a chamber called "The Second God's Passage which is at the Back of the House of Gold." It is not often found in KV tombs.

**Chamber M:** Found only in KV 17, of unknown purpose.

**Post-Pharaonic Use**

When KV was abandoned at the end of the New Kingdom, no further tombs were dug there, but it soon became a tourist destination. Greek and Roman traders traveled to Thebes from Alexandria and the Fayoum between 332 BC and AD 300. Graffiti were carved on monuments and hillsides and numerous graffiti have been found on KV tomb walls. KV tombs were used as campsites; the fires travelers lit and the food they cooked in the shelter of the tombs blackened walls and destroyed painted scenes.

The graffiti are not especially profound, but they are useful indicators of the kinds of tourists who visited Thebes two millennia ago. Their visits were motivated by the tales they heard of the wonderful Colossi of Memnon and the tombs in the Valley of the Kings. They would have agreed with Diodorus Siculus (ca. 59 BC) that Thebes, filled with "huge buildings, splendid temples, and other ornaments . . . [was a city] more opulent than the others in Egypt or anywhere else."[1] And they might have agreed, too, with Diodorus's disappointment that the opulent remains might originally have been even more so. He wrote that, "while the structures themselves have survived until our era, the silver, gold, and ivory, and a king's ransom in precious stones, were carried off by the Persians in the time when Cambyses burned the temples of Egypt."[2] (There is no evidence of this, however.)

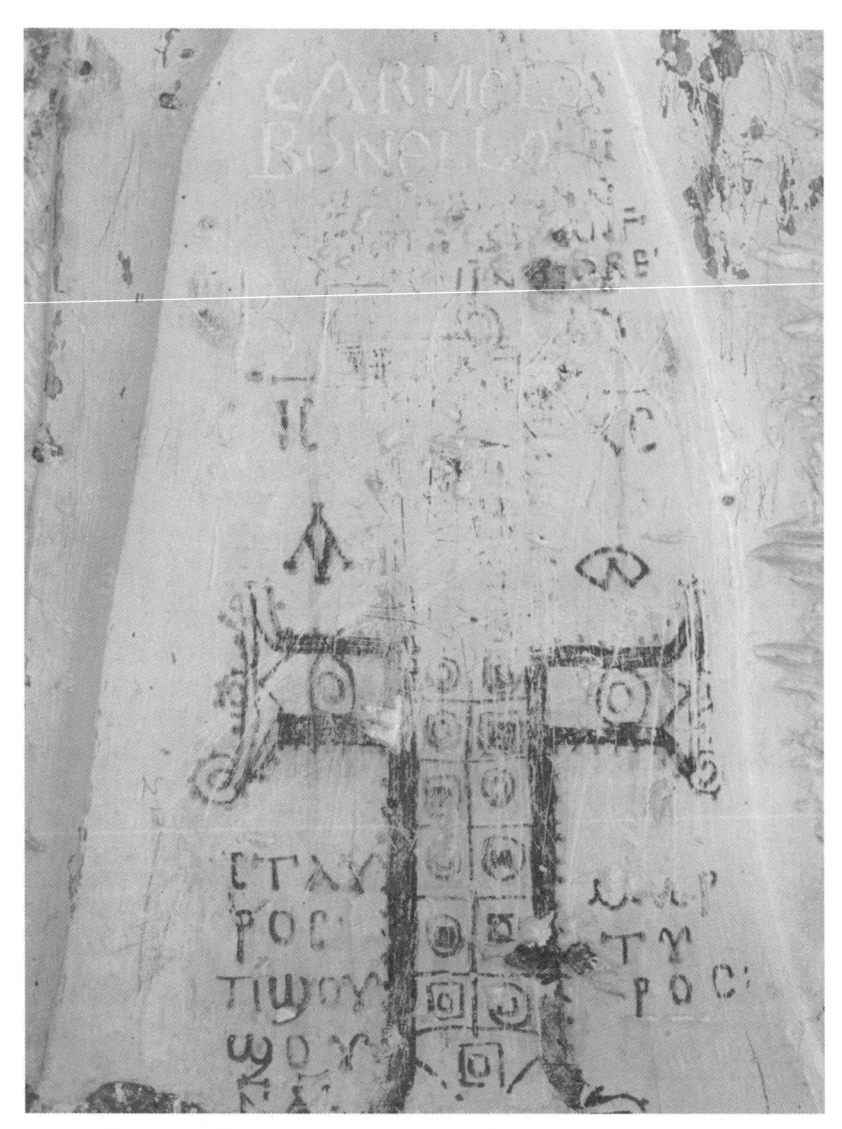

Fig. 15. Christian graffiti in KV 2, Ramesses IV. © Theban Mapping Project

These early travelers were followed by early Christians, who used the tombs as hermitages and sometimes defaced the figures of Egyptian gods, or replaced them with figures from Christian iconography. By the second century AD, Christianity was the predominant religion in Egypt, and between AD 451 and 1065, when a great famine hit Egypt and decimated its population, many Theban tombs and temples were converted to monasteries or churches, and statues and scenes of pagan gods were defaced. In AD 390, Constantine removed two obelisks from Thebes first to Alexandria, then on to the Circus Maximus in Rome and to Istanbul. These were among the first shipments abroad of Theban monuments. Many more shipments would follow.

**The Modern Era**

There is virtually no mention of Thebes in texts from antiquity until the eighteenth century, and even knowledge of its precise location was lost. The first modern European to 'rediscover' Thebes was the Jesuit priest, Claude Sicard, who came in 1726 and realized that the monuments he gazed upon were those of the fabled ancient city. Earlier travelers to Upper Egypt had mistaken Memphis, Antinoöpolis, and other sites for Thebes, but failed to recognize the town itself. Once rediscovered, however, it became a major source of antiquities for the European market. The number of European visitors to Thebes in the eighteenth century was small, but these travelers published journals and commentaries that contributed to the rise of nineteenth-century interest in ancient Egypt and to the rapidly increasing popularity of Nile Valley travel. Egyptian art and architecture became popular in Europe and interior decorators and architects clamored for drawings of ancient monuments and for the monuments themselves.

> At nine o'clock, in making a sharp turn round the point of a projecting chain of mountains, we discovered all at once the site of the ancient Thebes in its whole extent; this celebrated city, the size of which Homer has characterized by the single expression of with a hundred gates, ... this illustrious city ... the whole army, suddenly and with one accord, stood in amazement at the sight of its scattered ruins, and clapped their hands with delight, as if the end and object of their glorious toils, and the complete conquest of Egypt, were accomplished and secured by taking possession of the splendid remains of this ancient metropolis.
> Denon on first seeing the West Bank, 1803[3]

Fig. 16. KV map, as drawn by Pococke, 1743

Richard Pococke (1704–65) made the first map of the Valley of the Kings and drew plans of nine tombs there. He also sketched plans of the Ramesseum and the Ptolemaic temple at Deir al-Medina. James Bruce (1730–94), who discovered the tomb of Ramesses III in the Valley of the Kings, later called "Bruce's Tomb," also accurately described how the relief decoration in the temple of Medinet Habu had been carved.

The most important early attempt to record Theban monuments was prompted by Napoleon's desire to learn more about the country he sought to conquer. His army was in Egypt in 1799–1801, accompanied by over 130 scholars from all fields of science and the arts who set out to record everything from modern costume to natural history to ancient monuments. The results of their surveys, published as the *Description de l'Égypte*, appeared between 1809 and 1828. Two of the nineteen folio volumes of plates were devoted to the antiquities of Thebes and gave Europeans their first (mostly) accurate description of its monuments. Two members of this scholarly brigade, Prosper Jollois and Edouard de Villiers, prepared a remarkably accurate map of the Valley of the Kings, with plans of several tombs and many other Theban monuments.[4]

The *Description* and other nineteenth-century works on Egypt further whetted Europe's appetite for things Egyptian and encouraged large numbers of explorers, adventurers, merchants, and scholars to visit Thebes, both to study the monuments and to carry them home. So, too, did such popular books as Amelia Edwards's (1831–92) *A Thousand Miles Up the Nile*, and paintings of the Theban landscape (both real and imagined) by such artists as Alma Tadema (1836–1912), David Wilkie (1785–1841), Edward Lear (1812–88), John Frederick Lewis (1805–76), and especially David Roberts (1796–1864).

One of the most successful early travelers was Giovanni Battista Belzoni (1778–1859), who had come to Egypt to sell a water-lifting device to the government. He failed at this, but quickly found employment carting antiquities from Theban sites to Europe. A map drawn by Belzoni exists as one of the earliest attempts to record the tombs in KV (fig. 17). His most famous discovery was the tomb of Seti I (KV 17), often referred to as "Belzoni's tomb." Belzoni describes searching for private tombs and antiquities at al-Qurna:

Surrounded by bodies, by heaps of mummies in all directions . . . the blackness of the wall, the faint light given by the candles or torches for want of air, the different objects that surround me, seeming to converse with each other, and the Arabs with the candles or torches in their hands, naked and covered with dust, themselves living mummies, absolutely formed a scene that cannot be described.[5]

John Gardner Wilkinson (1797–1875), who worked at Thebes in 1824 and 1827–28, copied scenes and inscriptions in the private tombs that eventually led to his hugely successful study of life in ancient Egypt, *The Manners and Customs of the Ancient Egyptians*, a masterful ethnography of dynastic times. Wilkinson also surveyed the known tombs in the Valley of the Kings, assigning numbers to the twenty tombs then visible and establishing the numbering system still used today.

After Egyptian hieroglyphs were deciphered in 1822, the demand for accurate copies of Egyptian texts grew rapidly. Jean François Champollion (1790–1832), who was responsible for the decipherment, recorded texts and scenes at Thebes, and was the first to recognize that royal tomb inscriptions were religious texts, not autobiographical ones. Niccolo Francesco Ippolito Baldessare Rosellini (1800–43) worked with Champollion and published four hundred folio plates of Egyptian texts and scenes. Together with the *Description*, they were Egyptologists' principal reference works for many decades, and are still valuable sources today. Champollion's interest in Thebes was not entirely benign, however. He also worked to cut pieces of wall decoration from the tomb of Seti I and have them installed in the Louvre. In reply to a complaint from the English archaeologist Joseph Bonomi (1796–1878), Champollion wrote: "One day you will have the pleasure of seeing some of the beautiful bas-reliefs of the tomb of Osirei [Seti I] in the French Museum. That will be the only way of saving them from imminent destruction and in carrying out this project I shall be acting as a real lover of antiquity, since I shall be taking them away only to preserve and not to sell."[6]

The greatest of the nineteenth-century epigraphic expeditions was that of Carl Richard Lepsius (1810–84), which resulted in the *Denkmäler*

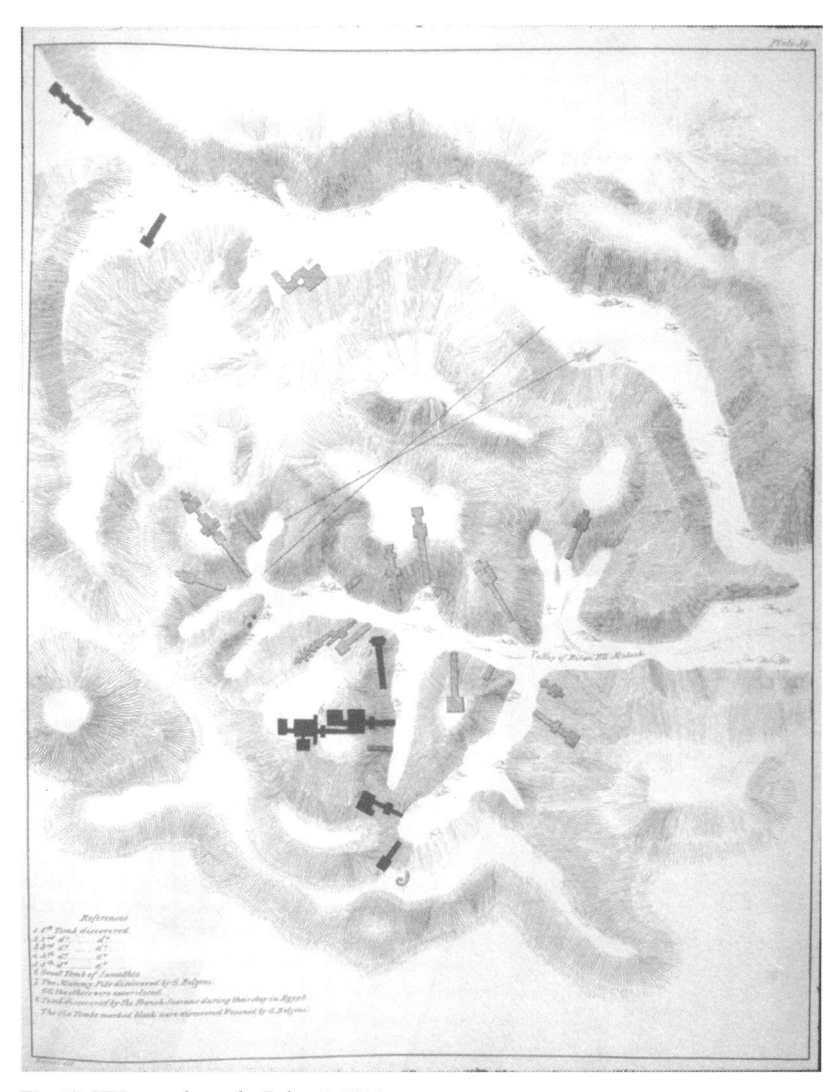

Fig. 17. KV map, drawn by Belzoni, 1821

*aus Ägypten und Aethiopien* (1859), 894 folio plates of Egyptian texts, reliefs, architectural drawings, panoramas, and maps, including two volumes on the monuments of Thebes. It is the largest Egyptological work ever published, and today, as Egyptian monuments deteriorate, it is an increasingly valuable record of ancient sites. Other epigraphers and artists who worked in Thebes include Edouard Henri Naville (1844–1926), who published four tombs in the Valley of the Kings in 1887 and, assisted by Howard Carter, the temple of Hatshepsut at Deir al-Bahari in 1894–1908.

Photography was used at Thebes by Maxime du Camp (1822–94), Francis Frith (1822–98), and other early photographers, but they did not try to produce systematic records of the monuments. Perhaps the first to do that was Felix Guilmant, who made a complete photographic record of the tomb of Ramesses IX. The Metropolitan Museum of Art's photographer, Harry Burton (1879–1940), was responsible for several major photographic surveys at Thebes, including complete coverage of the excavation of the tomb of Tutankhamun and its objects.

From the nineteenth century onward, Egyptian antiquities were much sought after by European collectors and museums. Many tales have been told about gun battles fought between rival expeditions, and violent diplomatic rows over objects. But by the early twentieth century, this 'Wild West Bank' image had ended, and the number of objects stolen or sold dramatically declined. It did not cease altogether, however: theft and vandalism still occur at Thebes in spite of the best efforts of authorities to prevent it. The passing of strict antiquities laws in Egypt has helped, as has the listing of Thebes in 1979 as a UNESCO World Heritage Site, and UNESCO declarations controlling international trade in antiquities. However, as long as there are customers, there will be people willing to supply the market.

Archaeological work in Thebes has varied greatly in methodology over the last 150 years, moving from the highly destructive, slipshod ransacking of tombs and temples to the meticulous analysis of even microscopic remains. Unfortunately, until recently, the former approach was by far the more common.

Excavations funded by the American businessman Theodore Davis (1837–1915) in the Valley of the Kings included work by Howard Carter, Edward Ayrton, and Arthur Weigall. Carter later cleared the tomb of Tutankhamun (discovered in 1922, worked on until 1932), an enormous undertaking that still is not fully published. Arguably, seven excavations have become the best known of the many conducted at Thebes and have thrust Thebes into international headlines that helped shape people's image of what ancient Thebes was like. They are: the discovery of the tomb of Seti I by Giovanni Belzoni (1817); the discovery of caches of royal mummies in 1881 (in Deir al-Bahari tomb 320) and 1898 (in the tomb of Amenhotep II); the discovery of the tomb of Nefertari by Ernesto Schiaparelli in 1903; James Quibbell's discovery of the tomb of Yuya and Thuya, the parents of Queen Tiye, in the Valley of the Kings in 1905; the 1922 discovery of the tomb of Tutankhamun by Howard Carter; and the 1995 discovery by the Theban Mapping Project of KV 5, a tomb of sons of Ramesses II. More recent discoveries of small tombs, labeled KV 63 and KV 64, continue to fire public imagination.

Interest in the protection of KV tombs, however, only came about in the 1990s. It has resulted in the careful excavation of KV 5, KV 10, KV 14, and KV 16, and in conservation studies of KV 17 and KV 62.

## A Move toward Conservation

One of the first visitors to express concern for the preservation of Theban monuments was Richard Pococke. He lamented that "they are every day destroying these fine morsels of Egyptian Antiquity, and I saw some of the pillars being hewn into millstones."[7] Auguste Mariette (1821–81), French Egyptologist and founder of the Egyptian Museum in Cairo, decried the all-too-common tourist who came to Thebes "with a pot of tar in one hand and a brush in the other, leaving on all the temples the indelible and truly disgraceful record of his passage." And he begged his colleagues to "preserve Egypt's monuments with care. Five hundred years hence Egypt should still be able to show to the scholars who shall visit her the same monuments that we are now describing."[8] Mariette's plea was largely ignored, however, and, if anything, the destruction of the monuments became even more common in the later nineteenth century.

Some notable exceptions, however should be pointed out. We have records of flood-prevention work in the Valley in the vicinity of KV 17 (Seti I) by J.G. Wilkinson, Robert Hay, and James Burton, when they cleared debris from earlier excavations by Belzoni.

> The science of observation, of registration, of recording, was yet unthought-of; nothing had a meaning unless it were an inscription or a sculpture. A year's work in Egypt made me feel it was a house on fire, so rapid was the destruction going on.
> 
> W. M. Flinders Petrie, 1931[9]

However, complete mapping, recording, and surveying of the Valley would not be completed until the twenty-first century. That work is summarized in chapter 5.

# 2 Current Risk Factors

In this chapter, we shall deal with the current threats to the Valley of the Kings and their underlying causes. Before any attempt can be made to remedy the problems of the site, we must have a clear idea of the condition of its fabric and the processes that have resulted in damage to KV. Only after we identify the threats that affect the sustainability of KV can we develop strategies for their removal or control. We distinguish between threats from the natural environment and threats due to human action.

## The Natural Environment
### Geology
The Valley of the Kings was cut into limestone bedrock by torrential rains and massive floods that poured over the African landscape millions of years ago. The limestone lies atop an underlying, discontinuous stratum of Esna shale, about 50 m thick. This shale is an unstable, weak, gray-looking stone that can expand up to 50 percent in volume when it is exposed to moisture. It can exert tremendous pressure on overlying strata, causing tombs cut within them literally to implode. Such damage has occurred in KV 7, the tomb of Ramesses II, for example, whose burial chamber was cut partly into an underlying Esna shale layer. When the shale expanded during various flood events, pressure caused the chambers' pillars and walls to fracture, and resulted in serious structural damage.

The thick layer of limestone is known as the Serai Formation of the Thebes Group. This formation consists of three major strata of limestone (fig. 18), varying in quality from fine, hard, solid stone, like that in KV 5 or KV 57, to the weak and fractured stone found in KV 7 and KV 11.

The lowest layer of the Thebes Group, called Member One (the Hamidat Member), is 120 m thick. Most KV tombs were cut into this stratum. Structurally, the stone varies in quality from poor to good. Tombs cut into the layer's lower parts have been affected by the underlying Esna shale even though they may not come into direct contact with it. The proximity of Esna shale and the variable quality of the limestone mean that the condition of the tombs dug here varies considerably. Some tombs, even after three thousand years, remain structurally sound. Others have suffered serious damage: pillars have fallen, walls have cracked, chambers have filled with flood-borne debris, ceilings have collapsed, and paint and plaster have disappeared. Tombs such as KV 7, 17, and 47, whose burial chambers graze the shale layer, have experienced serious damage. Others, such as KV 5 or 57, have experienced almost none.

Extensive fissures and fractures can be seen on KV hillsides where the lower parts of Member One are exposed. These were created about twenty thousand years ago by seismic activity, and can extend hundreds of meters below ground. They have acted as conduits allowing rainwater to seep into tombs, infiltrating the underlying Esna shale and causing structural problems. The TMP prepared a Valley-wide map of these fractures (figs. 19 and 20), and cleaned and sealed those in the hillside above KV 5 in 1997.

The middle layer, Member Two (the Dababiya), is up to 140 m thick. It is notable for the fossils it contains. Especially common are large bivalves *(Lucina thebaica)*, starfish, and nummulites, which can be seen in abundance along the footpath over the hill from KV to Deir al-Medina.

The upper layer, Member Three (the Shaghab), is up to 30 m thick and has a more yellowish color than the layers below. It can be seen in the upper reaches of al-Qurna as one walks from KV to the Village de Repos.

A preliminary study was made to evaluate the seismic risk in the KV/Luxor area. Although the archaeological literature occasionally refers to historic earthquake effects in ancient Thebes, this is poorly documented. A study of historic earthquakes was made based upon studies by Maamoun, Megahed, and Allam.[1] Earthquakes listed in this study that were

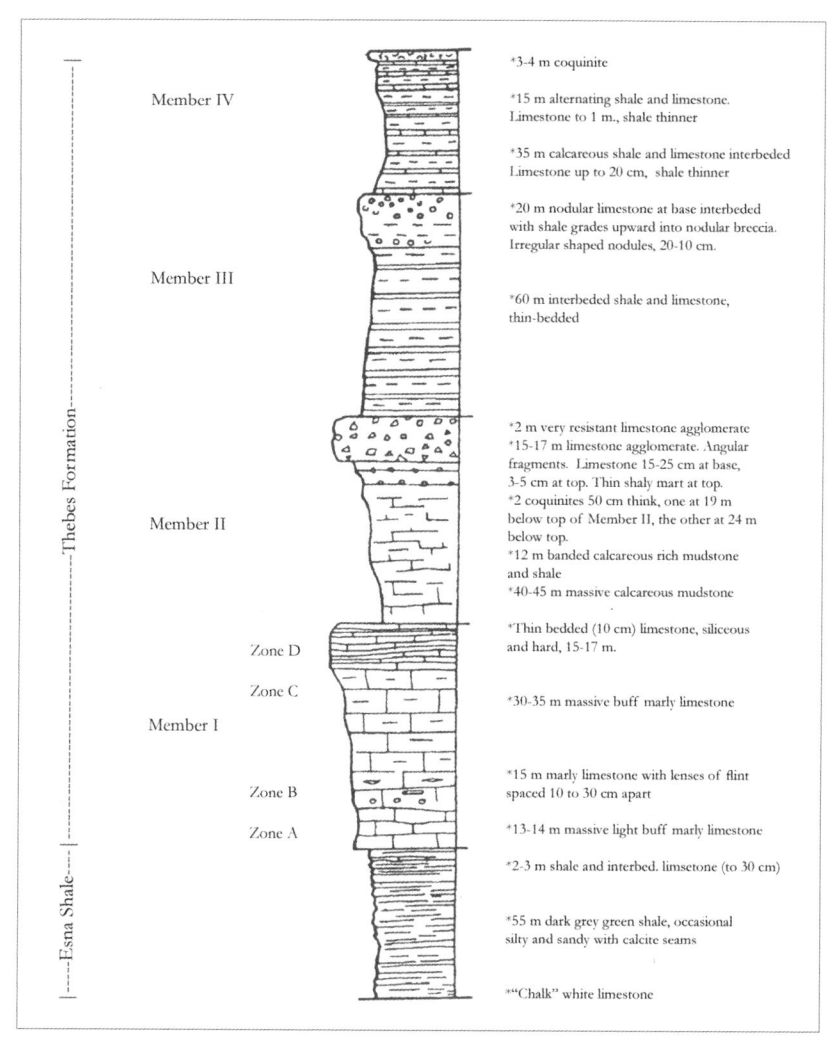

Fig. 18. Geology cross-section. © Thebes Mapping Project after Curtis

close enough to Luxor to have had any effect are shown in figure 21. Recorded earthquakes date from 600 BC to AD 1972. Figure 21 shows that most seismic events of any potential risk in Luxor were centered 200 km or more away. At this distance, even considering estimated Richter magnitude 6+ earthquakes, the local accelerations in Luxor would be less than 4–5 percent of the acceleration of gravity, consistent with the recommendations of the Egyptian Society for Earthquake Engineering (1988).

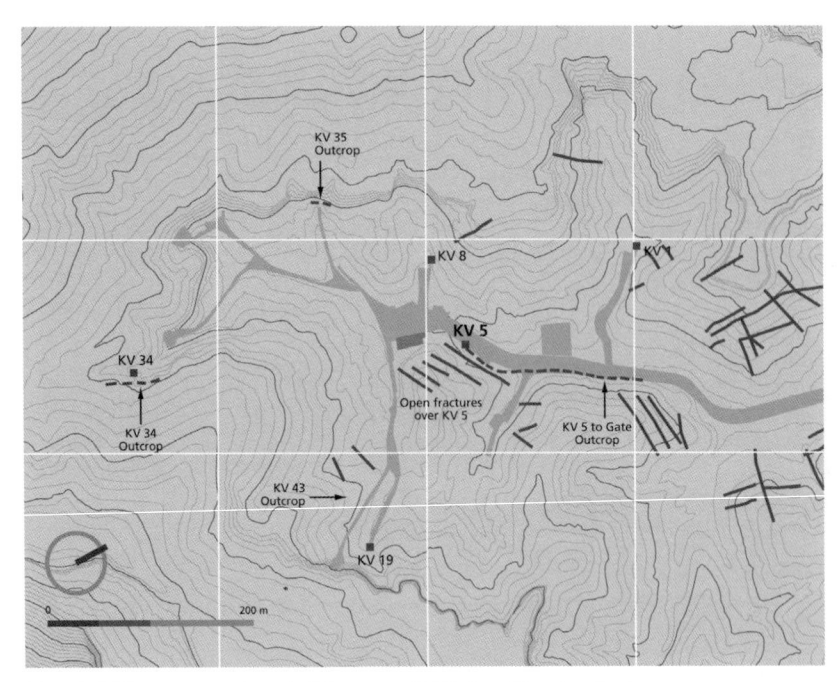

Fig. 19. KV outcrops and vertical fractures. © Theban Mapping Project

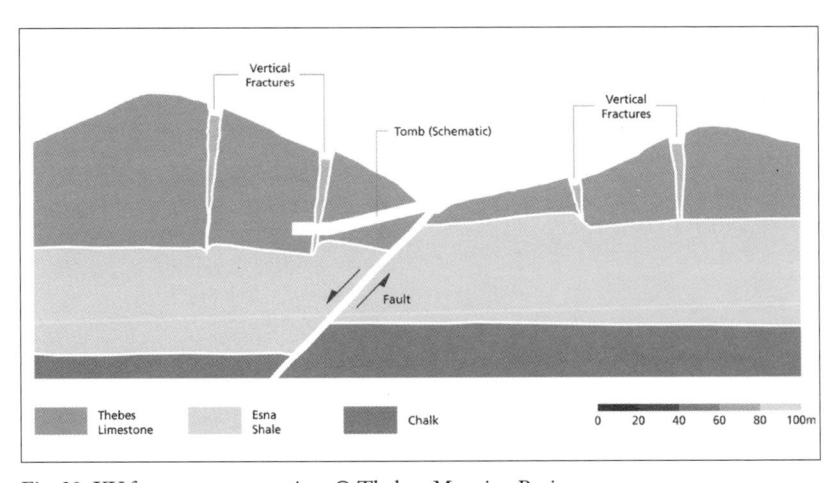

Fig. 20. KV fractures cross-section. © Theban Mapping Project

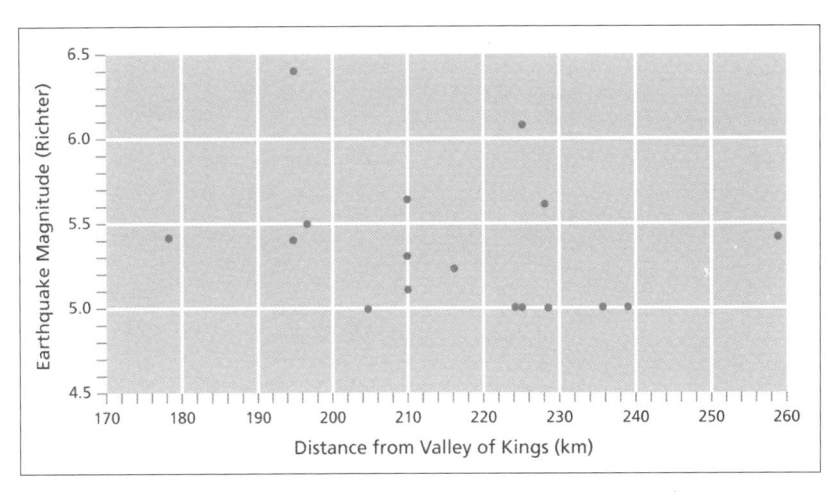

Fig. 21. Seismic activity, 300 BC to present. © Theban Mapping Project

## Topography

The central part of KV is clearly defined by sheer cliffs, 20 to 60 m high, extending around its eastern, southern, and western sides (fig. 22). Tombs were cut into these cliffs early in the New Kingdom. Later, they were dug into the low, rounded hills and steep slopes in the Valley. These low hills are separated from each other by natural pathways stretching like splayed fingers across the valley floor. The Valley's upper hillsides are covered by weathered chert nodules and fossils. The low-lying hills are covered with thick layers of limestone chips and sand. Some of this debris came from the ancient cutting of KV tombs; some came from nineteenth- and early twentieth-century excavations; some was debris dumped when KV pathways were widened and low retaining walls were built; and some was washed down from the hills high above KV during rainstorms and resulting flash floods that occur every few decades. The SCA has suggested that all of this debris should be removed down to bedrock, as was done a few years ago in the Valley of the Queens (QV). This will be an expensive and time-consuming project, and it must be done with great care if valuable data is to be recorded. Major aesthetic and hydrological concerns aside, such clearing will uncover extensive ancient workmen's huts, shrines, foundation deposits, and caches of funerary objects, all of which will require delicate archaeological excavation. The large amount of such material to be found here has been demonstrated by recent Swiss,

American, and British clearing operations. Further topographic studies are therefore needed before any further work is carried out.

In 2009–10, the SCA undertook such clearing operations in the central part of the Valley. Much of the excavated area was refilled to original levels, but the area between KV 62 (Tutankhamun) and KV 8 (Merenptah) has been left exposed to bedrock, making KV 8 inaccessible to tourists.

Fig. 22. Recent SCA archaeological work in the Valley of the Kings in front of KV 8.
© Theban Mapping Project

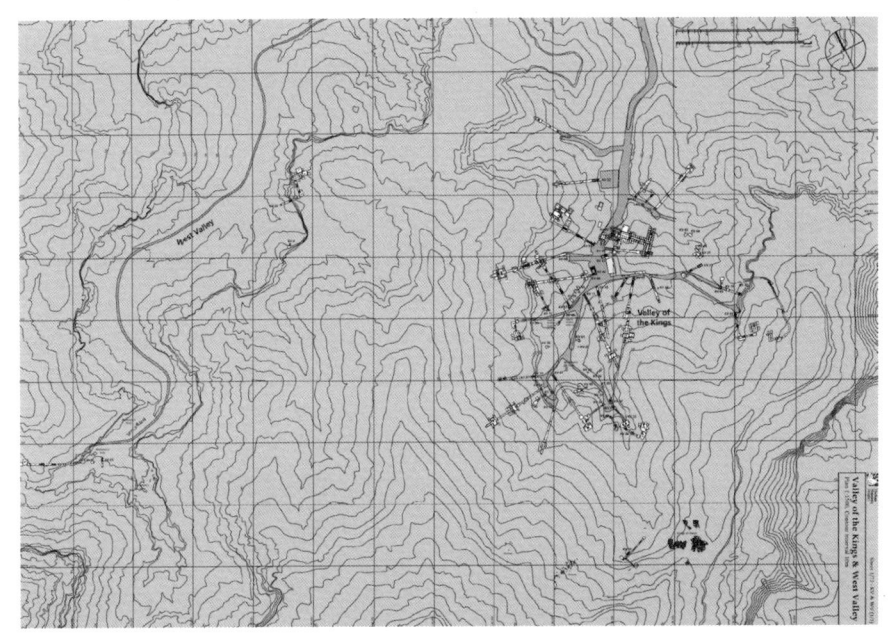

Fig. 23. KV topographical map. © Theban Mapping Project

Cursory examination of the work site indicates that substantial numbers of objects were found lying among numerous ancient constructions. What the SCA's ultimate plans for this area might be, and what kind of analysis and documentation of the work will be published, remains to be seen.

## Meteorology

Of all the threats to KV none is more serious (or more preventable) than the flooding caused by torrential rains that strike its watershed. In minutes, the flash floods these sudden cloudbursts create can wash tons of debris down the KV hillsides and into unprotected tombs. The floodwaters weaken bedrock in which the tombs are cut, destroy their decorated walls, deposit many meters of silt and stone in their chambers, and cause dramatic and damaging changes in the humidity levels within tomb chambers.

For example, the storms that struck Upper Egypt in October and November 1994 did terrible damage. In Upper Egypt generally, the government reported that over five hundred people were killed, eleven thousand homes were destroyed, and twenty-five thousand feddans of crops were ruined. In Thebes, too, there was considerable destruction to the monuments. In the Valley of the Kings, the storms caused the flooding of several tombs, and the Antiquities Inspectorate was forced to requisition pumps from neighboring villagers to remove the accumulated water. KV 13, the tomb of Bay, was the most heavily hit: inspectors measured 1.40 m of water in its lower chambers. KV 14, 15, 35, and 57, among others, received smaller amounts of rain and debris. During these storms, runoff from the KV watershed cut channels in the valley floor (through a deep layer of limestone chips), and damaged the asphalt road eastward from the new KV rest house. In the West Valley (WV), one can still see channels two meters deep and three meters wide that were cut through mounds of limestone and sand, and there is plentiful evidence of stones weighing 10 or 15 kg being rolled along the WV floor.

The floodwaters that rushed down the wadi from the KV and WV watersheds were joined by even heavier runoff from more northerly wadis. Near the house of Howard Carter, these streams joined forces, creating a wall of water that some residents of northern Thebes claim was as much as two meters high. This torrent rushed toward the temple of Seti I, seriously damaging the temple's enclosure wall and subsidiary buildings, turning limestone stelae and mud-brick walls into mush. A few meters

Fig. 24a and b. Flooding in KV, 1994. © Theban Mapping Project

Current Risk Factors

north, across the paved road from the temple, grave markers in a modern Muslim cemetery were demolished and the road itself buckled. Just east of the temple, homes in a mud-brick village were reduced to piles of rubble. The whole event took less than fifteen minutes. When it was over, several animals had been killed, scores of homes had been destroyed, and hundreds more were damaged. (It is important to note that the pattern of flooding at the northern end of the Necropolis in 1994 seems to have been very similar to a flash flood that struck in 1949.)

Over the past ninety years, archaeologists have slowly come to realize that flooding in KV is a recurring event that must be dealt with broadly if damage to the ancient monuments is to be prevented. The recent storms, and the historical pattern of storms that we are only now beginning to trace, lend a degree of urgency to this work. Most of these plans are still in elementary stages of design, and all have concentrated on the Valley of the Kings. But although KV forms a discrete watershed, it is nonetheless just one part of a broader area—the northern sector of the Theban Necropolis—that has been subject to rainfall and flooding for at least two centuries.

No one should have been surprised that heavy storms came to Thebes, or that their floodwaters damaged specific, localized areas. The storms of 1994 were only the most recent in a long history of storms, many of which have taken a heavy toll on Theban monuments. A review of the meteorological history of the West Bank (poorly known though that history is) indicates that the location of these storms is roughly predictable, and that the flooding they cause recurs in the same areas at the same intervals decade after decade. The topography of the West Bank dictates this pattern. This was reaffirmed by a heavy rain in 2005 that caused minor flooding in the same areas as the rains of 1994.

*The Regular Recurrence of Storms*
Figure 25, based on data prepared for the TMP by Dr. Sherif al-Didy, professor of hydrology at Cairo University, and supplemented with information provided to the TMP by the Egyptian Air Force, shows a partial history of storms in the Luxor–Thebes area since the first weather station was established in Luxor in the 1930s. These figures record data for Luxor, specifically the Luxor Airport weather station on the edge of the East Bank desert. Our interest is KV, another 19 km west. However, until

a weather station is installed on the West Bank (something the TMP is seeking permission to do), this is the best data available. (There was a station that operated in KV briefly in 1997–98, but it was dismantled and we have not been able to locate its records.) Figure 25 shows the occurrence, each year from the 1940s to the 1990s, of the storms that dropped the greatest amount of rainfall—at least 1 mm of rainfall—in a one-hour period. If there were several one-hour storms in a single year, only the storm with the heaviest rainfall is charted. The maximum amount of rain that fell in one hour is shown on the vertical scale (although, of course, the storm, if it continued with reduced intensity for more than one hour, may have dropped more than the one-hour amount). Note that the most significant storms seem to come in roughly three- or four-year clusters once every decade or so. Regular yearly patterns of rainfall have been noted in other parts of Egypt, too, although their intervals of recurrence differ from those seen here.

This pattern of three to four years of heavy rain per decade is not perfect, of course. However, each recent major storm dropping more than 5 mm of rain in one hour (in 1949, 1975, 1976, 1980, 1989, 1991, 1993, and 1994) usually has fallen within a three- or four-year storm cluster. That a greater number of heavy storms have occurred in more recent decades than in earlier ones may indicate that there is also a longer-term cyclical pattern of storms.

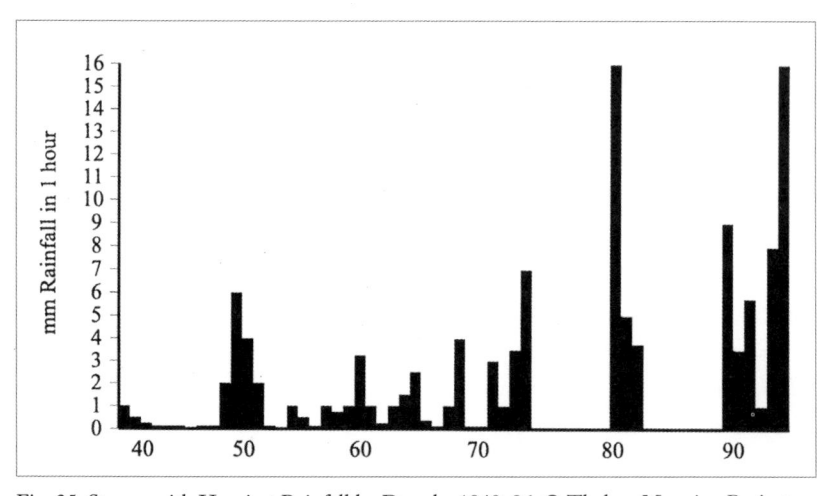

Fig. 25. Storms with Heaviest Rainfall by Decade, 1940–96. © Theban Mapping Project

> In a letter to his mother in October 1918, Howard Carter wrote: "For three successive Octobers we have had heavy downpours, and this time a peculiar phenomenon occurred. While we were as dry as a bone, the larger valleys suddenly became seething rivers. . . . The Valley of the Tombs of the Kings, joined by the Great Western valley, in a few moments became little short of mountain rivers . . . the torrent cutting out wide furows [sic] in the valley bed and rolling before it stones some two feet in diameter—natives returning home with their animals were unable to ford it, and thus were cut off from their homes."[2]

*The Seasonality of Storms*
It is also the case that virtually all of the recent heavy storms at Thebes (or at least those for which we have records) occurred in the months of October, November, or early December. Although much less frequent, rainfall has also been seen in Luxor in other months. Villiers Stuart *(The Funerary Tent of an Egyptian Queen)* noted that it rained in Luxor on 23 February 1882, but only a few drops.[3] A light rain also was reported in February 1896. If Dr. Abdel Aziz Sadek's interpretation of dates in Theban graffiti of the Ramesside period is correct,[4] rains heavy enough to leave ponds of water in the Valley of the Kings (events unusual enough to merit visits and comments by ancient scribes who brought their children to see the phenomena) fell on 18 March 1210 BC (in the reign of Merenptah), and again, less dramatically, on 6 June 1150 BC (in the reign of Ramesses IV). In the twentieth century AD, such rains were extremely rare. However, it did rain in March 2005. In the ancient Coptic calendar, the Gregorian months of October and November overlap the months of Tut, Phaophi, and Athyr (the three months of ancient *akhet*, the Egyptian season immediately following the recession of the Nile flood). In these months, the calendar warns that the weather will be intermittently but regularly windy, rainy, and stormy. There is a similar tradition of heavy October–November rains among the Bedouin of the Western Egyptian Desert.

*The Location of Storms*
Heavy rains in the Luxor area are remarkably limited in their geographical extent. One frequently hears of rains falling heavily in one village, while only a few hundred meters away another village remains dry (this

Fig. 26. Mold in KV 62, Tutankhamun. © Theban Mapping Project

is another reason why the Luxor Airport meteorological data is not the best indicator of West Bank weather.) Although there may be some rain falling throughout the Theban Necropolis during a storm, it is rare that the heaviest rains fall in more than a small part of it. In the 1994 storms, for example, light rain fell over the entire necropolis, but was not serious enough to do damage. Slightly heavier rains fell over parts of Malqata and Sheikh Abd al-Qurna (causing flooding in TT 139, Pairi). Very heavy rains fell in parts of KV, WV, and in the wadis north of these. In KV, the heaviest rains fell in those very limited areas of the watershed that drain into the southwestern-most part of the Valley—the hills above tombs KV 13, 14, 15, 31, and 32. There were only small to moderate amounts of water reported in KV 8, 35, 57, and 62. These tombs also lie below the western slopes of the Valley.

Tracing the scarce records of rainfall and flooding in KV in ancient graffiti, the diaries of nineteenth-century travelers, and the recollections of on-site inspectors and guards, this pattern seems almost always to be the case: there may be drops of rain falling throughout the Valley, but it is the western part of KV, and especially the southwestern part, that is subject to the most frequent and heaviest rainfall and consequently that receives the greatest amount of damage. The only KV tombs outside this quadrant that offer historical evidence of serious flooding are KV 5, 10, 17, and 18. None of these was affected by the 1994 storms.

The geographical split of rainfall is illustrated in a letter from Howard Carter to Lord Carnarvon:

> Towards the sunset, as the desert cooled, there was a great storm in the Northwest. No rain fell in the Valley, but from all the washes that ran down from the Theban hills, including the Valley of the Kings there was a torrent, which cut furrows four feet deep and rolled stones as big as two feet across. The locals were unable to ford the floods when returning from their work in the fields as the area was a vast lake. Yet no rain fell.[5]

**Flora and Fauna**

The Valley of the Kings is a desert wadi devoid of natural vegetation. Its only fauna are a few mice (lured by the detritus from tourists' lunch boxes) and occasional snakes (lured by the mice). There are also a few scorpions, insects, and small birds. In addition, beetles (family Dermestidae) and silverfish (family Lepsimatidae) have been observed in KV tombs. Bats were a problem several decades ago, but today, thanks to screened entrance gates, only KV 20 (Hatshepsut) is inhabited (its gate has been vandalized). The only other flora or fauna are microorganisms such as fungi and bacteria that infest a few KV tombs. These have had a deleterious effect on decorated walls and are to be seen, for example, on the walls of KV 62.

## Human Activity

Human activity has occurred at KV in one form or another almost continuously for the past half million years. Here, we provide an overview of these interventions.

### Prehistory

The hillsides surrounding KV were used in Upper Paleolithic and Mesolithic times (and in Dynastic times, too) as work stations where chert nodules embedded in the limestone bedrock were collected and used to fashion hand axes, knives, and scrapers. These work stations, first identified in the 1850s (they were the first evidence of the Paleolithic to be found in Africa), lie along the top of the sheer cliffs that define the Valley of the Kings, and along the footpaths that cross the hillsides.

### Dynastic Period

In the New Kingdom, Egyptians cut tombs for their pharaohs in KV and built numerous small huts and shelters near tomb entrances in which to house themselves during their work. Occasionally, ancient engineers were slipshod in their work, and were forced to dig in structurally weak bedrock, or accidentally broke into a pre-existing tomb. They were fully aware of the variable geology of KV, but time constraints, crowded conditions in KV, and the apparent absence of any overall KV map caused mistakes whose effects we are still trying to correct today.

In ancient times, perhaps only a few years after a tomb was sealed, thieves broke in searching for grave goods to be melted down or refashioned and sold. In their haste to acquire the treasure, the thieves showed no regard for the wall paintings, many times breaking through fragile constructions and damaging the walls.

However, attempts at conservation and restoration of what, even then, were ancient monuments were made during the Pharaonic Period, though not in the Valley of the Kings. Two examples of this are Thutmose IV, who cleared and conserved the Great Sphinx, and Khaemwese, son of Ramesses II, who had a special interest in Egypt's glorious past and restored several pyramids of Old Kingdom pharaohs in Memphis. Khaemwese has been called 'the first Egyptologist.'

## Late Antiquity

From Greco-Roman and early Christian times through the twentieth century, some KV tombs were used as temporary habitation sites by visitors, monks, or excavators. Often, the occupants left graffiti on tomb walls and on the Valley's cliffs. If ancient, such graffiti are considered a valuable part of the archaeological record; if recent, they are considered acts of vandalism.

## Nineteenth-century Rediscovery

From the Napoleonic invasion onward, interest in KV was rekindled, attracting visitors and looters alike. The Enlightenment of the nineteenth century placed Egypt firmly on the Grand Tour for the elites of Europe. A serious problem caused by these nineteenth-century visitors was the making of squeezes and rubbings of reliefs, and the use of fires to light their passage. Squeezes were made by pressing wet paper or soft wax against the walls, letting it dry, then pulling it off to use for cast-making. Unfortunately, the wall's painted surface was pulled off, too. Several tombs have been damaged because of squeezes, none more seriously than KV 17, the tomb of Seti I (fig. 27).

During this period, the grand museums of Europe, as well as opportunistic and wealthy private collectors, engaged in a campaign

Fig. 27. Damage to KV 17 from nineteenth-century squeezes. © Theban Mapping Project

of looting the antiquities of Egypt. The Valley of the Kings was not exempt from these ventures.

> Ours is probably the last generation which will be permitted to see the glory of Egyptian sculpture, as they were first revealed to the explorers at the beginning of the century.... the smoke of the travellers' torches and the disfigurement by travellers' spoliations, have rendered the "fine gold dim" in many of the paintings and inscriptions.
> William Howard Russell, 1869[6]

## Archaeology

Archaeological work in KV has also damaged the fabric of the site. Egyptology lags behind many other academic disciplines in its archaeological approaches and adoption of new ideas and was late in arriving at the notion of scientific archaeology. Only with the work of Flinders Petrie did the start of systematic recording, and what could be termed scientific archaeology, emerge. For over eighty years Egyptian archaeology has been dominated by the discovery of Tutankhamun's tomb; many Egyptologists have been guilty of feeling the "lure of gold" and until recent times have, regrettably, acted like treasure hunters.

Archaeologists are too often concerned with their own concession (the area defined by SCA in which they are allowed to work) and not the broader effects of their work on a site. In the past, ill-conceived clearing of tomb chambers has sometimes allowed floodwaters into chambers, which have destroyed fragile painted walls. The removal of debris around pillars has resulted in fractures in the bedrock and even the collapse of ceilings. The debris from excavations, often dumped on adjacent hillsides, has deflected rainwater into nearby tombs. More recently, archaeologists working in KV have failed to clean their work area, leaving behind unsightly piles of rubbish, stone, and gaping holes in the hillsides. Workers contracted to cart away excavation debris have dumped the debris alongside the road to the Valley instead of in more distant wadis in order to save time and money. As a result, the road to KV now offers tourists an unsightly, rubbish-lined drive to the site.

In addition, recent excavations in KV have significantly altered the topography of its watersheds, and hydrological studies conducted in the 1980s and 1990s need to be redone before the levels of pathways and the orientation of tomb entrances can be effectively changed and future floods diverted away from the tombs.

**Previous Conservation Attempts**
Modern attempts at cleaning, consolidating, stabilizing, or "restoring" KV tomb decoration have sometimes done more harm than good. This is also true of the installation of protective devices such as gates, glass panels (fig. 28), handrails, walkways, lights, and environmental controls. An early example of this is the lighting system installed in KV 9 (the tomb of Ramesses VI) by Howard Carter nearly ninety years ago. Carter drilled into walls at ceiling level and inserted wooden dowels to support the electric cables that he ran through the tomb to power lamps placed at intervals along its corridors. Original paint and plaster were damaged in the process.

In recent years, foreign missions have undertaken conservation work in 7, 9, 10, 14, and 16, and reports on these projects are available. Unfortunately, no records exist that document the much larger amount of past conservation activity conducted in the Valley by the SCA. No systematic survey of tomb conditions was even conducted until 2005, and most conservation work has proceeded in an irregular manner, governed by the availability of finances, labor, and materials, and the urgency of the needed work. The majority of

Fig. 28. Protective screens. © Theban Mapping Project

the work that has been done thus far is small-scale, such as the filling of cracks and fissures in tomb walls and ceilings, plastering over graffiti (even ancient ones), and the restoration of broken pillars. Fluorescent lighting, wooden stairs, ramps, walkways, and hand railings have been installed in many tombs, and large glass panels erected in front of decorated walls. Many problems, such as flaking pigment and the growth of fungi, have largely been ignored.

**Structural Changes to KV**

Structural changes to KV have been carried out for two main reasons: increased visitor access and flood protection schemes. The construction of pathways in KV, first undertaken in the 1920s and revised several times since, was done before hydrological studies had been conducted. This has resulted in an increased threat to tombs from flash floods. To widen pathways, for example, workers had to raise them to levels that deflected floodwater into nearby, low-lying tomb entrances. When the road from KV to Carter House was paved, it created a spillway that allowed floodwaters to pour out of KV in great quantity and with great force into areas like Dra Abu al-Naga, the temple of Seti I, and surrounding villages. As discussed above, in 1994 such a flood destroyed large parts of these areas, causing extensive damage. Recent construction of diversionary canals and barriers along the road is unlikely to help: the canals are not properly graded and the barriers do not cross the paved roadway.

Projects to prevent flash flooding within KV from damaging tombs or other parts of the archaeological zone have so far proved unsatisfactory. The hydrological studies on which they were based are outdated because continued excavations over the past decade have transformed the Valley's topography. Walls, recently constructed around some tomb entrances as flood barriers, are aesthetically inappropriate in KV (fig. 29).

**Tourism**

For the last two hundred years, KV has been an increasingly popular tourist destination. From a few dozen visitors each day in the mid-1960s to over seven thousand each day in 2005, the pressures on the tombs caused by mass tourism have grown to dangerous levels. Rapid changes in temperature and humidity in the tombs caused by hordes of hot, sweaty tourists pose serious threats to painted decoration. Lack of crowd control and traffic

Fig. 29. KV 17 flood walls. © Theban Mapping Project

Fig. 30. Visitor touching sarcophagus. © Theban Mapping Project

management make a visit to KV unpleasant for tourists and dangerous for monuments. Carelessly sited and poorly constructed tourist infrastructure—toilets, parking, lighting, etc.—threaten the aesthetic character of KV. Touching and accidental abrasion of tomb walls by visitors is an increasing problem. These will be dealt with in more detail below.

**Vandalism and Theft**

Major thefts have been perpetrated from antiquity onward (ancient texts detail some of them), but today such theft is extremely rare in KV, perhaps because of effective policing, harsh fines, and stiff prison sentences. (Antiquities theft is still a problem in Egypt, but most thieves concentrate on the many un-inventoried, unguarded nobles' tombs used as makeshift storerooms). In fact, very few artifacts or wall fragments from KV have been stolen in the past century. (One example of wall fragments that escaped detection is the pair of doorjambs taken from the tomb of Seti I that now reside in the Louvre and Florence). Increased tourism has itself helped to prevent theft, effectively keeping tomb interiors under scrutiny ten hours

Fig. 31a and b. Before and after attempted theft, KV 43. © Theban Mapping Project

54 | Current Risk Factors

a day. One of the few recent examples of attempted theft is the unsuccessful cutting out of a wall section in KV 43 in the early 1980s (fig. 31b). The attempt failed, but the wall was irreversibly damaged. Figures 32 and 33 graphically illustrate the changes to the fabric of KV over the last century.

Fig. 32a and b. Steps leading to KV 34, ca. 1910, 1999. © Theban Mapping Project

Fig. 33a and b. Entrance to KV 47, ca. 1910, 1999. © Theban Mapping Project

Human Activity | 55

## Summary of Risk Factors in the Valley of the Kings

**High Risk:**
- Flooding
- Tomb microclimate
- Inadequate site management and improper maintenance

**Medium Risk:**
- Fractures and structural instability of limestone bedrock
- Microorganism and animal intrusion
- Unsatisfactory conservation
- Inappropriate flood protection schemes
- Poorly sited and unaesthetic infrastructure
- Accidental abrasion and touching of walls by visitors
- Improper excavation

**Low Risk:**
- Landslides
- Seismic activity
- Theft and vandalism

# 3 Tourism and the Valley of the Kings

> The natural and cultural heritage, diversities and living creatures are major tourism attractions. Excessive or poorly managed tourism and tourism related development threaten their physical nature, integrity and significant characteristics. The ecological setting, culture and lifestyles of host communities may also be degraded, along with the visitor's experience of the place.
> International Council on Monuments and Sites (ICOMOS), 1999[1]

## Tourism in Egypt

Tourism has been an ingredient in Egypt's economy for about the last two hundred years. However, within the last generation, it has become an essential component that, until recently, generated 45 percent of the country's annual foreign currency earnings. Its contribution to the GDP is significant and readily quantifiable, but what is more difficult to calculate is the contribution tourism makes to employment levels and, particularly, its indirect effect on industries such as transportation, construction, food and beverage, and recreation.

In 1980, one million tourists visited Egypt and generated receipts of over US$300 million. By 2000, this had grown to 5.5 million tourists with total receipts topping $4.5 billion. In 2004, a record 8.1 million tourists visited Egypt, a 34.1 percent increase over the previous year, with revenues totaling around $6.1 billion (tables 5 and 6). It is the goal of the Egyptian government to increase the numbers of visitors to 9.5 million and raise cash receipts to $10 billion per annum within the next decade.

A very sizeable investment has been made by both public and private sectors in the infrastructure the tourist industry requires, and in all budgetary planning by the Egyptian government the assumption is made that this infrastructure will need to grow to accommodate an ever-increasing number of tourists. Millions of dollars are spent annually to encourage and promote tourism, most recently from neighboring Arab countries, which now represent a growing sector of the Egyptian tourist market. It has been argued that a few "high-end" tourists would maintain and increase tourism-based profits while imposing fewer pressures on the archaeological and natural resources. Egypt, however, has committed itself (due to ministerial decisions made decades ago) to the pursuit of mass tourism, and that pattern is unlikely to change in the near future. There is, however, a recognition of more diverse kinds of tourism that should be encouraged.

| The Egyptian Tourist Authority identifies sixteen categories of tourist attractions and types of tourism: ||
|---|---|
| Pharaonic Egypt | Natural Parks |
| Graeco-Roman Egypt | Resorts |
| Coptic Egypt | Golf |
| Islamic Egypt | Nile Cruises |
| Diving Resorts | Oases |
| Museums | Modern Egypt |
| Safari | Sports |
| Conferences | Therapeutic Tourism |

Table 4. Categories of tourism

### Tourist Statistics

As discussed above, the growth of tourism has progressed at an unprecedented rate. Despite some setbacks in 1997 with the terror attacks on tourists in Cairo and Luxor the market recovered fairly quickly. Again, a small downturn was felt after the September 11 attacks in the United States in 2001 and during the ensuing Afghanistan and Iraq conflicts. That said, the tourism industry in Egypt has shown itself to be very resilient. Recent events have caused tourist figures to decline, but recovery has been fairly

| Year | 1995 | 1996 | 1997 | 1998 | 1999 | 2000 | 2001 | 2002 | 2003 | 2004 |
|---|---|---|---|---|---|---|---|---|---|---|
| Total Arrivals (million) | 3.133 | 3.896 | 3.961 | 3.454 | 4.797 | 5.506 | 4.648 | 5.192 | 6.044 | 8.100 |
| % Increase | | 24.35 | 1.67 | -12.80 | 38.88 | 14.78 | -15.58 | 11.70 | 16.41 | 34.02 |

Table 5. Tourist arrivals, Egypt, 1995–2004

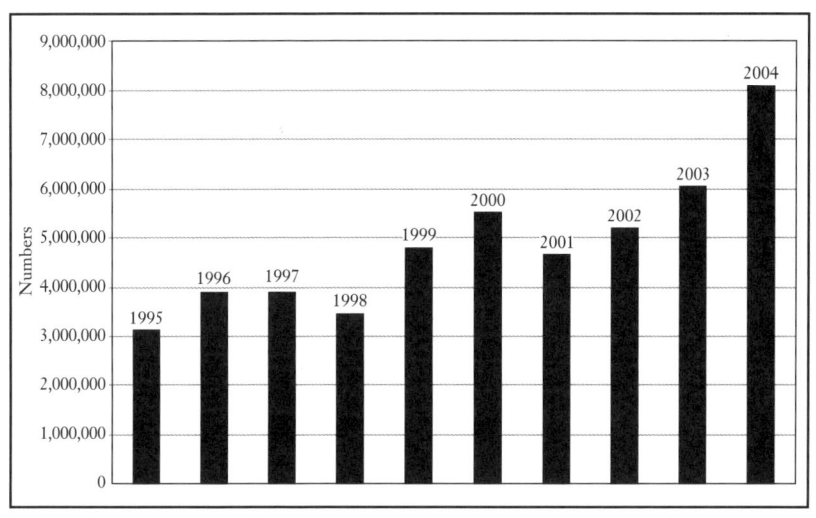

Table 6. Tourist arrivals, Egypt, 1995–2004

rapid. The Egyptian Revolution of 2011 is only the latest interruption to the regular increase in tourist numbers (tourism dropped by about 50 percent); this, too, is likely to be only temporary. Many have suggested that in light of global events, tourists are suffering from terrorism fatigue, and although concerned by these events, will not let them affect their holiday plans.

## Effects of Tourism

Until very recently, growth in tourism was thought to be achievable with no negative effects on Egypt's cultural heritage resources. Tourism was considered a non-consumable industry and was seen as an essential component of the country's development strategy with no downside. In fact, it was regarded as essential to the success of Egypt's economy. With hindsight, this turned out not to be true; tourism does consume resources of the host nation, not just natural and human-made resources, but cultural ones, too. Cultural resources are finite and have to be managed like any other scarce resource. This new reality is one with which the Egyptian authorities are now having to deal. The goal of previous administrations was to maximize

| Benefits of Tourism |
|---|
| Economic |
| General development and CH infrastructure |
| Social cohesion |
| Restoration and Conservation |
| Worldwide profile |
| **Negative Aspects of Tourism** |
| Degradation of CH, increase in conservatism, etc. |
| Neo-colonial nature of tourism |
| Access to sites |
| Security situation |
| Mass tourism |
| Reconstruction versus restoration |
| Disneyfication |
| Selling Egypt |
| Reliance on tourism: is it sustainable? |

Table 7. Tourism and cultural heritage (CH) in Egypt

revenue by the dual approach of opening more archaeological sites to visitors and promoting visits. This approach is now being challenged.

Until recently, Egypt has been slow to embrace change in the development of its tourism strategy. But now, many are calling for a revised approach and the implementation of a code of practice for tourism. The following is an example of a proposal compiled by the International Council on Monuments and Sites (ICOMOS), which could be revised and remodeled for the Egyptian market.

- Comprehensive tourist development plans are essential as the precondition for developing any tourist potential.
- It should be a fundamental principle of any tourist development plan that both conservation, in its widest sense, and tourism benefit from it. This principle should be part of the constitutional purpose of all national tourist agencies, and of local authority tourism and recreational departments.
- A significant proportion of revenue earned from tourism should be applied for the benefit of conservation, both nationally and regionally.
- The best long-term interests of the people living and working in any host community should be the primary determining factor in selecting options for tourist development.

- Educational programs should assist and invite tourists to respect and understand the local way of life, culture, history, and religion. Tourism policy should take these factors into account.
- The design of new buildings, sites, and transport systems should minimize the potentially harmful visual effects of tourism. Pollution controls should be built into all forms of infrastructure. Where sites of great natural beauty are concerned, the intrusion of human-made structures should be avoided if possible.
- Good management should define the level of acceptable tourism development and provide controls to maintain that level.[2]

## Tourism in Luxor

Luxor is a medium-sized town by Egyptian standards, with a population of approximately 150,000. Despite this, the town, because of its importance to the economy of Egypt, was declared a *medina* (city) by presidential decree in 1989.

Until this declaration, Luxor had been part of the al-Qurna administrative governorate. Administratively, the city of Luxor also includes the five adjacent villages (Karnak, Karnak al-Gadida, al-Qurna, Manshiya, and Awammiya), which swell the population to 360,000.

Fig. 34. Modern sign in Luxor. © Theban Mapping Project

The presidential decree granting Luxor city status gives its bureaucrats a unique position in Egyptian politics, in that they report directly to the office of the president of the republic, with authority over government ministries within the city's boundaries. This gives the governor a great deal of say in decisions affecting the future of Luxor's monuments.

The history of Luxor in many ways is also the history of international tourism in Egypt: as the tourist market expanded, so did Luxor. What was once a village has now become a city whose very existence is primarily dependent upon the continued growth in mass tourism. Luxor is one of Egypt's wealthiest cities. But it is unlike the rest of Egypt in that there is almost no industry other than tourism in Luxor's economic sector. A large proportion of the population works either directly or indirectly in the tourism industry. Yet most of the economic benefits from tourism in Luxor feed the national Egyptian economy, not that of Luxor or its residents.

Tourist accommodations and facilities are mainly situated on the East Bank of the Nile, in four- and five-star hotels, and an ever-increasing fleet of cruise boats (currently over three hundred boats operate on the Nile with a capacity of over thirty thousand beds). Recently, however, there has been a flurry of small hotel construction on the West Bank. These hotels cater mainly to independent travelers and archaeologists working in the area.

In 1976, the Council of Ministers issued Decree 134 designating Luxor a tourist zone, and requiring that all new construction be approved by the Ministry of Tourism. Two main rules of the order state that:

- No urban or hotel development shall take place on the West Bank of the Nile, except for the relocation of people living above or near tombs.
- Environmental protection/conservation zones shall be established around the monuments on both East and West Banks.

These rules have been applied arbitrarily: in some cases, construction is allowed close to the monuments; in others, buildings so situated are demolished when built illegally. This construction does not directly affect KV, but it has had a detrimental effect on other parts of the West Bank, particularly the area around its memorial temples. The first rule, referring to the relocation of people living close to the tombs, has been a contentious issue for many years. Several unsuccessful attempts have been made over the last century to move the inhabitants of Qurna, and recently, the Qurnawis have been moved to a new town in the northern part of Thebes and the old Qurna villages have been demolished.

> A more balanced interpretation of the archaeological past requires a management plan for the Luxor/West Bank archaeological zone which is sympathetic to the view that the ancient dynastic cemeteries were never the deserted places which notions of a national park or an open-air-museum attempt to invoke.
> Kees van der Spek, 2006[3]

Due to its importance to the overall economy of Egypt, Luxor has been the focus of many planning initiatives (fig. 35). Twenty years of planning for the future of Luxor have produced at least twelve separate plans for the city. These cover such diverse issues as poverty eradication, job creation, heritage protection, tourism, and urban planning. What they all have in common is a policy of segregation and specialization of districts and activities. One such concept is the goal of declaring Luxor an 'open-air museum' or 'heritage zone.' This is a principal goal of plan 12 in the list below, proposed by Abt Associates and being implemented in Luxor today. The plan has been actively promoted for the last five years, and its implementation is resulting in further isolation of visitors from the local community and the creation of 'enclave' tourism. Despite the fact that the stated goals of many of these plans and initiatives are to protect the cultural heritage, promote international tourism, and further the interests of the local community, it is only the second of these that has regularly received attention, and its primary goal has been to increase tourist numbers, not to properly manage their impact on Luxor's natural, social, and archaeological environment.

These projects require a high level of cooperation among stakeholders if they are to be successful, and should not be considered only on individual merit. Each project's broader implications for the community, the heritage, and the future of Luxor must be taken into account.

| |
|---|
| 1979: Shankland Cox Partnership. *Luxor-Ancient Thebes. A Report to UNESCO* |
| 1981: P. Mora, G. Torraca, E. Schwartzbaum, E. Smith. *Luxor West Bank Visitor Management Study: Possible Impact of Increased Tourist Numbers on the Tombs of the West Bank at Luxor.* ICCROM Mission Report: ICCROM, Rome |
| Arthur D. Little International, Inc., in association with Shankland Cox Partnership, William R. Fothergill, Sherif M. El-Hakim, and Associates. *Study on Visitor Management and Associated Investment on the West Bank of the Nile at Luxor*, interim report, 2 vols. Presented to the Ministry of Tourism and Civil Aviation. |
| 1987: Ministry of Housing. *Al-Imtidad al-'umrani li-madinat al-Uqsur* |
| General Organization for Physical Planning (GOPP). *Detailed Planning for the First Phase of Thebes New City* (in Arabic, undated) |
| High Council for the City of Luxor. *Luxor 21. Schedule for Development and Growth* (in Arabic, undated) |
| 1993: GOPP (Engineering and Consulting Office, APCO). *The Physical Extension of the City of Luxor*, fifth report, final report (in Arabic) |
| 1994: Luxor City Council/Engineering Consulting. *Mashru' dirasa tawatin ahali al-Gurna fi mantiqa al-taref al-gadida gharb madinat al-Uqsur* |
| 1995: Camp Dresser & McKee International Inc. *Secondary Cities Project, City of Luxor, Environmental Scoping Report* (Arabic & English) |
| 1994: Ministry of Housing. *Preliminary Report on the Conservation of the Cultural Heritage of Luxor* (in Arabic) |
| 1999: Ministry of Housing/United Nations Programme for Development. *Comprehensive Development for the City of Luxor Project, 1996–2003* |
| 2000: Abt Associates Inc and Ministry of Housing, Utilities and Urban Communities. *The Comprehensive Development of the City of Luxor, 2000* |

Fig. 35. History of urban planning proposals in Luxor.

## Tourism in the Valley of the Kings

The Valley of the Kings is by far the most visited SCA site in the Luxor area. (Karnak and Deir al-Bahari are the two runners-up.) Precise data is not available, but it would be safe to say that, of the tourists visiting cultural heritage attractions in the city, 90 percent visit KV. The site appears on almost all tourist itineraries and independent travelers invariably select the site for a visit. The figures for 2004 (table 10) show that 1.8 million visitors came to KV, an average of 5,000 per day. This is an increase of almost 40 percent over the attendance figures for 2003. Some of this reflects a recovery from the slump in tourism that followed 9/11, but the underlying trend is for continued growth.

## Tourist Statistics

|  | 2000 | 2001 | 2002 | 2003 | 2004 |
|---|---|---|---|---|---|
| January | 204,434 | 157,034 | 77,468 | 142,448 | 173,517 |
| February | 87,876 | 186,767 | 111,298 | 135,948 | 185,326 |
| March | 186,431 | 186,364 | 128,461 | 108,135 | 199,088 |
| April | 178,434 | 166,260 | 113,321 | 60,931 | 190,274 |
| May | 120,068 | 102,029 | 78,583 | 47,486 | 129,840 |
| June | 74,621 | 65,311 | 48,089 | 45,370 | 86,862 |
| July | 81,471 | 78,393 | 67,574 | 74,999 | 109,441 |
| August | 109,409 | 98,772 | 93,236 | 118,663 | 143,300 |
| September | 121,752 | 96,102 | 18,365 | 122,619 | 138,000 |
| October | 166,485 | 72,232 | 135,393 | 159,133 | 190,958 |
| November | 155,944 | 50,166 | 16,950 | 161,273 | 175,913 |
| December | 118,469 | 58,399 | 121,533 | 154,532 | 136,171 |
| Totals | 1,605,394 | 1,317,829 | 1,010,271 | 1,331,537 | 1,858,690 |
| % Change |  | -17.91% | -23.34% | 31.80% | 39.59% |

Table 8. KV visitor numbers by month, 2000–2004

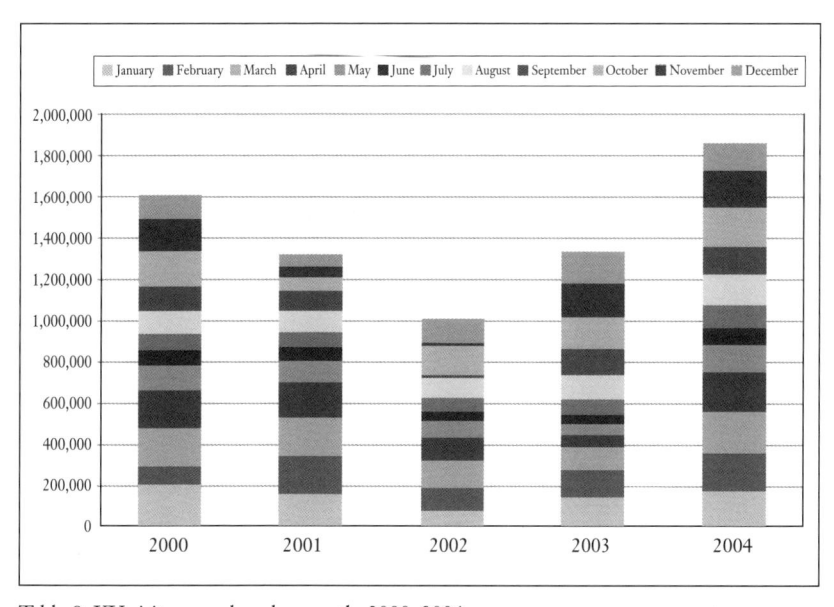

Table 9. KV visitor numbers by month, 2000–2004

Tourism in the Valley of the Kings

| Month | Egyptian | Foreign | Total |
|---|---|---|---|
| January | 19,927 | 153,590 | 173,517 |
| February | 18,302 | 167,024 | 185,326 |
| March | 10,462 | 188,626 | 199,088 |
| April | 7,169 | 183,105 | 190,274 |
| May | 1,817 | 128,023 | 129,840 |
| June | 1,462 | 85,400 | 86,862 |
| July | 2,440 | 107,001 | 109,441 |
| August | 3,511 | 139,789 | 143,300 |
| September | 2,624 | 135,376 | 138,000 |
| October | 1,683 | 189,275 | 190,958 |
| November | 5,463 | 170,450 | 175,913 |
| December | 6,478 | 129,693 | 136,171 |
| Total | 81,338 | 1,777,352 | 1,858,690 |
| Average Daily Figure | | | 5,092 |

Table 10. KV Visitor numbers, Egyptian and foreign, 2004

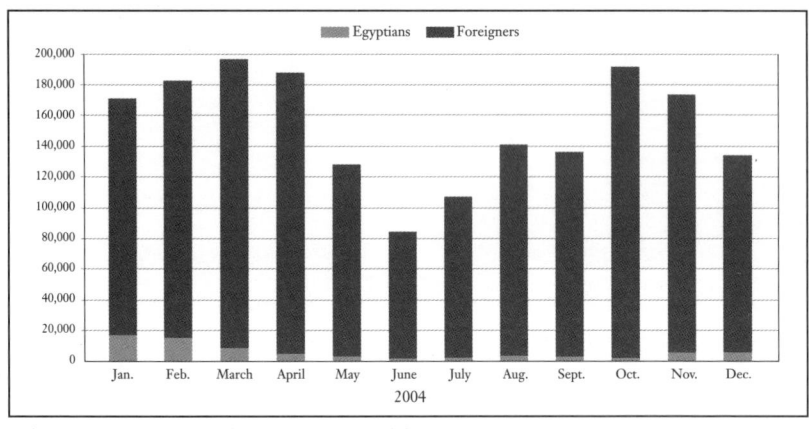

Table 11. KV visitor numbers, Egyptian and foreign, 2004

## Effects of Tourism

The Valley of the Kings has been dramatically altered in the last century. Mass tourism has had a huge impact on its physical and natural environment. The changes made to accommodate the rise in visitors have been substantial. These include:
- The widening of roads and pathways
- The construction of shelters, benches, rest houses, and toilets
- The provision of cafeterias, security points, and offices
- The erection of signage

In planning for tourism in the Valley of the Kings, we must assume that visitor numbers will continue to increase annually. Indeed, the Ministry of Tourism has stated that its goal is to have visitor numbers double and even triple within the next ten years. To prevent irreversible damage to the monuments, a KV management plan must assume that the current rate of seven thousand visitors per day in KV will reach fifteen to twenty thousand per day by 2015. Therefore, facilities designed today must have extra capacity built in at the design stage.

Fig. 36a and b. Entrance to KV, ca. 1910 and 1996. © Victor Loret, © Theban Mapping Project

# 4  Stakeholder Surveys

One of the first tasks in the initial research for the Valley of the Kings Masterplan was to identify and consult the stakeholders of the site. This had never been attempted at an Egyptian heritage site. The stakeholders, listed below, have an interest or stake in any future development of the Valley, and the inclusion of their views regarding any future development is essential for its successful implementation. Consequently, a comprehensive list of stakeholders was identified, and from this a two-stage strategy was devised to solicit their views. In Stage One, we targeted visitors, tour guides, site staff, and West Bank communities with ties to KV. In Stage Two, a questionnaire was placed on the Theban Mapping Project website at www.thebanmappingproject.com to collect the views of previous visitors to KV.

In 2007, the Getty Conservation Institute (GCI) conducted further work in this field in the Valley of the Queens (QV), using methodology similar to the KV survey. Some of their results are included in the tables and statistics below, and are identified as coming from their survey.

## Stakeholder Survey Stage One: Valley of the Kings Site Survey

In June 2004, we commissioned the Social Research Center (SRC) of the American University in Cairo to conduct a survey of the selected stakeholders.

## Methodology

*Valley of the Kings Stakeholders*

Fourteen major stakeholder groups were identified, and for the purposes of our survey the groups were subdivided by types.

- Archaeologists and scholars
- Egyptian Environmental Affairs Authority (EEAA)
- Tourists
  - Red Sea day trippers
  - Nile cruisers
  - Hotel groups
  - Solo/Individual/Backpackers
  - Repeat travelers
  - Egyptian nationals
- Tourism professionals
  - Tour operators
  - Tour guides
  - Taxi drivers
  - Bus drivers
- Merchants
- Site staff
  - Inspectors
  - Maintenance staff
  - Guards
  - Cleaners
  - Toilet staff
- Supreme Council of Antiquities (SCA)/Ministry of Culture
- Ministry of Tourism
- Security/Military
- Luxor City Council
- Local community
- World Heritage Organizations—UNESCO/ICOMOS, Getty Conservation Institute (GCI)
- World Monuments Fund (WMF)
- Donors/Sponsors

*Objectives of the Study*

The Valley of the Kings stakeholder consultation collected the opinions of tourists, tour operators, local vendors, KV staff, and local communities on the following issues facing the site:
- Congestion and crowding
- Quantity and quality of visitor services
- Maintenance
- Management
- Safety

The findings of the study were intended to assist in the design of the planned KV Visitors Center and the completion of the Valley of the Kings Masterplan.

**Study Design**

The study utilized both quantitative and qualitative approaches. The quantitative approach included self-administered interviews with visitors and tour guides. The study was conducted over the course of five days, from 13–19 June 2004. The interviews were conducted throughout the opening hours of the site (both morning and afternoon). A total of 610 interviews with visitors representing forty-four different nationalities were conducted. In addition, 208 interviews were conducted with tourist guides. The qualitative approach consisted of six focus-group discussions. Two focus-group discussions were conducted with merchants, two with KV staff, and two with local community residents.

*Study Instruments*

Two questionnaires were developed for the quantitative study: one for visitors, the other for guides. The questionnaires collected information on:
- Background characteristics (sex, age, nationality, etc.)
- Perceptions of visitor services available at KV (shops, toilets, 'tuf-tuf' train, parking, access to tombs, etc.)
- Suggestions to improve visits to KV

The questionnaires were developed by the TMP and the SRC and reviewed by Dr. Zahi Hawass of the Supreme Council of Antiquities. In addition to the English and Arabic versions, the visitor questionnaire

Fig. 37. Stakeholder survey staff. © Theban Mapping Project

was translated into French, German, and Italian. The GCI questionnaire (2007) included surveys in English, French, German, Russian, and Japanese.

The discussions with the focus groups covered the following points:
- The connection of participants to KV
- Participants' opinions on the benefits and problems with KV
- Suggestions to improve the present situation at KV

Three interviewers were involved in each focus group discussion: a supervisor, a moderator, and a note-taker. The discussions were recorded using a standard cassette recorder.

*Fieldwork*

Recruitment of Staff

Six interviewers and two supervisors were recruited to work alongside the conservation manager of the TMP. Fieldworkers and office editors were selected from those with past experience in such surveys.

## Training

Training of the interviewers took place in the first week of June 2004. The training course consisted of instructions regarding interviewing techniques, field procedures, and a detailed review of items on the questionnaires. An orientation session was held on the West Bank in Luxor prior to the start of fieldwork; this consisted of a tour of the antiquities area, an introduction to the Valley of the Kings, and a brief presentation regarding the issues affecting the site.

## Main Fieldwork

The field staff consisted of one team. During fieldwork, the team was arranged as necessary for quantitative and qualitative studies. Two supervisors were recruited for quality assurance. The fieldwork was conducted 13–19 June, 2004. Table 12 represents the number of completed questionnaires by language over the fieldwork period. (The 2007 GCI visitor survey in the Valley of the Queens was conducted in English, French, German, Russian, and Japanese.)

|         | June 13 | June 14 | June 15 | June 16 | June 17 | Total | %      |
|---------|---------|---------|---------|---------|---------|-------|--------|
| Arabic  | 42      | 0       | 2       | 9       | 1       | 54    | 8.85   |
| English | 87      | 74      | 21      | 69      | 28      | 279   | 45.74  |
| French  | 23      | 32      | 7       | 7       | 23      | 92    | 15.08  |
| German  | 27      | 30      | 20      | 19      | 20      | 116   | 19.02  |
| Italian | 0       | 0       | 34      | 35      | 0       | 69    | 11.31  |
| Total   | 179     | 136     | 84      | 139     | 72      | 610   | 100.00 |

Table 12. Completed questionnaires by language, 13–17 June 2004

### Data Processing

After the original data collection and field editing of questionnaires for completeness and consistency, experienced editors were recruited to carry out office editing and coding.

Data entry and verification started after one week of office data processing. The process of data entry—including editing, cleaning, and one 100 percent reentry—was facilitated using PCs and a computer database program developed specially for this survey. Data processing operations for the questionnaires were completed by the end of June 2004. The focus group discussions were analyzed by a specialist in qualitative approaches.

Quality Control Measures

The quality of the data collected was ensured by:
- Selecting qualified field staff
- Field editing (by supervisors)
- Field checks by general supervisors
- Office editing
- Reentry of 100 percent of questionnaires

*Limitations of the Study*

Because of time constraints, the study was conducted in mid-June 2004. The timing and limited nature of the survey may affect the survey results in the following ways:
- There are fewer visitors at this time compared to other months in the year, especially the cooler winter months (table 14a). The lower numbers of visitors influences visitor opinions regarding the adequacy and efficiency of available services at KV.
- A disagreement between guide and visitor opinion may occur. The guides' opinion reflects the satisfaction with services provided throughout the whole year, while the visitors' opinion is based only on one visit (in the majority of cases).
- A slight bias may result because this is a one-time survey. A less biased study design would have to represent all the months (or at least seasons) of the year.

Table 13 represents the visitor numbers during the period of the study and actual sample size and sample fraction of the visitors during each day of the fieldwork.

| Type | June 13 | June 14 | June 15 | June 16 | June 17 |
|---|---|---|---|---|---|
| Adult foreigners | 3162 | 3134 | 3842 | 2200 | 1300 |
| Student foreigners | 150 | 212 | 140 | 150 | 159 |
| Adult Egyptians | 72 | 74 | 37 | 28 | 46 |
| Student Egyptians | 2 | 22 | 7 | 9 | 0 |
| Visitor numbers/day | 3386 | 3442 | 4026 | 2387 | 150 |
| Visitors surveyed | 179 | 136 | 84 | 139 | 72 |
| Sample percentages | 5.29% | 3.95% | 2.09% | 5.82% | 4.78% |

Table 13. KV ticket sales, 13–17 June 2004

## Characteristics of Respondents

For all respondents, the study questionnaire included questions about the date and time of the interview, age and gender of the respondents, and size of the group they came with. The guide questionnaire included additional questions about languages fluently spoken, education, residence, and work experience. In contrast, the visitor questionnaire included questions about the number of visits to Egypt, the number of visits to KV, duration of visit to Egypt and to KV, type of travel (independent or with an organized group), the number of people accompanying the visitor, and the method of transportation to KV.

*Characteristics of Guides*
- **Gender:** The majority of guides were male (92%).
- **Age:** More than half of the guides (53%) were in their thirties; approximately 27% are younger, and 20% are older. The mean age of the sample is approximately thirty-four.
- **Languages fluently spoken:** More than 64% of the sampled guides speak English, 26% speak German, 21% speak French or Spanish, 13% speak Italian, and small percentages speak other languages.
- **Education:** Most of the guides have graduate or postgraduate studies in hotels and tourism (56%), languages (43%), or archaeology (9%).
- **Place of residence:** Many of the guides (38%) live in Luxor, 40% in Cairo or Giza, 13% in the Red Sea governorate or Aswan, and approximately 6% in Lower Egypt.
- **Work experience:** More than a quarter of the guides (26%) have work experience of less than five years; approximately 40% of them have ten or more years' work experience. The mean number of years of work experience is eight.
- **Number of visitors to KV per guide:** Many of the groups are small. Approximately two-fifths of the groups (39%) have fewer than ten members, and about one-fifth have thirty or more visitors. The mean group size was approximately seventeen visitors.

*Characteristics of Visitors*
- **Country of origin:** The distribution of sampled visitors according to their country of origin shows that the majority were Europeans,

and that Germany and Great Britain had the largest shares (17% and 14%, respectively).
- **Gender:** The results show that the sample is evenly distributed by gender (47% of the visitors are male and 53% are female).
- **Age:** The majority of visitors (about 70%) were in the range 20–49 years old. Only 4% are less than twenty years of old, and a quarter were fifty or more years old.
- **Number of visits to Egypt:** More than four-fifths (82%) of the visitors were visiting Egypt for the first time and only about 18% had visited Egypt more than once. The mean number of visits is 1.7.
- **Number of visits to KV:** Approximately 89% of the visitors were visiting KV for the first time and only 11% had visited it before. The mean number of KV visits is 1.5.
- **Alone or with family/friends:** Most of the visitors were visiting Egypt with their families or friends (47% and 40%, respectively). The mean number of persons accompanying the visitor is 5.4. Only 13% of the visitors came alone.

Fig. 38. Visitors completing survey. © Theban Mapping Project

| Background Characteristics of Visitors |||||||
|---|---|---|---|---|---|---|
| Country of Origin | TMP, 2004 (%) | GCI, 2007 (%) || Country of Origin | TMP, 2004 (%) | GCI, 2007 (%) ||
| | June | June | Feb | | June | June | Feb |
| Germany | 16.9 | 1.3 | 7.1 | Argentina | 0.5 | | |
| Great Britain | 14.1 | 33.7 | 18.8 | Colombia | 0.5 | | |
| Italy | 11.8 | 11.9 | 0.7 | Denmark | 0.5 | | |
| France | 10.8 | 8.4 | 17.0 | Iraq | 0.5 | | |
| Egypt | 7.2 | - | - | Malaysia | 0.5 | | |
| Australia | 4.3 | 2.5 | 0.8 | Sweden | 0.5 | | |
| Netherlands | 4.3 | 0.8 | 4.1 | Yugoslavia | 0.5 | | |
| USA | 4.1 | 11.1 | 12.2 | China | 0.3 | | |
| Spain | 3.4 | 3.9 | 0.7 | Greece | 0.3 | | |
| Belgium | 3.1 | 3.2 | 4.1 | Lebanon | 0.3 | | |
| New Zealand | 2.5 | | | Poland | 0.3 | | |
| Austria | 1.5 | | | Russia | 0.3 | 0.4 | 7.3 |
| Ireland | 1.5 | | | Bulgaria | 0.2 | | |
| Korea | 1.3 | | | Canada | 0.2 | | |
| Switzerland | 1.3 | | | Gambia | 0.2 | | |
| India | 1.0 | | | Kenya | 0.2 | | |
| Slovakia | 0.8 | | | Lithuania | 0.2 | | |
| South Africa | 0.8 | | | Morocco | 0.2 | | |
| Japan | 0.7 | 0.7 | 4.8 | Pakistan | 0.2 | | |
| Mexico | 0.7 | | | Portugal | 0.2 | | |
| Saudi Arabia | 0.7 | | | Serbia | 0.2 | | |
| Taiwan | 0.7 | | | Ukraine | 0.2 | | |

Table 14a. Background characteristics of visitors

- **Independent or with organized group:** More than four-fifths (83%) of the visitors come to Egypt as part of an organized group. The mean size of the group is 18.8 people. Approximately 17% of the visitors came to Egypt independently.
- **Duration of visit to Egypt:** Almost all visitors (97%) spent less than three weeks in Egypt. The mean duration of their visit was approximately twelve days.
- **Duration of visit to Luxor:** Approximately two-thirds of visitors spent only one or two days in Luxor. The mean duration of their visit to Luxor is 3.4 days.

| Background Characteristics of Visitors ||||
|---|---|---|---|
| **Gender** | | **Age Category** | |
| Male | 46.8 | <20 | 3.9 |
| Female | 53.2 | 20–29 | 32.7 |
| | | 30–29 | 21.5 |
| **Number of Visits to Egypt** | | 40–49 | 16.8 |
| 1 | 82.0 | 50+ | 25.0 |
| 2 | 10.0 | **Number in Group** | |
| 3 | 3.0 | <10 | 31.6 |
| 4+ | 5.0 | 10–19 | 21.3 |
| Mean = 1.7 | | 20–29 | 24.2 |
| **Number of Visits to KV** | | 30–39 | 15.2 |
| 1 | 89.0 | 40–49 | 5.1 |
| 2 | 6.2 | 50+ | 2.7 |
| 3 | 1.6 | Mean =18.8 | |
| 4+ | 3.1 | **Duration of Visit to Egypt (days)** | |
| Mean = 1.5 | | | |
| **Alone or with Family/Friends** | | <7 | 4.1 |
| Alone | 13.0 | 7–13 | 44.5 |
| Family | 47.3 | 14–20 | 48.8 |
| Friends | 39.7 | 21–27 | 0.7 |
| **Number of Relatives/Friends** | | 28+ | 2.0 |
| 1 | 23.5 | Mean =12.1 | |
| 2 | 40.0 | **Duration of Visit to Luxor (days)** | |
| 3 | 10.2 | 1 | 33.3 |
| 4 + | 26.3 | 2 | 33.1 |
| Mean = 5.4 | | 3 | 12.3 |
| **Independent or Organized Group** | | 4 | 4.4 |
| Independent | 17.0 | 5+ | 16.9 |
| Organized group | 83.0 | Mean = 3.4 | |

Table 14b. Background characteristics of visitors

In its 2007 survey of visitors to the Valley of the Queens, GCI asked which sites each of its interviewees had visited on their current trip to Luxor (based upon two samples, one in February and one in June 2007, each with 748 international visitors participating):
- Valley of the Kings          90%
- Karnak Temple                88%
- Luxor Temple                 82%

- Deir al-Bahari           61%
- Colossi of Memnon        54%
- Luxor Museum             38%
- Tombs of the Nobles      32%
- Deir al-Medina           16%
- Medinet Habu             15%
- Ramesseum                14%
- Mummification Museum     13%

(Since the survey was conducted in the Valley of the Queens, 100% of the participants were visitors to that site.)

## Perceptions of the Valley of the Kings

Visitors and guides were asked their opinion of services inside KV. Both the visitor questionnaire and the guide questionnaire collected respondents' views concerning shopping, transportation, management of visits to tombs, toilets, and crowding inside KV.

|  | Visits to KV One | Visits to KV 2+ | Visitors Ind. | Visitors Group | Total | Guides |
|---|---|---|---|---|---|---|
| **Is the shopping area in an appropriate location?** | | | | | | |
| Yes | 81.6% | 75.4% | 83.0% | 80.3% | 80.9% | 57.5% |
| No | 18.4 | 24.6 | 17.0 | 19.7 | 19.1 | 42.5 |
| **Is the number of shops appropriate?** | | | | | | |
| Yes | 81.1 | 74.6 | 80.2 | 80.3 | 80.4 | 89.9 |
| No | 18.9 | 25.4 | 19.8 | 19.7 | 19.6 | 10.1 |
| **Is the merchandise available appropriate?** | | | | | | |
| Yes | 80.9 | 78.6 | 82.6 | 80.1 | 80.6 | 60.2 |
| No | 19.1 | 21.4 | 17.4 | 19.9 | 19.4 | 39.8 |
| **Is the size of shops appropriate?** | | | | | | |
| Yes | 82.9 | 81.0 | 80.7 | 82.9 | 82.7 | 60.8 |
| No | 17.1 | 19.0 | 19.3 | 17.1 | 17.3 | 39.2 |
| **Did you enjoy the shopping area?** | | | | | | |
| Yes | 71.1 | 64.4 | 67.4 | 70.9 | 70.4 | - |
| No | 28.9 | 35.6 | 32.6 | 29.1 | 29.6 | - |
| **Do you think that the shopping area is appropriate?** | | | | | | |
| Yes | - | - | - | - | - | 42.2 |
| No | - | - | - | - | - | 57.8 |

Table 15. Opinions about retail outlets at KV

*Shopping*
Table 15 presents the visitors' and guides' views regarding the shopping area, number of shops, availability of merchandise, size of shops, and the experience of shopping in KV. The findings indicate that the visitors were more satisfied with the shopping situation in KV than were the guides. Approximately four-fifths of visitors found the shopping area, number of shops, availability of merchandise, and the size of shops to be appropriate. Despite this result, only 70 percent of visitors enjoyed the shopping area. Regarding guides' opinion on shopping at KV, slightly more than 40 percent of guides found the shopping area appropriate. These results imply that satisfaction with shopping area at KV is related to the length of experience with KV. Guides, with more experience than visitors, are less satisfied; visitors who visited KV more than once are also less satisfied with shopping in KV than first-time visitors.

*Transportation*
Visitors were asked how they came to KV on the day of the survey. Table 16 indicates that the majority (71.3%) came by bus and that 11% used a taxi. A noticeable percentage (17.7%) used other means of transportation such as bicycles, donkeys, or private vehicles. The results also indicate that visitors who traveled independently are more likely to use a taxi (34.6%) or other means of transportation (35.6%) than a bus (29.8%).

Both visitors and guides were asked their opinion on the bus parking location and the 'tuf-tuf' (a small train used inside KV at the time of

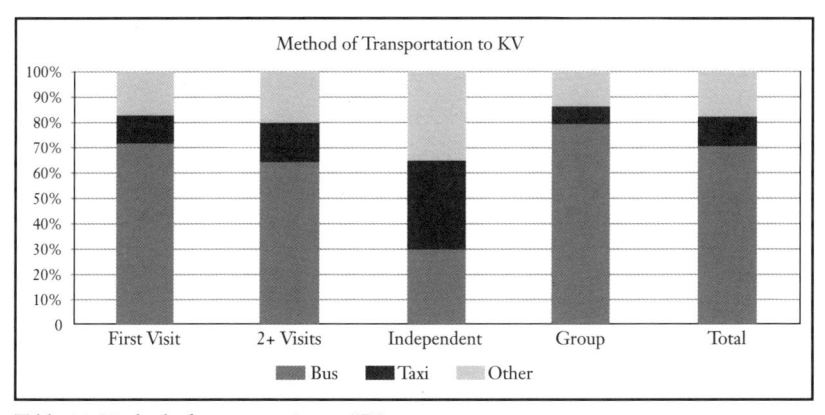

Table 16. Method of transportation to KV

the survey). Table 17 presents these results. The findings indicate that guides had more problems with transportation than visitors. When asked about the suitability of the bus parking location, slightly more than half of guides and 92% of visitors said it was in a suitable position. Around 75% of guides and 35% of visitors said that the parking lot has an environmental impact on KV (pollution and/or noise). The results also indicate that the majority of guides (77.8%) and visitors (94.3%) saw the 'tuf-tuf' train as an appropriate service for KV.

Despite these results, 53.8% of guides and 11.1% of visitors thought that the appearance of the 'tuf-tuf' train is not appropriate for KV. Moreover, slightly less than a quarter of visitors and two-thirds of guides said that the 'tuf-tuf' train caused pollution and/or noise in KV. Minor differentials are observed in the visitors' responses by the number of visits to KV and the type of visitor (alone or with a group).

|  | Visits to KV Once | 2+ | Visitors Ind. | Group | Total | Guides |
|---|---|---|---|---|---|---|
| **Is the bus park location appropriate?** | | | | | | |
| Yes | 92.8% | 88.7% | 88.6% | 93.1% | 92.4% | 52.1% |
| No | 7.2 | 11.3 | 11.4 | 6.9 | 7.6 | 47.9 |
| **Does the bus park cause noise and pollution?** | | | | | | |
| Pollution | 28.5 | 32.2 | 29.8 | 29.0 | 28.9 | 58.1 |
| Noise | 15.4 | 18.6 | 11.7 | 16.9 | 15.4 | 49.7 |
| No | 65.2 | 59.3 | 63.8 | 64.4 | 65.2 | 26.7 |
| **Is the 'tuf-tuf' train an appropriate service for KV?** | | | | | | |
| Yes | 94.8 | 90.5 | 94.0 | 94.2 | 94.8 | 77.8 |
| No | 5.2 | 9.5 | 6.0 | 5.8 | 5.2 | 22.2 |
| **Is the appearance of the 'tuf-tuf' train appropriate?** | | | | | | |
| Yes | 82.5 | 88.8 | 88.7 | 89.6 | 46.2 | |
| No | 17.5 | 11.2 | 11.3 | 10.4 | 53.8 | |
| **Does the 'tuf-tuf' train cause pollution and noise?** | | | | | | |
| Pollution | 15.1 | 18.6 | 11.6 | 16.6 | 15.1 | 50.5 |
| Noise | 12.1 | 10.2 | 11.6 | 12.4 | 12.1 | 50.5 |
| No | 77.7 | 78.0 | 80.0 | 77.0 | 77.7 | 33.7 |

Table 17. Opinions about transportation at KV

*Management of Visits to Tombs*

Visitors were asked about the number of tombs they visited on the day of the survey and the time they spent inside KV. Table 18 shows that the majority of visitors (69%) visited three tombs and around one-fifth of visitors visited four or more tombs. The mean number of tombs visited was 3.35. However, repeat visitors were more likely to enter four or more tombs compared with first-time visitors (30.2% compared to 20.9%).

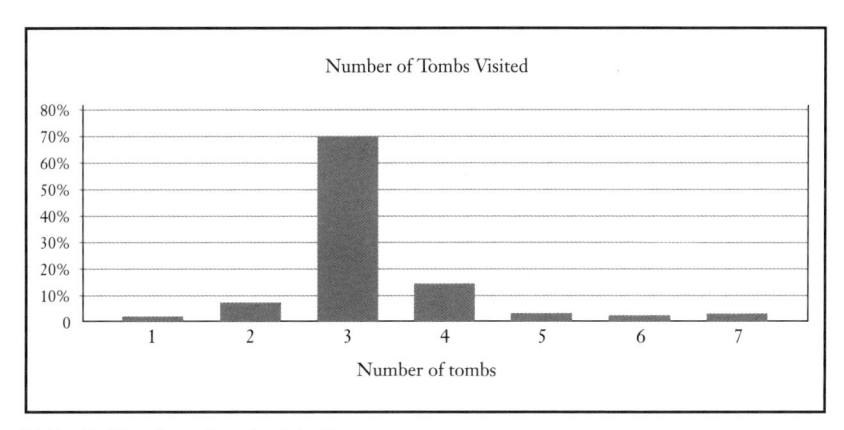

Table 18. Number of tombs visited

Slightly less than one-third of visitors spent between ninety minutes and two hours in their visit to KV. In addition, table 19 reveals that less than 2% stayed less than half an hour and 17.2% stayed more than two hours. On average, the visitor stayed 108.6 minutes inside KV.

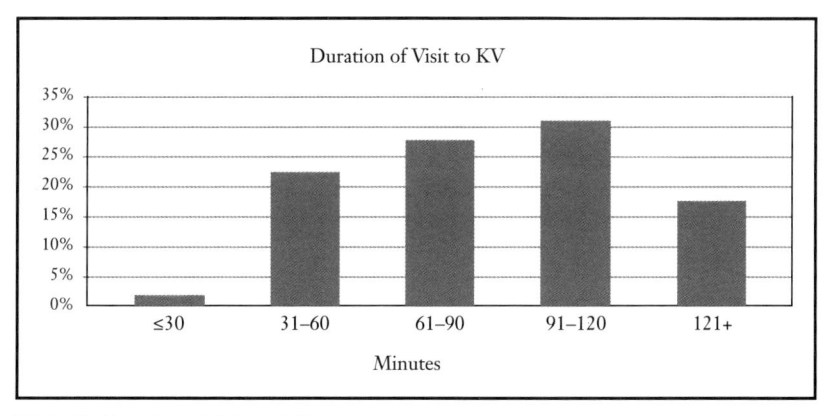

Table 19. Duration of visit to KV

|  | Visits to KV |  | Visitors |  |  | Guides |
|---|---|---|---|---|---|---|
|  | One | 2+ | Ind. | Group | Total |  |
| Are the opening hours of the tombs appropriate? ||||||||
| Yes | 93.6% | 91.4% | 92.9% | 93.5% | 93.4% | 83.9% |
| No | 6.4 | 8.6 | 7.1 | 6.5 | 6.6 | 16.1 |
| Are the tombs crowded? ||||||||
| Yes | 45.2 | 60.3 | 34.4 | 49.3 | 46.8 | 86.2 |
| No | 54.8 | 39.7 | 65.6 | 50.7 | 53.2 | 13.8 |
| Were the tombs hot and humid or comfortable? ||||||||
| Comfortable | 45.1 | 53.1 | 63.0 | 42.5 | 46.0 | 13.7 |
| Hot | 43.0 | 34.4 | 28.0 | 44.9 | 42.0 | 68.4 |
| Humid | 25.2 | 25.0 | 17.0 | 27.0 | 25.2 | 55.3 |

Table 20. Opinions on visit to KV

Guides and visitors were asked about the opening hours, the number of visitors, and the environment inside the tombs in KV. Around four-fifths of guides and slightly more than 90% of visitors said that the opening hours of the tombs were appropriate (table 20). When asked their opinion on the numbers present in the tombs, 86.2% of guides and 46.8% of visitors said the tombs were crowded. The internal climate in the tombs was considered uncomfortable (hot and/or humid) by 86.3% of guides and 54% of visitors.

*Toilets*

The toilets in KV at the time of the survey consisted of one mobile porta-loo. Visitors and guides were asked questions regarding the suitability of the system, the location of the porta-loo, and whether they experienced queues at the toilets. The findings (table 21) indicate that the guides had more complaints about the toilets than the visitors had. Partially, this result is due to the time of the survey. The survey was conducted in June, a month when the number of visitors is low. Two-thirds of the guides and one-quarter of the visitors found the porta-loos and their location unsuitable. The majority of guides (86.5%) and one-third of visitors experienced queues at the toilets. Again, this result is partly due to visitor opinion being based on their limited experience (and the day of their visit), while guides' answers reflect a longer experience of the site.

|  | Visits to KV | | Visitors | | | |
|  | One | 2+ | Ind. | Group | Total | Guides |
|---|---|---|---|---|---|---|
| **Is the porta-loo toilet suitable?** | | | | | | |
| Yes | 74.5% | 61.8% | 78.4% | 71.8% | 73.1% | 34.2% |
| No | 25.5 | 38.2 | 21.6 | 28.2 | 26.9 | 65.8 |
| **Is the location of the toilet suitable?** | | | | | | |
| Yes | 80.5 | 74.1 | 76.7 | 80.6 | 79.8 | 38.3 |
| No | 19.5 | 25.9 | 23.3 | 19.4 | 20.2 | 61.7 |
| **Is there a queue of persons for the toilet?** | | | | | | |
| Yes | 32.2 | 41.5 | 38.4 | 32.0 | 33.2 | 86.5 |
| No | 67.8 | 58.5 | 61.6 | 68.0 | 66.8 | 13.5 |

Table 21. Opinions of toilet facilities in KV

In 2009, the location of this porta-loo was changed from adjacent to KV 5 to the pathway leading to KV 1. We have no data indicating that this move has had an impact on visitor responses, but since neither the porta-loo itself nor the long queues of tourists has changed, any impact is probably minimal.

*Visits to Tombs*

Guides were asked about the tombs they visited on the day of survey to assess the tombs more likely to be visited and, therefore, under pressure from visitor numbers. The majority of guides (82.9%) visited the tomb of Ramesses V/VI (KV 9) (table 22). Two-thirds of guides (65.2%) visited the tomb of Ramesses III (KV 11), and slightly more than half (51.9%) visited the tomb of Ramesses IX (KV 6). More than a third of guides (38.1%) visited Ramesses IV (KV 2). Other tombs were visited by minor percentages of guides. Over 7% of visitors claimed to have visited closed tombs, probably because of misremembered tomb numbers or pharaohs' names.

Since 2008, guides have been prohibited from accompanying their groups into KV tombs and no lecturing inside is allowed. Tourists are simply handed the standard three-tomb ticket by their guide, who offers some recommendations about which tombs are available (usually KV 2, 6, and 11—the closest and easiest to access) and given one hour in which to visit them and return to the shelter in the center of the Valley. In addition, KV 9 now requires a separate ticket (LE 80) to enter, as does KV 62 (Tutankhamun, LE 100).

| KV 9 | Ramesses V and VI | 82.9 % |
|---|---|---|
| KV 11 | Ramesses III | 65.2 % |
| KV 6 | Ramesses IX | 51.9 % |
| KV 2 | Ramesses IV | 38.1 % |
| KV 15 | Seti II | 16.0 % |
| KV 16 | Ramesses I | 8.8 % |
| KV 62 | Tutankhamun | 8.3 % |
| KV 14 | Tawosret and Setnakht | 6.1 % |
| KV 1 | Ramesses VII | 3.3 % |
| KV 4 | Ramesses XI (currently closed) | 2.2 % |
| KV 43 | Thutmose IV | 2.2 % |
| KV 5 | Sons of Ramesses II (currently closed) | 1.1 % |
| KV 17 | Seti I (currently closed) | 1.1 % |
| KV 35 | Amenhotep II (currently closed) | 1.1 % |
| KV 3 | Son of Ramesses III (currently closed) | 0.6 % |
| KV 8 | Merenptah (currently closed) | 0.6 % |
| KV 10 | Amenmesse (currently closed) | 0.6 % |
| KV 47 | Siptah | 0.6 % |

Table 22. Tombs visited by guides during survey

Table 23 summarizes the answers of guides when asked, "What was the most enjoyable part of your group's visit to KV?" and the answers given by visitors. A significant percentage of guides and visitors gave general answers, such as "the tombs" (around 30% of visitors and 23% of guides). Complementing what was observed in table 19, Ramesses V and VI (KV 9) was mentioned by a high percentage of guides and visitors: just over half of the guides (51.8%) and about one-third of visitors (29.7%). Eight percent of visitors and 25% of guides felt that the tomb of Ramesses III was the most enjoyable part of their visit to KV. Table 19 shows that parts of KV were mentioned by some visitors but were not mentioned by guides. There were limited responses from visitors about certain surprising aspects of their experience, such as "the guides are very good," "going to the Valley by donkey," "walking around the Valley and visiting the ancient theater."

|  | Visits to KV | | Visitors | | | |
|---|---|---|---|---|---|---|
|  | Once | Two+ | Ind. | Group | Total | Guides |
| Visitor: Which part of the visit did you enjoy most today? | | | | | | |
| Guide: Which part of the visit do you think the tourists enjoyed the most? | | | | | | |
| KV 1 Ramesses VII | 0.4% | - | - | 0.5% | 0.4% | - |
| KV 2 Ramesses IV | 5.4 | 9.6 | 5.7 | 5.8 | 5.8 | 15.9 |
| KV 5 Ramesses II | 0.4 | 1.9 | - | 0.7 | 0.6 | - |
| KV 6 Ramesses IX | - | - | - | - | - | 8.7 |
| KV 7 Ramesses II | 2.5 | 1.9 | 1.1 | 2.7 | 2.4 | - |
| KV 8 Merenptah | - | - | - | - | - | 2.6 |
| KV 9 Ramesses V and VI | 30.2 | 25.0 | 20.6 | 31.6 | 29.7 | 51.8 |
| KV 10 Amenmesse | 0.2 | - | - | 0.2 | 0.2 | 2.1 |
| KV 11 Ramesses III | 8.5 | 5.8 | 8.0 | 8.2 | 8.2 | 24.6 |
| KV 14 Tawosret and Setnakht | 0.4 | - | - | 0.4 | 0.4 | 4.1 |
| KV 15 Seti II | 1.8 | 3.8 | 3.4 | 1.7 | 2.0 | 6.7 |
| KV 16 Ramesses I | 3.6 | 7.7 | 1.1 | 4.6 | 4.0 | 5.6 |
| KV 17 Seti I | 0.4 | - | - | 0.5 | 0.4 | 7.2 |
| KV 20 Thutmose II | 0.2 | - | - | 0.2 | 0.2 | 0.5 |
| KV 34 Thutmose III | - | - | - | - | - | 11.3 |
| KV 35 Amenhotep II | - | - | - | - | - | 3.1 |
| KV 43 Thutmose IV | - | - | - | - | - | 0.5 |
| KV 47 Siptah | 0.4 | - | 2.3 | - | 0.4 | 2.1 |
| KV 57 Horemheb | - | - | - | - | - | 2.1 |
| KV 62 Tutankhamun | 8.0 | 13.5 | 4.6 | 9.4 | 8.6 | 8.7 |
| Tombs in general | 31.5 | 17.3 | 40.2 | 27.7 | 29.9 | 23.6 |
| Tombs that are now closed | - | - | - | - | - | 1.5 |
| Tombs containing mummies | 0.2 | - | - | 0.2 | 0.2 | - |
| "Unspecified Ramesses tomb" | 1.1 | 1.9 | 1.1 | 1.2 | 1.2 | - |
| Reliefs and colors | 2.7 | 1.9 | 3.4 | 2.7 | 2.8 | 7.2 |
| "The walk around the Valley" | 0.2 | - | - | 0.2 | 0.2 | - |
| "Going to Valley by donkey" | 0.4 | 1.9 | 2.3 | 0.2 | 0.6 | - |
| All of the Valley | 16.1 | 17.3 | 17.2 | 15.9 | 16.1 | 10.8 |
| The guides | 1.6 | 5.8 | 4.6 | 1.4 | 2.0 | - |
| The Ramesseum | - | - | - | - | - | 2.6 |
| Boat trip to West Bank | 0.4 | - | - | 0.5 | 0.4 | - |
| Egyptian people | 0.9 | - | 1.1 | 0.7 | 0.8 | - |
| Stories and history | 0.9 | - | 3.4 | 0.2 | 0.8 | - |
| Building and design | - | 1.9 | - | 0.2 | 0.2 | - |
| "Tomb no. 3" | - | 1.9 | 1.1 | -0.2 | - | - |
| "Ancient theater" | - | 1.9 | - | 0.2 | 0.2 | - |

Table 23. Most enjoyable aspects of visit

## Stakeholder Suggestions

The final question on both the visitor and guide questionnaires was deliberately phrased as an open-ended question to allow participants to contribute their own views regarding the future direction of the Valley of the Kings. We asked, "In your opinion, how could we improve a visit to the Valley of the Kings?" The number of responses received was staggering and covered many diverse areas in the operation of the site. In order to assess these suggestions, we subdivided the responses into five main categories and one miscellaneous section:

- Visitor Services
- Site Infrastructure
- Visitor Management
- Site Information
- Tombs and Ticketing
- Miscellaneous

*Visitor Services*

Table 24 presents suggestions for improving general services in the Valley. What is overwhelmingly demanded by both guides and visitors are improved or new facilities for refreshments: a cafeteria, snack shop, or sale of cold water. In fact, 44% of the guides raised this as a particular concern, and among visitors, 25% noted the lack of any refreshment facilities. The harsh environmental conditions at the site, not only in June, when the survey took place, but also throughout the year, strongly influenced the suggestions for the improvement of the visitor experience. Furthermore, some visitors suggested making umbrellas and hats available (1.9%; whether these were to be sold or rented was not made clear.) However, it should be noted that the provision of goods and services such as drinks, umbrellas, and hats could be a lucrative source of income for vendors and the SCA alike.

Other noteworthy areas of concern included a higher profile for the Valley through promotional campaigns, the provision of enhanced medical services—which was particularly singled out by the guides (5.1%)—and the overall improvement of visitor services throughout the site.

Since 2007, many of the problems raised by tourists and guides have been addressed (not always successfully) by the SCA. The new Visitors Center, bazaar, parking area, and tramline to KV seem to have improved the visitors' experience.

|  | Visitors | Guides |
|---|---|---|
| Reopen the cafeteria to provide refreshments | 13.7% | 42.4% |
| Provide medical services | 0.3 | 5.1 |
| Improve the general services | 1.1 | 3.5 |
| Make water available | 11.3 | 2.5 |
| Improve cleaning of KV, spraying insects | 0.3 | 2.5 |
| Promotion campaign for KV | 0.5 | 0.5 |
| Sell mobile cards/film | - | 0.5 |
| Provide visitors with umbrellas and hats | 1.9 | - |
| Provide and improve transportations | 1.1 | - |
| Provide staff for services and protection | 0.5 | - |
| Reinstate the car ferry | 0.3 | - |
| Provide free tissue in toilets | 0.3 | - |

Table 24. Stakeholder suggestions: visitor services

*Site Infrastructure*
Options suggested for improving the infrastructure of the site, from both the guides' and the visitors' points of view, focused in the main on the provision of effective sun protection and clean and readily available toilets (table 25). Over 45% of the guides felt that the provision of more and/or larger rest houses and shelters would improve the visitor experience. Concern about protection from the sun was also expressed by almost one-fifth (19.4%) of the visitors. In second place was the desire for clean and accessible toilet facilities. Over one-third of guides (35.9%) mentioned this and over one-eighth (13.2%) of the visitors felt improvement was needed.

Additional concerns raised by the guides were the need to find a replacement for the 'tuf-tuf' train (8%) and the need to redesign entrance gates to deal with large numbers of visitors (3.5%). Visitors, however, were more concerned with the lighting systems in the tombs, with approximately 4% of the visitors asking for an enhanced system of illumination, compared with just half a percent of guides. This is probably due to the recently introduced guiding ban within the tombs, which means that the guides no longer enter the tombs. The effect of this ban is felt by about 1% of visitors, who suggested that an audio guide system be made available for the tombs—something for which, unsurprisingly, no guide felt a need.

Finally, a more radical solution was suggested by some to negate the impact of large numbers of visitors to the site. This was the provision of replicas of key tombs or a complete copy of the entire Valley. The kind of replicas that might be built, the choice of tombs to be replicated, and the location of such replicas have been much discussed in recent years. Factum Arte, a Spanish cultural preservation firm, presented an exact replica of KV 62 (Tutankhamun) to the SCA in 2012, proposing to install it on the West Bank, near Carter House, in 2013–14. A decision on their proposal has not been reached yet.

Since 2007, small, shaded seating areas have been built adjacent to several KV tomb entrances (e.g., at KV 1, 2, 6, 11, 14, 34, 35, and 47). In 2010, the large shaded seating area in the center of KV across from KV 62 and adjacent to KV 55 was converted into a cafeteria selling bottled

|  | Visitors | Guides |
| --- | --- | --- |
| Provide clean toilets | 13.2% | 35.9% |
| Provide shaded places | 14.3 | 32.8 |
| Provide waiting places/larger rest houses | 5.1 | 12.6 |
| Improve frequency of train/select more suitable place/improve it | - | 8.1 |
| Replace the 'tuf-tuf' train with an electric train | 0.3 | 8.1 |
| Open new entrance gates to avoid overcrowding | - | 3.5 |
| Pave roads to tombs | 0.5 | 3.5 |
| Larger and more organized parking area | - | 2.0 |
| Provide machines to absorb humidity in tombs | - | 1.5 |
| Widen the entrance and exit gate | - | 1.0 |
| Construct two-way path network for the disabled | 0.3 | 1.0 |
| Improve lighting system in tombs | 3.8 | 0.5 |
| Improve quality of merchandise in shops | 0.5 | 0.5 |
| Provide mains supply of water | - | 0.5 |
| Build a replica to decrease the number of visitors | 0.3 | 0.5 |
| Construct a wooden path | - | 0.5 |
| Reposition shops to car park for improved access | 0.5 | 0.5 |
| Audio guides in tombs needed | 0.8 | - |
| Train should enter valley | 0.8 | - |
| Bazaars should sell Egyptian products/with appropriate prices | 0.5 | - |
| Decrease number of shops | 0.3 | - |
| Provide public utilities and infrastructures | 0.3 | - |
| Install security cameras | 0.3 | - |

Table 25. Stakeholder suggestions: site infrastructure

water and soft drinks. The cafeteria is an eyesore, filled with commercial signs, refrigerator cases, and numerous small metal tables and chairs, and is especially noisy during the busiest morning hours. It seems to be especially popular with tour guides, who wait here for their clients to visit the three tombs their KV ticket entitles them to see.

*Visitor Management*

The treatment of visitors while at the Valley of the Kings is a pressing concern to many of the guides, with almost a quarter (23.8%) concerned at the way in which merchants, freelance traders, and site staff interact with the visitors (table 26). This concern, however, does not appear to be shared by the visitors; less than 5% of visitors (4.1%) raised issues relating to negative interaction with traders, staff, and local people. In addition, the future location of the bus parking in relation to the electric-train starting point is an important consideration to some of the guides (2.5%).

|  | Visitors | Guides |
|---|---|---|
| Stop sellers and hawkers from annoying visitors | 0.5% | 16.2% |
| Stop guards accepting money from visitors for photography | 0.3 | 6.6 |
| Provide drop-off point closer to train | 0.5 | 2.5 |
| Control prices in shops | 0.3 | 2.0 |
| Reduce presence of armed forces | - | 1.0 |
| Educate sellers on how to deal with visitors | 0.8 | 1.0 |
| Ban smoking for all, including staff | 0.3 | 0.5 |
| Prevent guards from annoying visitors | 2.2 | - |
| Prevent commissions | 0.8 | - |
| Improve customer service | 0.3 | - |

Table 26. Stakeholder suggestions: site management

*Site Information*

The need to improve the present signage in the Valley was raised by many of the guides (table 27). The key areas of concern are the numbers of boards currently available for guiding, with almost one-fifth (19.7%) suggesting more information panels were needed. However, the visitors were less concerned with the provision of information panels, with only 3% raising the matter, along with only 2% expressing any concern with the level of general signage throughout the Valley. Interestingly, some visitors (2.2%) suggested the need for information panels in multiple languages, a concern the guides did not share. A small percentage of guides (1%) suggested providing additional information for the visitors in the form of site information leaflets.

Metal signs installed at the entrance to each of the KV tombs open to the public were installed by the TMP and have proved highly successful. Guides use them as a visual aid while delivering short talks on the KV tombs, and many visitors photographed the signs (until all photography in KV was banned in 2010) to remind themselves of what they had seen on their visit.

|  | Visitors | Guides |
| --- | --- | --- |
| Increase number of information panels outside tombs | 3% | 19.7% |
| Improve signage in the valley | 2.2 | 9.6 |
| Provide information booklets | 0.5 | 1.0 |
| Provide guides for Egyptian visitors | 2.2 | - |
| Make the information panels available in different languages | 1.9 | - |
| Ensure guides are of a high standard | 1.3 | - |
| Provide information film in different languages | 0.3 | - |
| Provide library | 0.3 | - |

Table 27. Stakeholder suggestions: site information

*Tombs and Ticketing*

Issues surrounding access to the tombs are an obvious concern to many guides and visitors, and they produced a large number of suggestions and comments (table 28). The main proposal was to open more tombs, both those currently closed for restoration and those that have never been made available for the public to visit. This was cited by 22% of guides and 6% of visitors. In addition, longer opening hours, especially in the summer months, were suggested by 13% of guides and 5% of visitors.

The interior conditions of the tombs were also of concern, with the provision of environmental controls suggested by 4% of guides and 7% of visitors. Other suggested tomb-protection strategies included the control of visitor numbers within a tomb (4% of guides, 1.3% of visitors), protecting all the opened tombs with glass screens (5.1% of guides, 0.5% of

|  | Visitors | Guides |
|---|---|---|
| Open more tombs/reopen closed tombs | 6.5% | 22.2% |
| Increase the opening hours for tombs particularly in summer | 5.4 | 13.6 |
| Enforce camera ban inside tombs | 5.6 |  |
| Protect all opened tombs with glass screens | 0.5 | 5.1 |
| Better ticket design/tomb entry system | 0.5 | 5.1 |
| Install air-conditioning systems in all tombs | 7.0 | 4.0 |
| Control visitor numbers | 1.3 | 4.0 |
| Arrange tourist schedule between tourism companies | - | 3.0 |
| Allow the use of cameras/video without payment | 6.5 | 3.0 |
| Organize visitor flow in tombs | 0.5 | 3.0 |
| Increase number of ticket windows available | - | 2.5 |
| Construct a two-way path network | - | 1.5 |
| Change kiosk place to be in front of KV/Tutankhamun | - | 1.5 |
| Decrease number of tombs per ticket | - | 1.0 |
| Pre-select tombs when buying tickets | - | 1.0 |
| Provide time-coded tickets | - | 1.0 |
| Allow guides in tombs | 1.9 | 1.0 |
| Increase number of tombs per ticket | 1.6 | 1.0 |
| Provide better mobile telephone network coverage | - | 0.5 |
| Improve security inspection | - | 0.5 |
| Tickets should include price of train | - | 0.5 |
| Raise the price of tickets and allow entry to all opened tombs | - | 0.5 |
| Ticket should include Tutankhamun tomb | 1.1 | - |
| Ticket should include all tombs | 1.1 | - |
| Egyptians should pay same ticket price as foreigners | 0.8 | - |
| Reopen the tomb of Seti I, KV 17 | 0.3 | - |
| Allow the purchase of permits | 0.3 | - |
| Reduce the price of tickets | 0.3 | - |
| Provide different ticketing levels | 0.3 | - |
| Prevent talking inside tombs | 0.3 | - |
| Reduce queues | 0.3 | - |
| Arab visitors should pay reduced price for tickets | 0.3 | - |

Table 28. Stakeholder suggestions: tombs and ticketing

visitors), and enforcement of the camera ban within the tombs (5.6% of guides). In contrast, 6% of visitors felt that they should be allowed to use cameras and video cameras without further payment.

Concerning the current ticketing system in the Valley (at the time of the survey), several suggestions were made to change the present procedures. These included: redesigning the current tickets (5.1% of guides, 0.5% of visitors); the inclusion of the tomb of Tutankhamun on the current entry ticket (1.1% of visitors); and an increase in the number of tombs available on one ticket (1.6% of visitors).

Three percent of tour guides felt that the present schedules of tour companies would benefit from an arrangement of schedule sharing in order to avoid overcrowding at certain times of the day and particular days of the week. The issue of controlling visitor flow was also raised by 1% of the guides, who suggested the use of timed tickets.

In 2009, a single general ticket entitled a visitor to see any three of the KV tombs open to the public. Extra tickets were required to visit KV 9, 35, and 62. A separate charge was made for the tramline running from the Visitors Center to KV and back. As of 2010, no special ticket was required for photography, since all cameras (including cell phones) are banned from the Valley, the result of several tourists being caught ignoring an earlier ban on flash photography inside KV tombs.

*Miscellaneous*

The responses in table 29 were difficult to categorize and have therefore been placed under the heading "miscellaneous." However, they do offer several insights into the workings of the Valley, including the sentiment shared by one-tenth (10.8%) of visitors, who feel that the site is perfect as it is and should be left unaltered; only 0.5% of the guides shared this view.

|  | Visitors | Guides |
|---|---|---|
| **Ensure high standards among all KV staff** | - | 8.6% |
| **Improve conservation of tombs** | - | 2.5 |
| **Enforce ban on foreign guides** | - | 1.5 |
| **Stop the 'tuf-tuf' drivers selling postcards** | - | 1.5 |
| **Improve salary and work conditions of guards** | - | 1.5 |
| **Stop police intervening in guides' work** | - | 0.5 |
| **Ensure that guides follow the rules** | - | 0.5 |
| **No improvement needed** | 10.8 | 0.5 |
| **Leave it natural and do not modernize it** | 0.5 | - |
| **Close the Valley to visitors** | 0.5 | - |
| **Facilitate traveling to Egypt** | 0.3 | - |
| **Plant palm trees** | 0.3 | - |
| **Reduce the temperature of the water in the toilet** | 0.3 | - |
| **Reduce pollution and noise** | 0.3 | - |

Table 29. Stakeholder suggestions: miscellaneous

## Analysis of Qualitative Data

As discussed in the introduction, six focus-group discussions were conducted, two with merchants, two with workers at KV, and two with local community residents. In general, the focus-group discussions investigated the experience of the participants with KV and their suggestions to improve services there.

*The Merchants*

Two focus-group discussions were conducted with merchants. Ten sellers participated in the two groups (five in each one). On average they have been working in these jobs for eleven years; one had worked as a souvenir seller for thirty years. All of the traders working at the Valley operate on annual contracts from the Luxor City Council.

Fig. 39. Merchant area. © Theban Mapping Project

The following questions were asked during the discussion:

### A. Are you satisfied with your business?

A common feeling of dissatisfaction about work conditions was recorded among all the respondents. Some of the complaints and suggestions were:
- There is no cafeteria
- The toilets are too far away from the shopping area

- Vendors are not allowed to sell bottled water and soft drinks
- The shelters over their outlets are insufficient
- Mosquitoes are a persistent problem and the city council should use insecticide early in the morning before the site opens
- The retail area is not clean
- The area is not sheltered from the sun
- Tourist guides mistreat the sellers and advise the tourists only to buy from shops whose owners the guides like
- The authorities impose a fine if a trader exceeds his unit's defined area
- The authorities take traders handcuffed like criminals to jail if the fines are not paid

> Typical quotations from merchants:
> "The tourism police treat us like drug dealers if they find a bottle of water with us."
> "FIFA was right to refuse our request to organize the Football World Cup 2010; I can't find anything well organized in Egypt to be proud of."

### B. What are the changes you have noticed in the last few years?

The traders in the focus-group discussions found conditions in previous years better than the present day because previously they were allowed to sell water and soft drinks. Furthermore, visitors now buy goods directly from local factories and not from the retail shops; as a result, the merchants' goods are often left in the sun for long periods and are ruined. The respondents also mentioned the constant harassment from tourism police who are posted outside the Valley.

### C. Is the market suitable, and how can it be improved?

As seen from the above responses, the market is thoroughly unsuitable. It needs such basic services as toilets, a cafeteria, umbrellas, regular spraying of insecticide, regular cleaning, and specific times set aside by guides for tourists to shop before or after their visit in the Valley.

### D. Are you satisfied with your income? What are the problems you face with the tourists, and how can they be solved?

With regard to income, the merchants all claimed to be satisfied. They say they have no problems with the tourists; their problems are with the guides, who always hurry their groups past the retail area. One of the respondents said, "I overheard one of the guides tell his group in English to be wary of the shopkeepers, because they are all thieves and have infectious diseases. He thought that we are uneducated and couldn't understand him."

Some of the participants said their income in the past was higher than now. They observed that tourist guides take the groups directly to factories, which then pay guides commission on sales, but point out that the factories are illegal, while the retail shops at KV are legal. One respondent suffers monetarily because he and his partner cannot work at the same time, as the authorities do not allow two persons in a shop.

**E. What does KV represent for you?**
KV is very important for the merchants and represents for them:
- The only source of income and work for those without industrial or agricultural opportunities
- Their national heritage, historical civilization, and impressive ancient history
- A great landmark to be proud of

**F. How can the increasing number of tourists be dealt with in the future?**
The antiques sellers in the focus-group discussions mentioned numerous ways to improve KV in the future. Some of these suggestions are:
- The parking lot should be widened and expanded
- All the shops should be of the same size and appearance
- Shops should specialize, one selling gallabiyas, another drinks, etc.
- The shopping area should be covered
- The bazaars should be parallel to each other
- The conditions of the shop licenses should be designed more in the sellers' favor
- The area should be clean and tidy
- Toilets should be available
- The Valley should be opened at night
- A sound and light show could be produced

The construction of a new covered bazaar adjacent to the new KV Visitors Center addressed many of these concerns and has been very favorably received by both the vendors and the tourists.

*Valley of the Kings Staff*

Two focus-group discussions were conducted with workers at KV, one group containing seven supervisors and the other with seven workers. The supervisors' focus-group discussion included the guards' supervisors, cleaning supervisors, and inspectors. The workers' focus group discussion included restorers, restorers' assistants, guards, cleaning staff, and an electrician. The following points were covered during the discussions:

**A. Are you satisfied with your job? How could the work conditions be improved?**

*Supervisors:*

Although the supervisors were generally satisfied, they had a few complaints and suggestions:
- They work long hours
- The number of guards is inadequate
- Restorers lack necessary chemicals and trained assistants

Fig. 40. KV staff. © Theban Mapping Project

Stakeholder Surveys

- Tombs need cooling systems
- As white cement is now prohibited, they are forced to use lime and the natural powder from the hills, which is more difficult, and harkens back to the time of the pharaohs
- The janitorial supervisor asked for more equipment and ashtrays

> One supervisor remarked, "Here we deal with tombs, which is totally different from temples; tombs need special treatment, but we can't find the appropriate materials or trained workers."

*Workers:*

The workers harbor the following concerns:
- They work long hours
- They are exposed to dangerous materials
- The system of awarding bonuses is unfair
- Some work without contracts and therefore have no benefits
- They have no official papers from the tourism authority
- They have no medical insurance or pension plan
- There are no vacations; they must gain permission from the supervisors for days off
- Some go unpaid for several months at a time
- They lack tools and equipment
- The ventilation system in the tombs borders on being dangerous
- The system of rotating guards is inadequate

> The following are two representative quotes from workers in KV:
> "I went to Luxor city to receive my new government ID card, but they told me you have to stamp your papers; the authority in Cairo told me that they can't stamp my papers because I'm a temporary worker. Is that fair?"
> "I have been working as an antiquities restorer for twenty-one years now; I know everything about my work, wooden scaffolds, ceilings, walls, ladders, chemicals, and the repair mixture. We work in very bad conditions: the depth of the tomb could be 300 m, and the amount of oxygen is not sufficient. But if we talk about our rights or complain, they threaten us. We just need some fairness, we just need our rights."

## B. How many hours do you work?
*Supervisors:*
A guards' supervisor does not have specific working hours. They usually inspect the tombs every two or three hours. The other respondents typically work for about nine hours a day.
*Workers:*
Guards do not have specific working hours; they are on duty for twenty-four hours, and then rest for twenty-four hours. The rest of the respondents work for about nine hours a day.

## C. Are you satisfied with your income, and how has the Valley changed over time?
*Supervisors:*
The supervisors claim to be satisfied with their income. Of the changes that have occurred in the Valley over time, the supervisors mentioned:
- The new shelters
- The restorers now have a laboratory and work more scientifically
- There are glass walls in the tombs to protect the walls
- The tombs' gates are now well designed
- There is now a computer in the inspector's room
- The road to the tomb of Thutmose III is now wider
- Technical improvements: electricity in the tombs now working on three lines, not just one as before
- Two inspectors pass by daily and report on the restorers' work

*Workers:*
None of the workers are satisfied with their salaries; they consider the income insufficient. The changes that have taken place in the Valley mentioned by the workers include:
- Glass protection screens in the tombs
- The wooden scaffolds
- Improved electricity supply
- Improved cleanliness
- The area is now highly secured

## D. What problems concern you in the work?
Both supervisors and workers mentioned the lack of transportation for the

employees to KV as the main problem. In addition, workers again cited the low salaries.

**E. Do you notice any increase in the number of tourists?**
Supervisors and workers both observed an annual increase in the number of tourists to KV.

> One respondent remarked, "There are more tourists in winter than in summer, but generally speaking there is an increasing number of tourists every year, and there are many new nationalities."

**F. How do you deal with the tourists, and do you have problems with them?**
*Supervisors:*
Three of the respondents had no direct contact with the visitors, but the rest mentioned that the main problem with the visitors is the use of photography, particularly flash photography inside the tombs. They feel this is the fault of the guides, who do not tell their groups that flash photography is prohibited. The solution they suggest is to prohibit all cameras inside the tombs. The respondents also mentioned the fact that the guides do not tell their groups that Tutankhamun's tomb requires a separate ticket, forcing people to go all the way back to the main gate to get tickets. This is an avoidable inconvenience, which is particularly hard on elderly people.
*Workers:*
None of the respondents has direct contact with the visitors.

**G. How can the increasing number of tourists be dealt with in the future?**
*Supervisors:*
The supervisors discussed many points, some technical, and made the following suggestions:
- A cooling system is needed inside the tombs
- Limit number of visitors for each tomb per day
- Open more tombs
- Widen the parking area

- Have more coordination between the East and West Bank tourist convoys
- With regard to the Japanese project (Visitors Center) and its services: toilets, cafeteria, panorama, and so forth

**H. Do you think that the number of open tombs is adequate?**
The respondents agreed that the visiting hours are adequate. They commented on the future Visitors Center's large screen production that will provide information about the Valley and its tombs, enabling the tourists to decide which tombs they want to visit (planned but not installed). *Workers* suggested that more tombs be opened in the winter.

**I. What would you like accomplished in KV?**
*Supervisors:*
- Make the tourists feel comfortable
- Find a good solution for the ticketing system, either writing details of a visit on the ticket, or making guards punch a small hole in it instead of tearing it
- Have a first-aid station

*Workers:*
- A cafeteria
- Shelters with more fans
- More protective glass walls inside the tombs
- Cooling inside the tombs
- Modern cleaning equipment

*Local Community Residents*

> One essential element in improving the encounter between tourists and local populations lies in the participation in and, ultimately, control over the protection and management of sites by the local people themselves, as well as their sharing in the profits which derive from tourism.... Ways must be found to develop tourism so as to preserve both the cultural and natural resources, whilst also inviting the substantive participation of local communities; that is, a tourism which can be part of sustainable development.
> —UNESCO, 1996[1]

Two focus-group discussions were conducted in two hamlets: al-Hassasna and al-Sawalem, both in al-Qurna. Five villagers attended each of the focus-group discussions. The participants were farmers, alabaster sellers, traders, and the like. None of the participants worked in KV. The following points were discussed:

**A. Do the tourists who visit KV come to your village?**
Most tourists visit the village, the alabaster factories, and the agricultural area. Some eat lunch in small restaurants, take photographs, buy gifts, and walk around the village. A small number ride horses and camels.

These visits are considered an important source of the participants' income. They also know about the tourists' ideas, culture, and attitudes.

> One of the shop owners said, "Tourism generates a lot of job opportunities; in my shop I hired five or six people. They find jobs away from governmental authorities [public sector], which is good for the national economy."

**B. Have you ever visited the Valley and the tombs?**
In the al-Hassasna focus group discussion, only one of the respondents had visited the Valley and the tombs before. The rest had seen the Valley from outside, but had never been to the tombs.

In the al-Sawalem focus group discussion, all of the participants had visited the Valley more than once, either with their families and relatives or to meet tour guides and drivers. One of the traders, an archaeology student, had visited the Valley more often than the others.

**C. Do the tour buses affect your village?**
Some respondents said that tour buses have a positive effect on their village and they want more of them. Others mentioned the effect of bus exhaust fumes, noise, and general environmental safety.

**D. What can be done to enhance visitor satisfaction in KV?**
When asked to suggest ways to improve the situation at KV, the participants mentioned many necessary services and more general suggestions:

- Cafeteria required
- Toilets improved
- First-aid center needed
- Phone booths should be installed
- Road signs needed
- Fire station needed
- Lining the road with trees
- Extending the working hours into the night
- Sound and light show
- Determining specific times to have tourists visit the alabaster factories and bazaars

**Conclusions and Recommendations**

As discussed above, the purpose of this study was to analyze the views of the stakeholders of the Valley of the Kings. The study successfully recorded the views of over six hundred visitors and two hundred guides and included in-depth discussions with over thirty site workers and community residents. We can happily state that we have achieved our goals. But more than that, we received remarkable support and enthusiasm for the masterplan from a large percentage of the stakeholders we consulted.

Furthermore, nearly all the consultations indicated the high regard in which the Valley is held by visitors and the local community alike. The overwhelming majority of visitors had positive things to say about KV. This can be seen in table 30, which shows that over 80 percent of visitors would pay a return visit.

|  | Visits to KV Once | Visits to KV Two+ | Visitors Ind. | Visitors Group | Total |
|---|---|---|---|---|---|
| Would you visit the Valley of Kings again? | | | | | |
| Yes | 80.4% | 93.7% | 82.3% | 81.9% | 81.9% |
| No | 19.6 | 6.3 | 17.7 | 18.1 | 18.1 |

Table 30. Visitor satisfaction

The groundswell of goodwill highlighted by this survey is a valuable tool in the successful implementation of the Valley of the Kings Masterplan. The utilization of this resource will result in a more successful implementation and guarantee the long-term success of the plan.

The main proposals extracted from the site survey can be summarized as:
1. The provision of a cafeteria
2. Improved toilet and shelter facilities
3. Opening the site at night
4. Improvements to the retail facilities
5. Improved conservation of the tombs
6. Improved cleaning of the site
7. Amendment of ticketing procedures
8. Improvement of visitor flow

As of 2010, the first of these proposals had been, we believe, badly implemented with the installation of a drinks stand in the central KV seating area, which was recently closed; the second had not been dealt with; the third was under discussion (and permission had been given by the Egyptian Ministry of the Interior); the fourth had been dealt with; the fifth, sixth, seventh, and eighth had yet to be implemented.

## Stakeholder Survey Stage Two: Online Survey

In October 2004, we launched the second part of our stakeholder consultation. This took the form of an online survey placed on the Theban Mapping Project website at www.thebanmappingproject.com. The following announcement was also made on the front page of the TMP website, soliciting contributions (the website receives an average of five million hits monthly, and was therefore ideally suited to attract repeat visitors to KV and other interested parties).

> **TMP Website Announcement:**
> Last year (2003), the Theban Mapping Project was asked by Dr. Zahi Hawass, Secretary General of the Supreme Council of Antiquities, to take the lead role in developing a masterplan for managing the Valley of the Kings.
> In antiquity, the Valley was the burial place of the Egyptian elite for over five hundred years, and for the last three thousand years it has been the focus of attention from scholars, travellers, and tourists. Today, after centuries of damage and looting, the Valley is facing its most severe challenge: its future preservation hangs in the balance. Unless swift, radical, and all-encompassing action is undertaken, we may see the

> destruction of this site within the next twenty-five years. The problems facing the Valley today come predominantly from human intervention, but in addition, there are natural threats that have to be managed. The sheer number of visitors brings countless problems, ranging from damage to the fabric of the site to issues surrounding the provision of tourist facilities appropriate to the site and the visitors.
>
> The first stage of developing this masterplan is a consultation process involving as many interested parties as possible and we are particularly interested in the views and suggestions of previous visitors. Therefore, we invite you to take part in our online survey.

## Methodology

Fourteen stakeholder groups were identified above. The goal of the online survey was to target the academic community, repeat visitors to KV, visitors to the Theban Mapping Project website, and the wider international community.

The opinion of these stakeholders was sought on the following issues facing the site:

- Perceptions of KV
- Quantity and quality of visitor services
- Role of the Visitor Center
- Recommendations for the future

The study by its nature (online self-administered questionnaire) was only quantitative. We encouraged participation in the survey by placing announcements on various email and web-based communities, including the Egypt Exploration Society (EES), Egyptologists Electronic Forum (EEF), Amun Yahoo Group, and university mailing lists, including University College London (UCL) and the American University in Cairo (AUC). We also mailed requests to TMP newsletter subscribers.

The survey instrument contained twenty-five questions, some closed-ended but in the main with open-ended answers, and appeared in English, the language of the TMP website. The study remained on the website approximately six months and, when it was closed, 504 questionnaires had been submitted. Coding of the data was carried out in the Cairo office of the TMP by intern Joseph Lehner.

Throughout the following results from the online survey, we have given typical examples of comments and suggestions received.

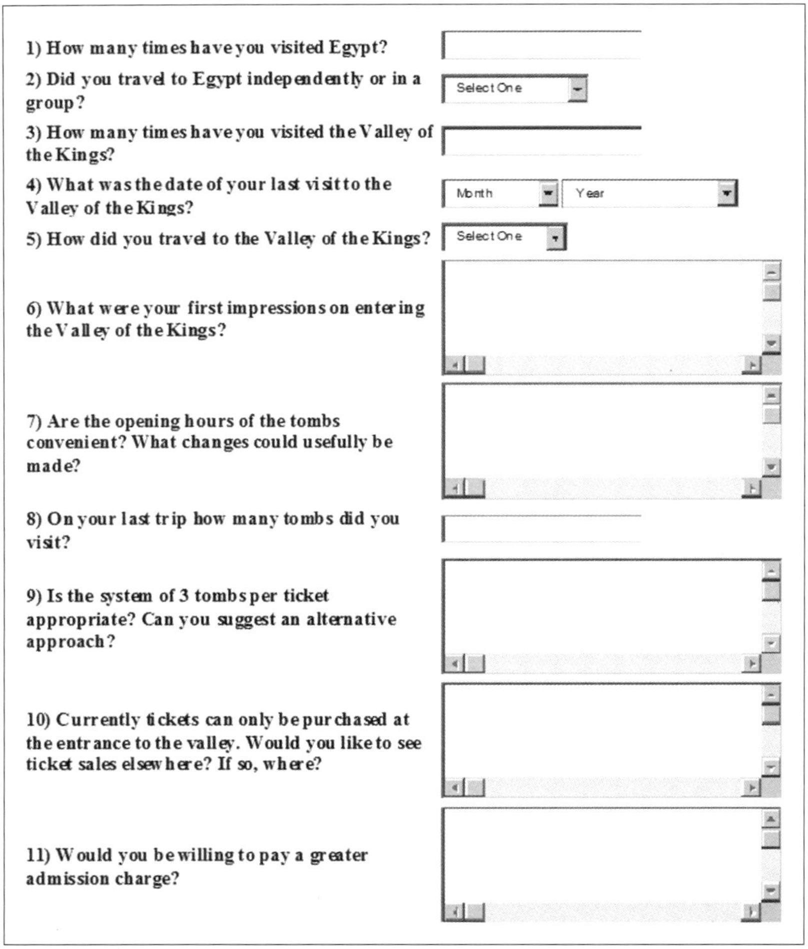
1) How many times have you visited Egypt?

2) Did you travel to Egypt independently or in a group? Select One

3) How many times have you visited the Valley of the Kings?

4) What was the date of your last visit to the Valley of the Kings? Month Year

5) How did you travel to the Valley of the Kings? Select One

6) What were your first impressions on entering the Valley of the Kings?

7) Are the opening hours of the tombs convenient? What changes could usefully be made?

8) On your last trip how many tombs did you visit?

9) Is the system of 3 tombs per ticket appropriate? Can you suggest an alternative approach?

10) Currently tickets can only be purchased at the entrance to the valley. Would you like to see ticket sales elsewhere? If so, where?

11) Would you be willing to pay a greater admission charge?

Fig. 41. Online survey. © Theban Mapping Project

## Background Characteristics of Respondents

*Country of Origin*

The geographic spread of contributors to the online survey covered thirty-nine countries (table 31). Of these, the United Kingdom (47.62%) and the United States of America (15.48%) dominated the responses received. This is to be expected as both the questionnaire and the TMP website are written in the English language. Other English-speaking nations also figure highly, with Australia and Canada each contributing 4.76% and New Zealand 0.99% of the completed

| | | | | | | |
|---|---|---|---|---|---|---|
| United Kingdom | 240 | 47.62% | Israel | 2 | 0.40% |
| United States | 78 | 15.48% | Japan | 2 | 0.40% |
| Netherlands | 26 | 5.16% | Norway | 2 | 0.40% |
| Australia | 24 | 4.76% | Portugal | 2 | 0.40% |
| Canada | 24 | 4.76% | Russia | 2 | 0.40% |
| Germany | 14 | 2.78% | American Samoa | 1 | 0.20% |
| France | 11 | 2.18% | Chile | 1 | 0.20% |
| Italy | 11 | 2.18% | Croatia | 1 | 0.20% |
| Belgium | 8 | 1.59% | Dominican Republic | 1 | 0.20% |
| Spain | 6 | 1.19% | Hungary | 1 | 0.20% |
| Denmark | 5 | 0.99% | Latvia | 1 | 0.20% |
| New Zealand | 5 | 0.99% | Malta | 1 | 0.20% |
| Sweden | 5 | 0.99% | Mexico | 1 | 0.20% |
| Egypt | 4 | 0.79% | Slovenia | 1 | 0.20% |
| Ireland | 4 | 0.79% | Switzerland | 1 | 0.20% |
| Poland | 3 | 0.60% | Turkey | 1 | 0.20% |
| South Africa | 3 | 0.60% | Uruguay | 1 | 0.20% |
| Afghanistan | 2 | 0.40% | Zimbabwe | 1 | 0.20% |
| Czech Republic | 2 | 0.40% | Blank | 4 | 0.79% |
| Greece | 2 | 0.40% | **Total** | **504** | |

Table 31. Background characteristics: country of origin

surveys. This gives the English-speaking nations a total share of over 73% of responses. This must be taken into account when considering the data. However, the fact that so many other nations contributed is encouraging, and further studies could target the underrepresented language groups.

*Gender*
The sample is slightly skewed in the representation of females: 56% of respondents were female and 43% of the responses were male. The remaining 1% left the question blank.

*Age*
The majority of respondents were in the age ranges 26–45 (42%) and 46–65 (43%). This is consistent with the community that we targeted.

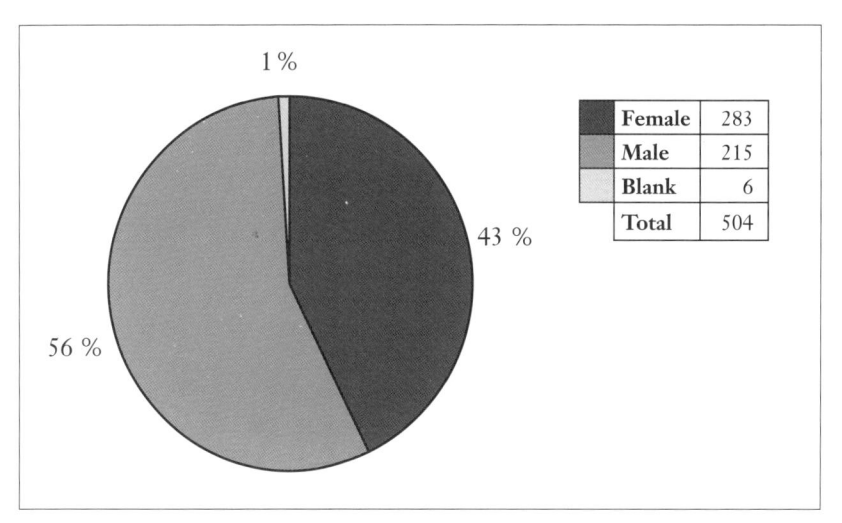

Tables 32a and b. Background characteristics: gender

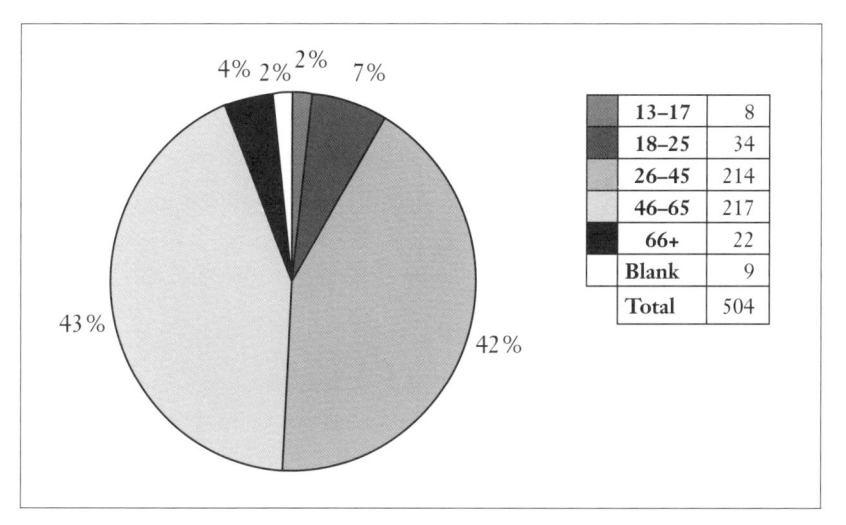

Tables 33a and b. Background characteristics: age

*Number of Visits to Egypt*
A large number had only visited Egypt once, but many respondents had made multiple visits, including nineteen individuals (3.77%) who had been over twenty times. The number who have visited more than ten times is over 10%. This is clearly an audience who will have strong views on any plans for KV.

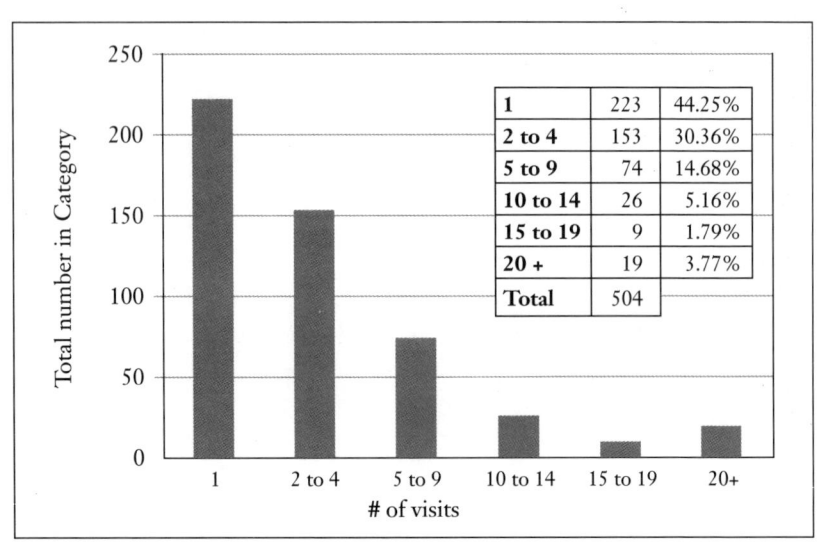

| 1 | 223 | 44.25% |
|---|---|---|
| 2 to 4 | 153 | 30.36% |
| 5 to 9 | 74 | 14.68% |
| 10 to 14 | 26 | 5.16% |
| 15 to 19 | 9 | 1.79% |
| 20 + | 19 | 3.77% |
| Total | 504 | |

Tables 34a and b. Background characteristics: visits to Egypt

| 0 | 8 | 1.59% |
|---|---|---|
| 1 | 226 | 44.84% |
| 2 | 81 | 16.07% |
| 3 | 48 | 9.52% |
| 4 | 28 | 5.56% |
| 5 | 28 | 5.56% |
| 6 to 10 | 53 | 10.52% |
| 11 to 15 | 13 | 2.58% |
| 16 to 20 | 7 | 1.39% |
| 21+ | 12 | 2.38% |
| Total | 504 | |

Table 35. Background characteristics: visits to KV

*Visits to Valley of the Kings*

These results mirror the findings for visits to Egypt. Overwhelmingly most respondents had only visited KV once (44.84%). However, we also had a significant group (6.35%) who had been more than ten times.

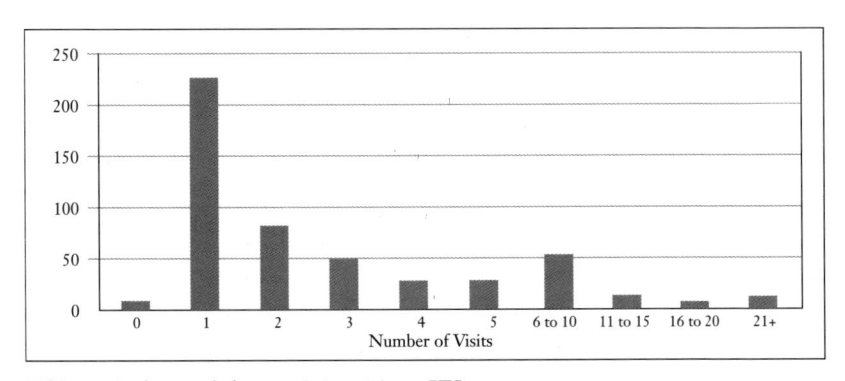

Table 36. Background characteristics: visits to KV

108 | Stakeholder Surveys

| | | |
|---|---|---|
| 2005 | 16 | 3.17% |
| 2004 | 208 | 41.27% |
| 2003 | 64 | 12.70% |
| 2002 | 42 | 8.33% |
| 2001 | 36 | 7.14% |
| 2000 | 20 | 3.97% |
| 1999–1990 | 73 | 14.48% |
| 1989–1980 | 14 | 2.78% |
| 1979–1970 | 2 | 0.40% |
| 1969–1960 | 1 | 0.20% |
| 1959–1950 | 2 | 0.40% |
| Blank | 26 | 5.16% |
| Total | 504 | |

Table 37. Background characteristics: last year of visit

*Last Visit to Valley of the Kings*
For the majority the last visit to KV was within the last two years (57.14%); however, a sizeable number had not visited for over five years (18.26%). This is important to consider, as a considerable change in visitor numbers has occurred over this time, along with the resulting visitor experience.

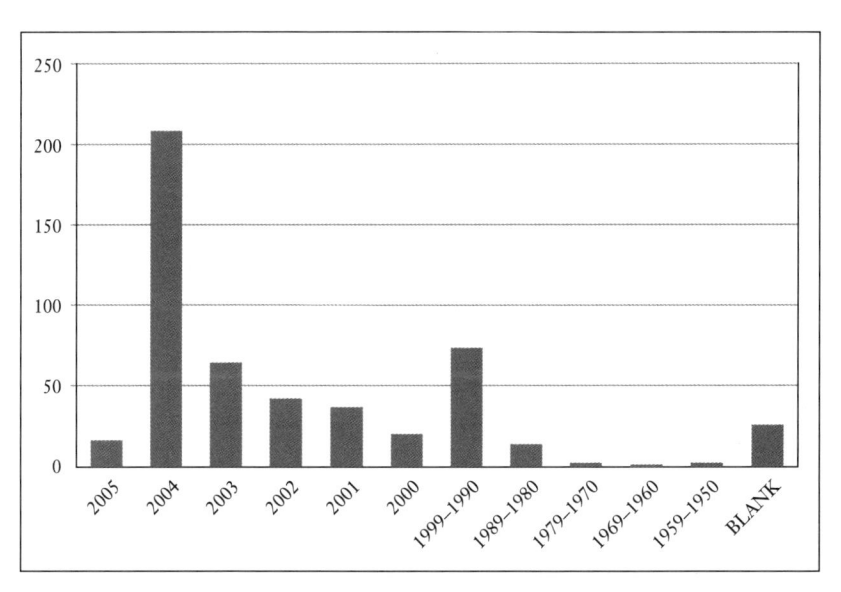

Table 38. Background characteristics: last year of visit

*Type of Traveler*
This is the principal difference between the stakeholder survey carried out in KV and the online survey. Here we have a roughly even split between independent travelers (51%) and group travelers (47%), compared with 17% and 83% respectively in the previous study in KV. Again, this is due to the nature of the target audience.

|  | Independent | 255 |
|---|---|---|
|  | Group | 238 |
|  | Blank | 11 |
|  | Total | 504 |

Independent: 51%
Group: 47%
Blank: 2%

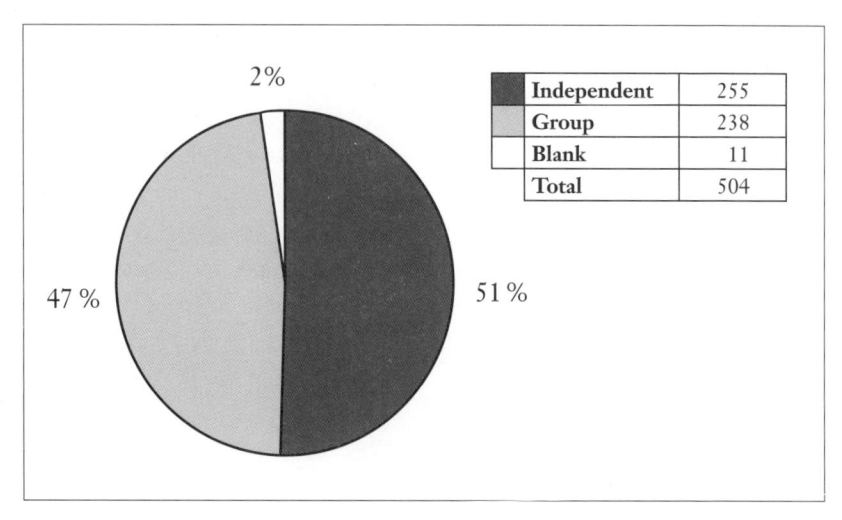

Table 39a and b. Background characteristics: type of traveler

*Mode of Transport to Valley of the Kings*

Visitors were asked how they traveled to KV on their last visit. Only 48% did so by bus, compared to 71% in our onsite survey. This change is due to the large sample of independent travelers in this survey. What is encouraging is that some 12% of visitors used a non-polluting alternative to the motor vehicle—foot, bicycle, or donkey.

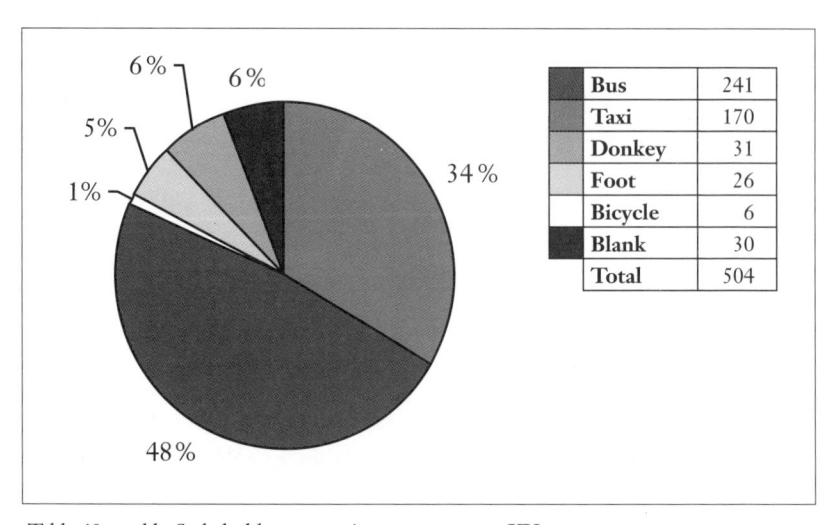

|  | Bus | 241 |
|---|---|---|
|  | Taxi | 170 |
|  | Donkey | 31 |
|  | Foot | 26 |
|  | Bicycle | 6 |
|  | Blank | 30 |
|  | Total | 504 |

Bus: 48%
Taxi: 34%
Donkey: 6%
Foot: 5%
Bicycle: 1%
Blank: 6%

Table 40a and b. Stakeholder perceptions: transport to KV

## Perceptions of the Valley of the Kings
*First Impressions*
Overwhelmingly, the responses are positive. Visitors are overcome by awe, feel enthused, and feel that the reality of their experience exceeded their expectations. However, negative issues and statements arise as well. Typical responses include:
- "Desolate and barren when you block out the tourists."
- "What a difference between 1978 and 2004. What a crowd!"
- "I'd wanted to go there all my life. I just stood in amazement. It was wonderful and everything that I had expected."
- "Everything I had ever imagined and more. However, it was swamped by large organized tour groups, and I was worried about their impact on the tombs and surrounding landscape."
- "While some parts definitely looked wild and untamed, a great portion of it seemed to have been modified for the convenience of visitors. The West Valley, however, seemed almost totally wild."

*Shopping Area*
A large percentage (45%) disliked this area and the experience of walking through it to reach the tombs. This was mirrored in many comments

Fig. 42. KV vendors and tourists. © Theban Mapping Project

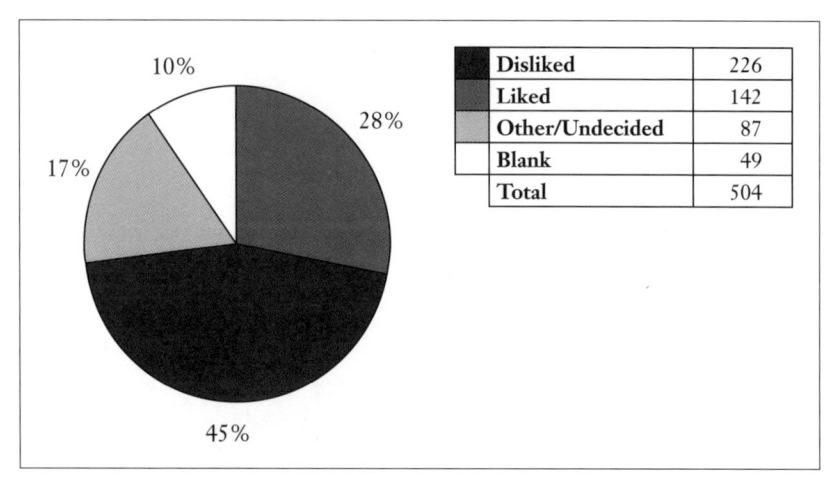

| Disliked | 226 |
|---|---|
| Liked | 142 |
| Other/Undecided | 87 |
| Blank | 49 |
| Total | 504 |

Table 41a and b. Stakeholder perceptions: shopping area

received about the level of harassment and intimidation experienced when passing through the vendors. This should be compared to the 70% who enjoyed the shopping area in the previous poll.

*Parking Area*

There is a definite pattern of like and dislike among the visitors; however, many of the individuals appear to recognize the "necessary evil" of

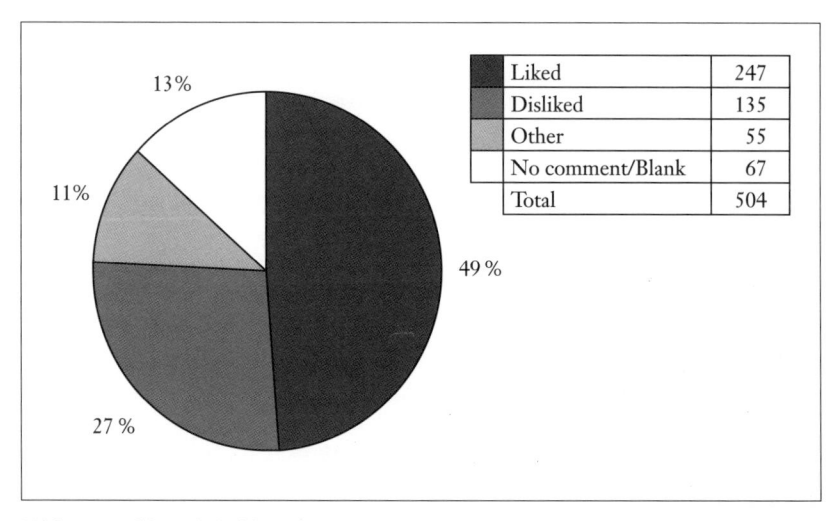

| Liked | 247 |
|---|---|
| Disliked | 135 |
| Other | 55 |
| No comment/Blank | 67 |
| Total | 504 |

Table 42a and b. Stakeholder perceptions: parking area

having a parking area. Some people focused on the fact that the parking lot should not detract from the experience of the visit, but that without the parking area the visit may not have been possible. Many suggested moving the area farther away to protect the Valley and enhance the sense of place. Those individuals with responses marked as "other" chose to answer the question with suggestions irrelevant to the asked questions, or experienced the parking area but with no real feelings toward it—neither liking nor disliking the parking. Overall, 49% of those surveyed liked it.

*Transport within Valley of the Kings*
A pattern similar to the responses on parking emerges here with the views on the 'tuf-tuf' train that transports visitors from the parking area to the security entrance. Most respondents were unconcerned with it (32%) or in fact approved of it (57%). However, those who did not approve (18%) were very vocal in their condemnation, as illustrated below.
- "Visitors should be strongly encouraged to walk the short distance. I appreciate there are those unable to walk for whom transport may be needed but there is a big difference between 'can't walk' and 'can't be bothered to walk.'"
- "Diesel train is a novelty but a little electric tram on rails would be better for the environment it's in, i.e., fumes and vibrations."
- "Too touristy. Should remove Disney style trains and hawkers stands. No respect for history or cultural importance of site. Dirty. Too much litter."

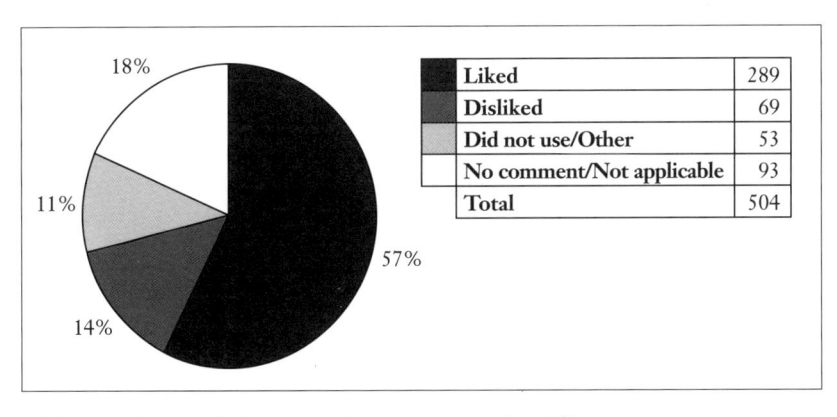

| | | |
|---|---|---|
| | Liked | 289 |
| | Disliked | 69 |
| | Did not use/Other | 53 |
| | No comment/Not applicable | 93 |
| | Total | 504 |

Table 43a and b. Stakeholder perceptions: transport within KV

## Visitor Management

> "I would hate to see more tourist buildings. Part of what I loved about my visit, was how you can imagine how it (KV) was in the past."
> —One visitor's opinion

*Ticketing and Admissions*
Ticket Sales Location

We posed the question: "Currently tickets can only be purchased at the entrance to the Valley. Would you like to see ticket sales elsewhere? If so, where?" Fifty-one percent of respondents felt that ticket sales would be beneficial in other areas. Their suggestions included:
- An additional booth within KV
- Main ticket office on West Bank
- Ferry terminal, East or West Bank
- In Cairo, Luxor, etc., at other antiquities sites and museums
- In hotels and cruise boats
- Travel agents
- On the Internet
- Tourist information centers in Egypt and/or overseas

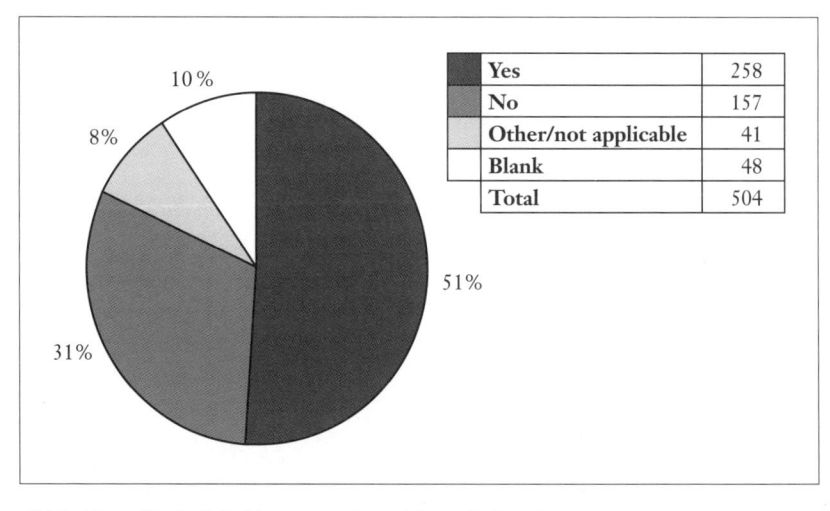

| | |
|---|---|
| Yes | 258 |
| No | 157 |
| Other/not applicable | 41 |
| Blank | 48 |
| Total | 504 |

Table 44a and b. Stakeholder perceptions: ticket sales location

| Yes | 353 |
|---|---|
| No | 52 |
| Undecided | 73 |
| Blank | 26 |
| Total | 504 |

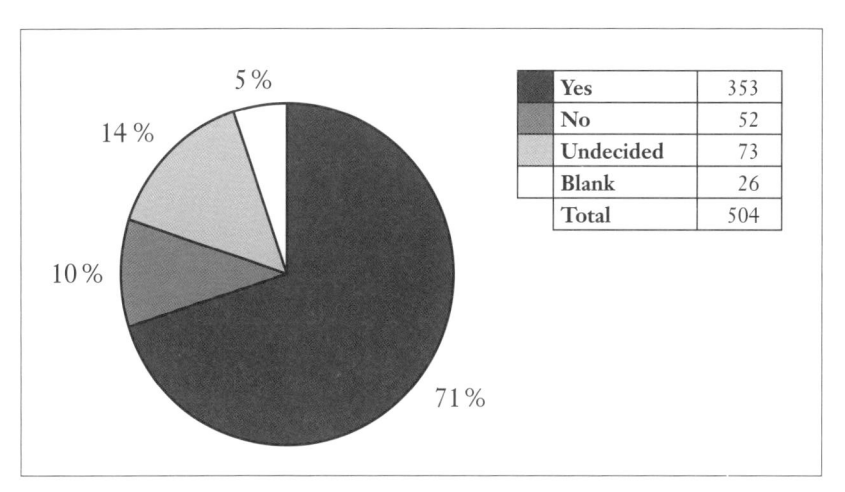

Table 45a and b. Stakeholder perceptions: admission charge increase

We also asked: "Would you be willing to pay a greater admission charge?" A large majority (71%) were happy to do this, although many added the caveat that the increased charges should go toward the conservation of the site.

On the matter of the opening hours we asked: "Are the opening hours of the tombs convenient? What changes could usefully be made?" Sixty-seven percent were happy with the current system; however, many asked for increased hours in the evenings, especially through the hot summer months.

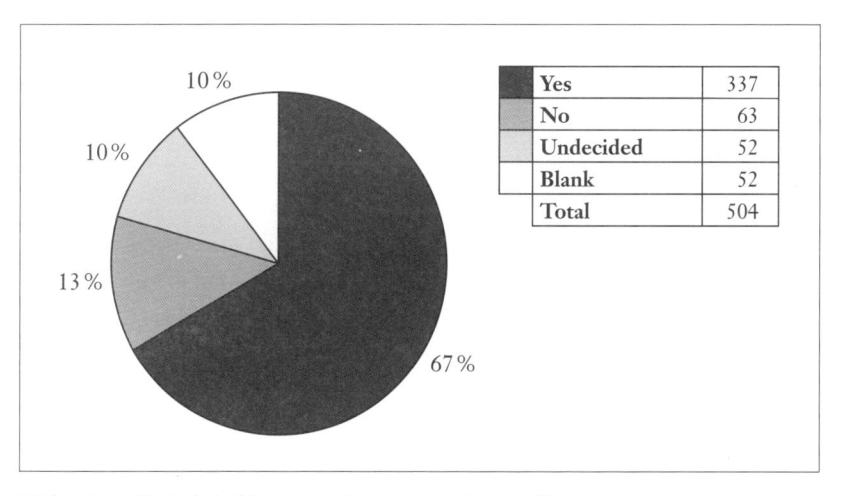

| Yes | 337 |
|---|---|
| No | 63 |
| Undecided | 52 |
| Blank | 52 |
| Total | 504 |

Table 46a and b. Stakeholder perceptions: opening hour sufficiency

Stakeholder Survey Stage Two: Online Survey | 115

| | | | | | |
|---|---|---|---|---|---|
| 0 Tombs | 4 | 0.79% | 9 Tombs | 18 | 3.57% |
| 1 Tomb | 11 | 2.18% | 10 Tombs | 5 | 0.99% |
| 2 Tombs | 17 | 3.37% | 11 Tombs | 1 | 0.20% |
| 3 Tombs | 230 | 45.63% | 12 Tombs | 8 | 1.59% |
| 4 Tombs | 89 | 17.66% | 14 Tombs | 1 | 0.20% |
| 5 Tombs | 44 | 8.73% | 15 Tombs | 1 | 0.20% |
| 6 Tombs | 53 | 10.52% | 20 Tombs | 1 | 0.20% |
| 7 Tombs | 14 | 2.78% | **Total** | **504** | |
| 8 Tombs | 7 | 1.39% | | | |

Table 47. Stakeholder experience: number of tombs visited

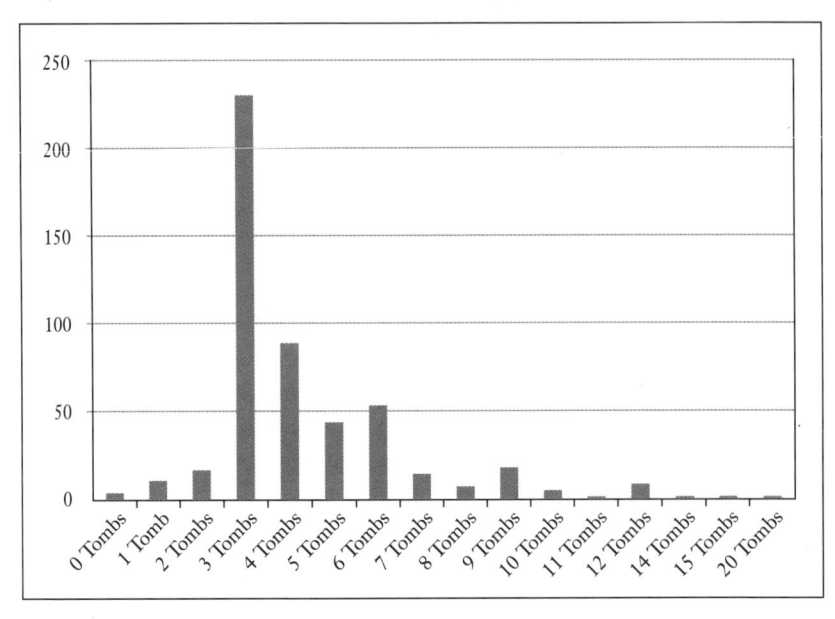

Table 48: Stakeholder experience: number of tombs visited

*Tomb Visits*

We asked: "On your last trip, how many tombs did you visit?" Just over half the sample (52%) visited three or fewer tombs. This is in contrast to 69% who visited three or fewer tombs during our onsite survey.

Length of Visit

We asked: "How long did you stay in the Valley of the Kings?" Here we found a large difference from our KV sample, with 42% of respondents spending over three hours in KV compared with an average visit of 108

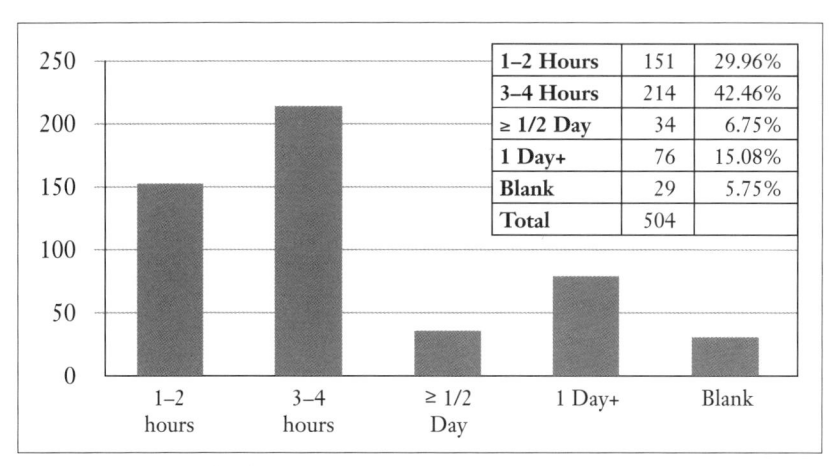

| 1–2 Hours | 151 | 29.96% |
|---|---|---|
| 3–4 Hours | 214 | 42.46% |
| ≥ 1/2 Day | 34 | 6.75% |
| 1 Day+ | 76 | 15.08% |
| Blank | 29 | 5.75% |
| Total | 504 | |

Table 49a and b. Stakeholder experience: length of visit to KV

minutes for the on-site respondents. Furthermore, 21% of those answering the online questionnaire spent more than half a day visiting KV. Here we are dealing with a core of regular, well-informed, enthusiastic visitors.

Crowded Tombs

We asked: "Did you find the tombs crowded?" The responses here show a clear split in opinions. The number of those who felt the tombs were crowded was almost equal to the number who considered them not

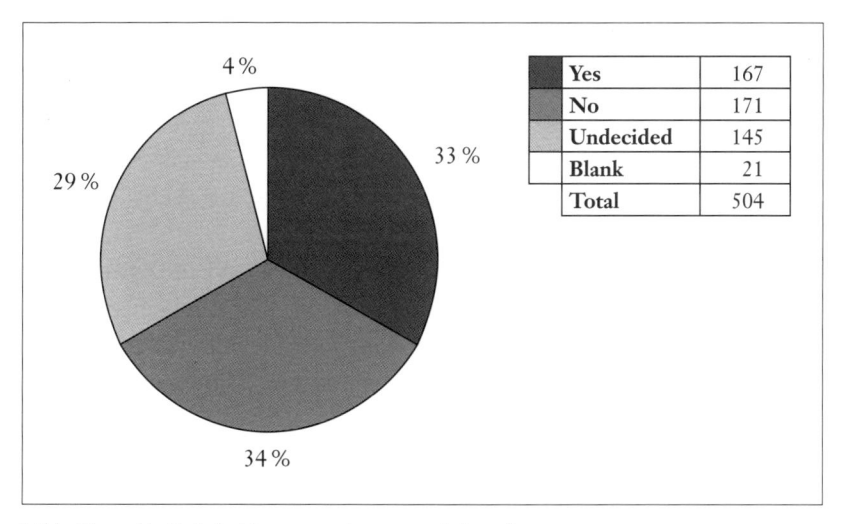

| Yes | 167 |
|---|---|
| No | 171 |
| Undecided | 145 |
| Blank | 21 |
| Total | 504 |

Table 50a and b. Stakeholder perceptions: crowded tombs

crowded or were undecided in their opinion. Some typical responses from visitors who had found the tombs crowded were:
- "Everyone is clustered around about three tombs—where the large groups go."
- "Crowded—too many in a given tomb at one time."

Tomb Conditions

We asked: "Did you find the tombs hot and humid, or comfortable?" Here again we see opinion almost evenly split between those who found the tombs comfortable (46%) and those who found them hot and humid (44%). What we are seeing here is a result of the views expressed over a long period of time by both first-time visitors and the more experienced visitor who will avoid the peak periods.

| Comfortable | 235 |
| Hot | 144 |
| Humid | 77 |
| Undecided | 28 |
| Blank | 20 |
| Total | 504 |

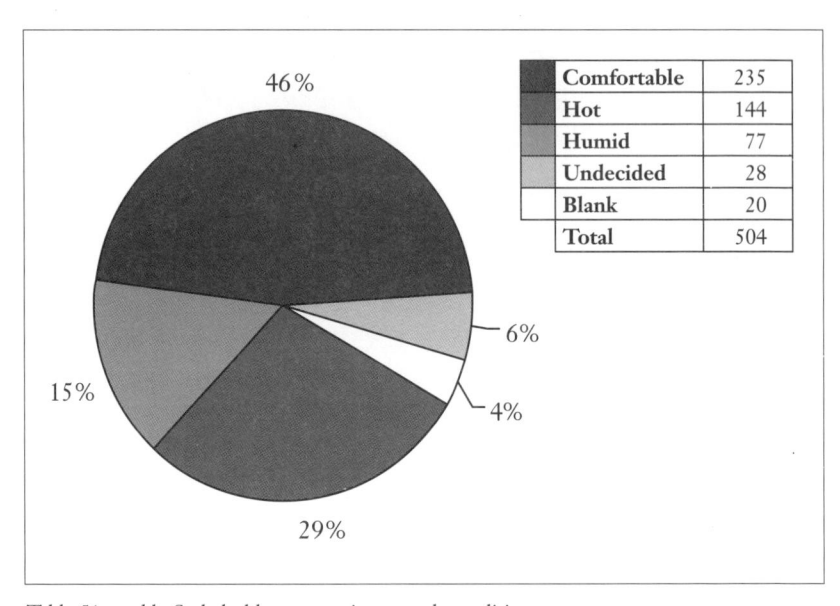

Table 51a and b. Stakeholder perceptions: tomb conditions

Lecturing

We asked: "Guides are not permitted to lecture in the tombs. Do you approve of this restriction?" This restriction, which was first brought into force in 2002 in order to keep visitor traffic moving and to protect the tombs, has the seal of approval of 64% of the responders.

| Yes | 335 |
|---|---|
| No | 119 |
| Undecided | 34 |
| Blank | 16 |
| Total | 504 |

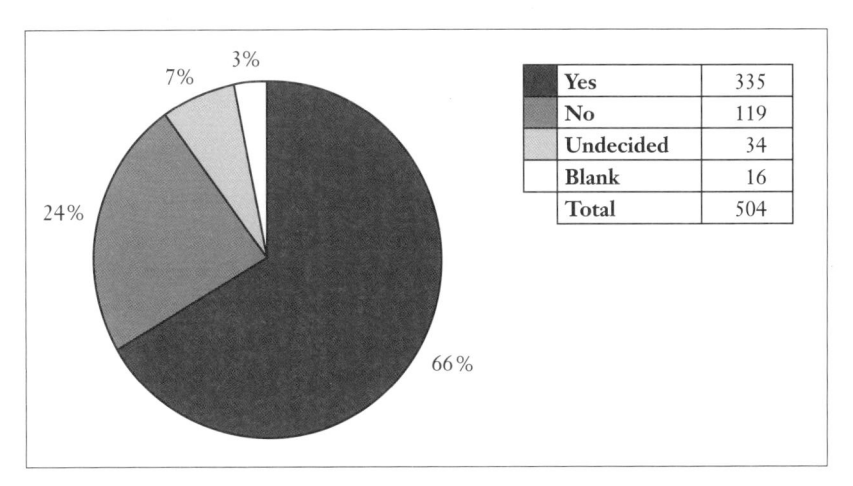

Table 52a and b. Stakeholder experience: guide ban

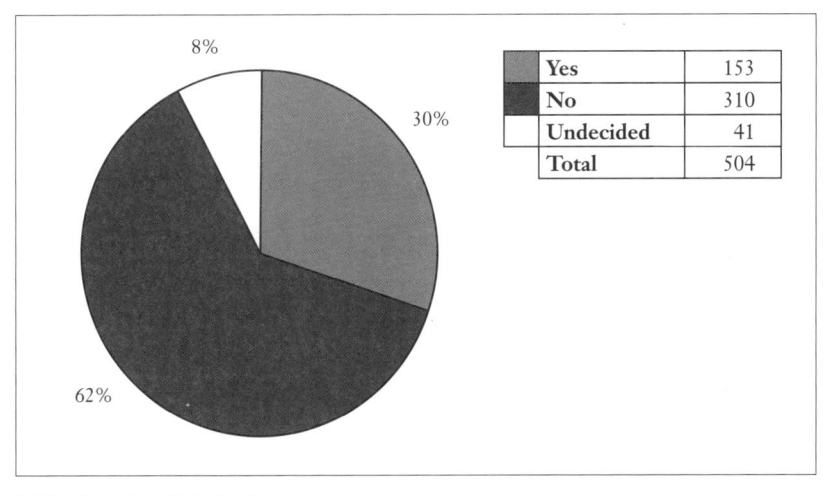

| Yes | 153 |
|---|---|
| No | 310 |
| Undecided | 41 |
| Total | 504 |

Table 53a and b. Stakeholder experience: photo ban

Photo Ban

We asked: "Did the photography ban in the tombs affect your visit?" Again we see that the ban has general approval, with 62% saying it did not affect their visit. However, many felt that the rules were easily broken, as evident from the following comments:

- "For a few euros to the attendant you can take all the photos you want."
- "It seemed to me that the tourists took very little notice of the guards and continued with flash and touching walls."

Stakeholder Survey Stage Two: Online Survey | 119

*Site Facilities*

Security

We asked: "Were security procedures appropriate?" Sixty-seven percent felt that site security was appropriate.

Bathrooms

We asked: "Were the bathroom facilities suitable?" Of those that used them, a majority felt that the bathrooms were not suitable and need replacing as well as a change of location. However, a large number (32%) did not see or use them.

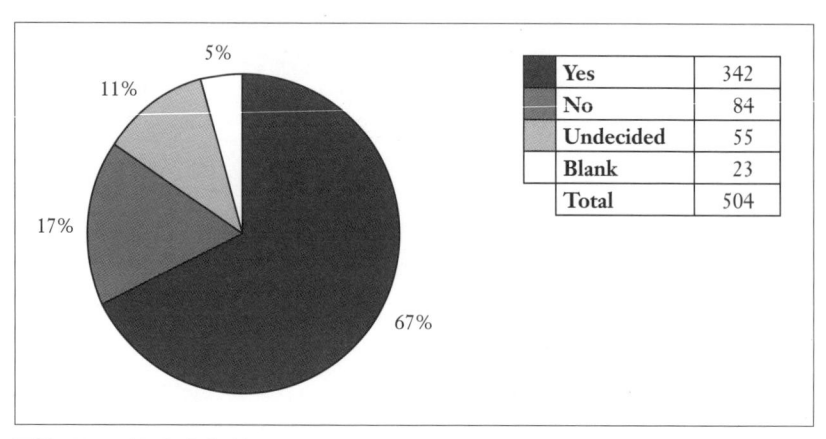

| Yes | 342 |
| No | 84 |
| Undecided | 55 |
| Blank | 23 |
| Total | 504 |

Table 54a and b. Stakeholder perceptions: appropriate security

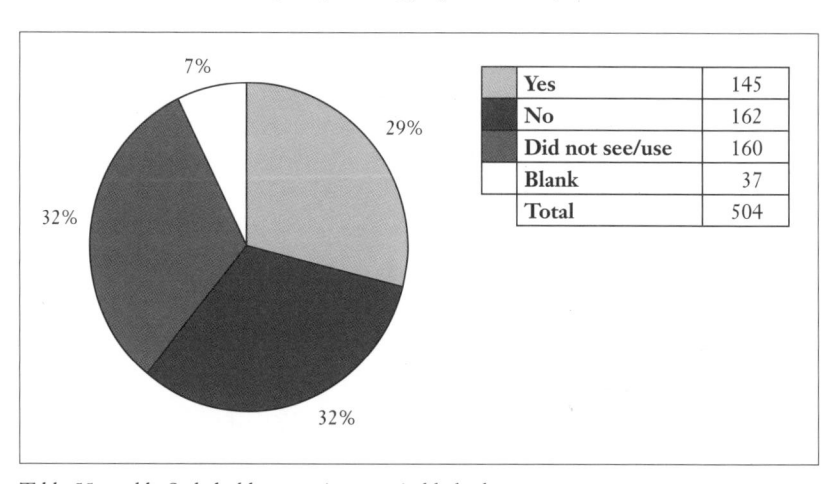

| Yes | 145 |
| No | 162 |
| Did not see/use | 160 |
| Blank | 37 |
| Total | 504 |

Table 55a and b. Stakeholder experience: suitable bathrooms

## Conclusions and Recommendations

Many of the suggestions and comments received in the online survey mirror the concerns of the participants in our earlier KV study described above. They call for better site facilities including a new cafeteria, new toilets, and improved shelter for visitors. They want to see extended opening hours in the summer months and a solution to running the gauntlet of the vendors in the present retail area. They want new options for the purchasing of tickets and a guarantee that funds will be used for conservation of the site. However, the responses we received were more detailed than previously and have, therefore, given us a greater insight into the views and wishes of the many stakeholders of KV. One recurring request is that information about KV and the tombs currently open should be made available on the Internet and at selected locations in Luxor, and that site-specific information should be made available in KV.

---

Typical Comments on Visitors' Most Frequent Recommendations
- "Lack of shade and lack of official guidebooks."
- "After the car park, etc., KV is beautiful. In places, it remains almost desolate even when busy. Do not spoil this impression!"
- "Fantastic for ruins but signage and control over site rather lacking."
- "How intrusive the tarmac can be."
- "Need more signage encouraging people to visit tombs at the end of the Valley."
- "Explanations on signs and tickets why numbers must be restricted to save the tombs."

---

Considering all this, it is positive to note that, when asked whether they would consider returning to the Valley, an overwhelming 92% of the population surveyed says they will "absolutely," "definitely," "surely" be coming back; many had, in fact, already booked tours or trips.

## Other Stakeholders

There are many stakeholders involved in the future of KV. Due to time and financial constraints this report has not been able to solicit the views of all of the organizations and individuals connected with KV. What follows is a brief review of these bodies and their relationship with KV.

| Yes | 467 |
| No | 18 |
| Blank | 19 |
| Total | 504 |

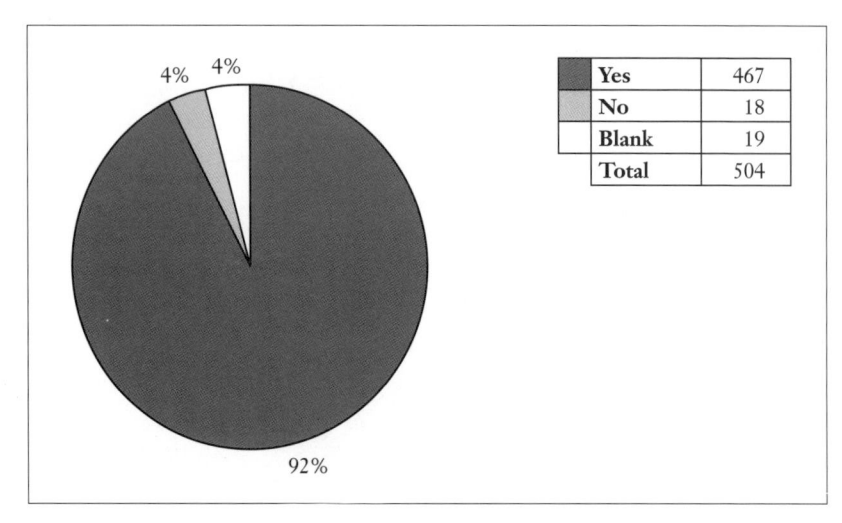

Table 56a and b. Stakeholder experience: return visit

The Ministry of Culture, of which the Supreme Council for Antiquities is a part, bears the primary responsibility for Egypt's monuments. The SCA is a large, bureaucratically complex organization that currently employs over nineteen thousand people. Many of its administrators believe that only by making the SCA a separate ministry (as is done in several other archaeologically rich countries), substantially scaling down the size of its staff, and introducing regular, professional programs of training, will it rise to the task of protecting Egypt's rich patrimony.

The Ministry of Tourism is responsible for encouraging and managing tourism in Egypt, and as such, its primary goal has been to bring as many tourists to Egypt's monuments as possible. There is nothing inherently antithetical about the goals of the SCA and the Ministry of Tourism if there is close cooperation between them, but this has not usually been the case.

The governor of Luxor City Council is responsible for the coordination of the activities of government ministries in Luxor. He sits with representatives of the ministries on the High Council of Luxor. Its decisions on road building, water, sewage, electrical supplies, and the growth of local villages directly affect the archaeological monuments.

The Ministry of the Interior controls the Tourism and Antiquities Police, who are responsible for the security of tourists on archaeological sites and the protection of archaeological monuments from theft and vandalism. They have a direct say in matters such as opening hours of sites and crowd control within sites.

International organizations such as UNESCO, while appearing to have no direct role in the management of KV, have a powerful role to play in influencing public perceptions of cultural heritage and in brokering responsible behavior in government ministries. Pressure can be brought to bear if inappropriate decisions are made, and training and guidance can be provided for site staff.

Tour agencies, both within and outside of Egypt, are a powerful lobbying group, often with direct access to government ministries. They can have a huge impact on site conservation, and they are an essential part of any future planning of visitor numbers and access controls.

# 5     Valley of the Kings Condition Survey

> There were several reasons why we began our Theban survey in the Valley of the Kings and not elsewhere in the necropolis. The rapid increase in mass tourism that had begun in the late 1970s seemed likely to continue. It was especially heavy in KV, and careful planning would be required to keep the tourist threat to a minimum. Nonetheless, tourism and archaeological preservation are not necessarily antagonistic, so long as tourism is properly controlled.[1]
>
> —Kent Weeks, 1998

Eighteen KV tombs are suitable for opening to the public (table 57), but usually only eleven at a time are available on a rotating schedule. The other forty-four tombs in the Valley are closed to visitors, some because of the need to protect them, some because they have not been cleared, some because they are undergoing restoration, and some because they are of no interest except to specialists. The condition surveys undertaken by the TMP have focused on the eighteen open tombs.

## Current and Recent Archaeological Intervention in the Valley of the Kings

As discussed above, archaeological work has had and continues to have a deep and lasting effect on the condition of KV. People have been digging

| KV 1    | Ramesses VII      | KV 17*  | Seti I            |
|---------|-------------------|---------|-------------------|
| KV 2    | Ramesses IV       | KV 19   | Mentuherkhepeshef |
| KV 6    | Ramesses IX       | KV 34   | Thutmose III      |
| KV 8    | Merenptah         | KV 35*  | Amenhotep II      |
| KV 9**  | Ramesses VI       | KV 43   | Thutmose IV       |
| KV 11*  | Ramesses III      | KV 47   | Siptah            |
| KV 14   | Tawosret/Setnakht | KV 57*  | Horemheb          |
| KV 15   | Seti II           | KV 62** | Tutankhamun       |
| KV 16   | Ramesses I        | WV 23   | Ay                |

\* = Tombs closed to the public as of December 2010
\*\* = Tombs open but requiring a separate ticket

Table 57. KV tombs accessible to tourists

in the Valley of the Kings since antiquity, and the story of this work is told in some detail in Nicholas Reeves and Richard Wilkinson's book, *The Complete Valley of the Kings*. However, the history of conservation work, touristic development, and recent archaeology in KV has yet to be written. In recent years, there have been from five to ten missions working annually in KV. In 2010, for example, there were seven missions working in the Valley: a French group in the tomb of Ramesses II; a Swiss team in the various habitation sites dotting the East Valley; Finns in the hilltop Village de Repos; Americans in the tomb of Amenmesse; British in the area between KV 9 and KV 57; the Theban Mapping Project in KV 5 and preparing a general Valley management plan; and the Egyptians in Seti I, in front of Merenptah, around Amenmesse and Mentuherkhepesh, and in the West Valley.

## Previous Work by the Theban Mapping Project

The Theban Mapping Project (TMP) was established in 1979 to prepare a detailed archaeological map and database of the Theban Necropolis. Its goal is to establish a historical and contemporary record of all the monuments in this ten-square-kilometer World Heritage Site, beginning with the Valley of the Kings. It firmly believes that if these ancient remains are to be preserved, the first and most essential step is to make detailed studies that record every archaeological, geological, and ethnographic feature at Thebes and regularly monitor the condition of its monuments.

Fig. 43. Surveying in KV 5. © Theban Mapping Project

To date, the TMP has achieved the following goals:
- It has compiled copies of all known maps, published and unpublished, of the Valley of the Kings. Together, these maps document the Valley's changing topography over the past 250 years.
- It has compiled an archive of historical photographs and engravings from the late eighteenth century onward that document changes in the Valley's appearance and track the history of touristic developments (such as footpaths and retaining walls) and the patterns of previous flash floods.
- It has acquired aerial photographs of the Valley. The earliest dates from 1918, but the most important are the 1949 survey made by the RAF, the 1969 survey of the French Centre national de la recherche scientifique (CNRS), the 1980 photographic survey made for the TMP by Egypt's Academy of Scientific Research, a 1986 Egyptian Air Force survey, and the 1992 survey made for Waseda University. In addition, new satellite imagery of the West Bank was acquired by the Center of Documentation in 2003. The TMP has also made extensive use of hot-air balloons to obtain oblique color photographs of all the significant features on the West Bank.

- It commissioned two photographers to prepare color images of all decorated walls in all KV tombs open to the public (except for KV 17, which is being photographed by the SCA; KV 62, which is being photographed by the GCI; and KV 19, which could not be photographed because it proved impossible to safely remove the huge glass panels in front of its walls.) This imagery is now available online on our website.
- It has collected existing topographic maps of the area and has prepared its own topographic map of the Valley of the Kings. The TMP map was published, together with detailed plans, sections, and axonometric drawings of all accessible KV tombs, in its *Atlas of the Valley of the Kings* (2000, 2002, 2003, 2005; available online at www.thebanmappingproject.com).
- It has conducted extensive geological, hydrological, and structural surveys of the Valley of the Kings, and these reports have been published in its *KV 5: A Preliminary Report on the Excavation of the Tomb of the Sons of Ramesses II in the Valley of the Kings* (2000, reprinted 2002, revised edition 2005).
- It has developed plans for the protection of tombs in case of future flash flooding and rainfall (published in the *KV 5* volume).
- It has designed and installed interpretive signs for visitors: general maps of the Valley; signs indicating which tombs are open to the public; and detailed signs specific to individual tombs, describing their most important features, illustrated with photos and tomb plans. The signs are laser-printed on aluminum sheets to withstand the harsh environment of the Valley.
- It has published an Arabic-language booklet on the Valley of the Kings intended for native Arabic-speaking students who visit as part of their school history courses. An initial printing of five thousand copies has sold out and is being reprinted by the SCA.
- It has made several KV tombs wheelchair-accessible by constructing ramps over sills in chamber doorways. Wheelchair-accessible tombs are identified on TMP signs.
- It rediscovered the entrance to KV 5, the tomb of the sons of Ramesses II, and has discovered over 130 chambers inside. It has devoted over fifteen years to the clearing and preservation of this

tomb. It discovered that the tomb was the largest ever dug in the Valley of the Kings, one of the largest ever found in Egypt. It was published in the *KV 5 Preliminary Report* and is updated regularly on the TMP's website. The discovery made headlines around the world and appeared on the cover of *Time* magazine in 1995.

- It has developed a website, www.thebanmappingproject.com, on which it publishes all the information it has assembled, including detailed maps, plans, photographs, and descriptions of all KV tombs, articles on Valley-related subjects, and 'zoomable' aerial photographs of the entire Theban Necropolis. The site, which receives over a million hits each month, is the recipient of over a hundred awards for excellence in content and design, and has been chosen as a website of the year by the *New York Times*, the *Times* of London, the *Guardian*, the *Christian Science Monitor*, *Popular Science*, and many other publications.

> The protection of our archaeological heritage must be based upon the fullest possible knowledge of its nature and extent. General surveys of archaeological resources are essential working tools in developing strategies for site protection. Consequently, archaeological survey should be a basic obligation in the protection and management of the archaeological heritage.
> —UNESCO, 1996[2]

## Current Tomb Condition Reports

In 2004–2005, documentation surveys of all accessible KV tombs were undertaken by means of detailed photographic and condition assessments and compiled by Dina Bakhoum, Lamia al-Hadidy, and Lotfy Khaled. These serve several purposes. The photographs taken by the TMP throughout the years form a valuable historical database of the tombs and provide a detailed record of their condition. Historical images are being collected to provide even more historical depth to these records, and we propose that the tombs be photographed periodically (every ten years, for example) in order to monitor changes in their condition. It is important to note that this condition survey has been carried out

Fig. 44. Dina Bakhoum, conservator. © Theban Mapping Project

visually. Only in KV 9 have monitoring devices been installed (described below), although such devices will eventually be installed in all open tombs, as funding permits.

The completed condition reports deal with each tomb individually. In some reports, each type of damage was given a symbol that is shown in figure 46. Figure 45 is from Corridor C in KV 15, showing the left and the right walls and the pictures taken of them. (Other detailed photos were taken but are not indicated on the general layout.)

The level of detail in the documented condition is enough to provide knowledge of the problems in a tomb, and forms an important record and survey of the tombs. On the other hand, it is important to note that before any restoration work is to take place, a more detailed survey should be carried out. The photographs taken by the TMP are useful in comparing the condition of tomb painting before and after restoration.

Fig. 45. KV 15: an example of TMP survey photographs. © Theban Mapping Project

## Methodology

The surveys undertaken by the TMP were conducted and laid out according to conventions adopted by international conservation bodies.

*The structural condition*

Most of the tombs in the Valley of the Kings are in a structurally stable condition. Cracks and fissures observed in the bedrock do not represent a danger to most tombs. In some cases, the cracks have resulted in the loss of plaster layers. The loss of plaster in such parts must have taken place shortly after the tomb was decorated. During recent restoration activities, replastering was done when plaster has fallen (due to its lack of cohesion to the substrate; see "The plaster layers," below). Such replastering serves to protect the remaining plaster from falling. A major disadvantage of much modern replastering is that it hides the real cause of the deterioration.

*The plaster layers*

Ancient Egyptian tombs show different techniques of decoration. In some cases, the decoration was carved or drawn on plaster; in other cases it was carved in bedrock. If the tomb was to be plastered, then, after cutting the tomb, a plaster layer would be applied, then scenes drawn in red lines (often later corrected in black ones). The plaster was then carved and painted. When reliefs were to be carved in stone, a very thin plaster layer was applied, and then the same procedure of drawing first in red lines, then correcting in black, then carving was followed. The choice of the technique might be related to the dynasty when the tomb was cut, and also depended in some cases on the quality of the bedrock.

In tombs that were plastered, the plaster was usually applied in two or more layers: a thick layer as the main base, and another, thinner layer as the base for the colors. When the bedrock was uneven, it was often necessary to apply two thick layers of plaster. The material used for mortar was in some cases clay with straw, ashes, or, in other cases, gypsum or lime. The types of damage and deterioration observed on the plaster layer and/or the carved stone surface include the following:

    a. The loss of the thick and thin plaster layers. The bedrock is visible, but in many cases recent restoration has replastered over the lost areas (further discussion below in "Interventions").

b. The loss of the thin plaster layer, while the background layer is still visible.
c. Powdering of the plaster layer.
d. Decay of the plaster.
e. Cracks or micro-cracks in the plaster layer or the bedrock. Often these cracks are related to cracks in the bedrock behind the plaster. In some cases, they are caused by the natural shrinkage of the plaster; in other cases, they are due to the detachment of the plaster layer from the substrate bedrock.
f. Detachment of the plaster layer from the background surface. This type of damage is very serious and can cause the plaster to fall away. In order to record this type of damage, one raps gently on the plaster and, according to the sound, hollow areas in the background can be identified. Detachment of plaster is also often indicated by micro-cracks, and in many areas where numerous cracks were found it could be assumed that the plaster is detaching. Many such areas had already been injected during previous restoration activities.
g. Human-made damage: scratches or hacking. In many tombs, scratches damaged the decoration and removed a substantial part of the plaster layer. Much of this damage can be attributed to ancient visitors.
h. Human-made damage: graffiti. Another form of human intervention is graffiti. This exists in numerous tombs in various forms over several centuries. In some cases, the graffiti are painted, drawn, or written on the plaster or stone surface. In others, they are carved in the plaster or stone. Numerous graffiti are the work of early travelers to the valley and give their names, the place they come from, and the date of their visit. In tombs where Christian monks lived, crosses and symbols were drawn on the walls. Beside ancient graffiti that has historical value, there is also some modern graffiti done by visitors during the twentieth century.
i. Wasp nests. Wasps built their nests on the walls and ceilings of many tombs. The problem with such nests is that they adhere to the surface of the painting and cannot be easily removed.

## The paint layer and the surface

The paint is the final layer applied to the surface of the plaster. Its deterioration, flaking, and detachment depend on the type of pigment, the binding material, and the grain size. The main types of damage are the following:

- a. Loss of the paint layer. In numerous tombs, paint was lost mainly in the upper parts of walls and in the corners of ceilings. This is perhaps due to the higher humidity in those areas.
- b. Flaking and detachment of the paint layer.
- c. Chromatic alterations, such as the fading of the colors.
- d. Abrasion of the paint layer.

Some damage, although not directly related to the paint layer, is found on its surface and is therefore included here.

- a. Soot blackening. In many tombs, the upper corners and upper parts of walls in corridors and chambers show blackening on the surface. In historical photographs, the black appears to be more intense than today. This black soot is most probably due to fires used in antiquity to provide light and heat. Much of this soot has been cleaned during recent restoration activities, but it has not been completely removed. For example in corridor D of KV 6, the soot has not been removed and looks today as it does in the historical images. In some recent restoration interventions, paint was applied over the black soot in order to hide it.
- b. Blackening due to humans touching the surface. People tend to touch areas where special scenes are indicated, and corners of gates or pillars while going up or down a corridor. This constant touching blackens tomb walls and, in some cases, fragile parts of the paint or the plaster have been knocked off.
- c. Dust accumulation. On almost all walls in the tombs, dust is accumulating and causing colors to appear darker and less intense than they really are. As there is no regular maintenance of the tombs and the dust is not regularly removed, it accumulates, sticking to the paint due to the high humidity in the tombs. This is very damaging, as it becomes heavy and causes underlying painting to detach. This phenomenon appears on almost all of the walls. It was therefore not

marked on each photograph but indicated only where the conditions were especially bad.
   d. Incrustations on blue and green pigments. A strange black incrustation appears on much of the blue and green pigments. It does not appear on any other colors. More analysis should be carried out to understand why it appears here. It may be the result of a chemical reaction with certain ancient consolidants.
   e. Salt efflorescence.

Interventions

Walls were thoroughly checked not only for damage but for any modern intervention. Although some interventions clearly prevented the tomb's decoration from being lost, others resulted in serious problems.
   a. Replastering of missing parts. Modern plaster has been applied to almost all lacunae.
   b. Stains due to chemicals used for injections and consolidation. In numerous areas of the ceiling and the walls, injections were used to strengthen the adhesion of plaster or paint to the substrate surface. The holes used for such injections are still visible, and show staining around them. In some cases, a kind of blackening or yellowing appears in areas at the center of the wall. It is not due to dust accumulation, fire, or bats. Due to its odd location, and the way it affects pigments, it is assumed that it is due to certain chemical consolidants that reacted badly with the background materials. Samples of plaster in such areas should be analyzed to learn what materials were applied there. In other areas, there are incrustations, blackening, or chromatic alterations that might be due to the application of chemicals. It was also noted that the injections were not done carefully enough to avoid leakage lines and stains.
   c. Paint over black soot.
   d. Retouching. In some tombs, there was retouching of areas where the plaster has fallen. Modern plaster was applied, then retouched.
   e. Wooden inserts for electricity cables. In some tombs, rounded wooden inserts were found at intervals in the upper part of the wall. In KV 6 these inserts still carry the old electrical cables used for the lighting of the tomb.

f. Glass panels. Glass panels have been installed in many tombs to protect the paintings from touching, scratching, or other damage. For this purpose, the glass panels are very effective. For example, in some tombs the plaster and paint layers are very fragile and would be easily detached if touched. But, despite the advantages of the glass panels, they do also have serious disadvantages that can result in worse deterioration of paintings. These panels are not fixed, as for museum objects where the environment is completely controlled. The glass does not reach the ceiling and accordingly the dust gets in and remains on the walls. The heat and humidity that accumulate behind the glass are also dangerous to the painted surfaces.

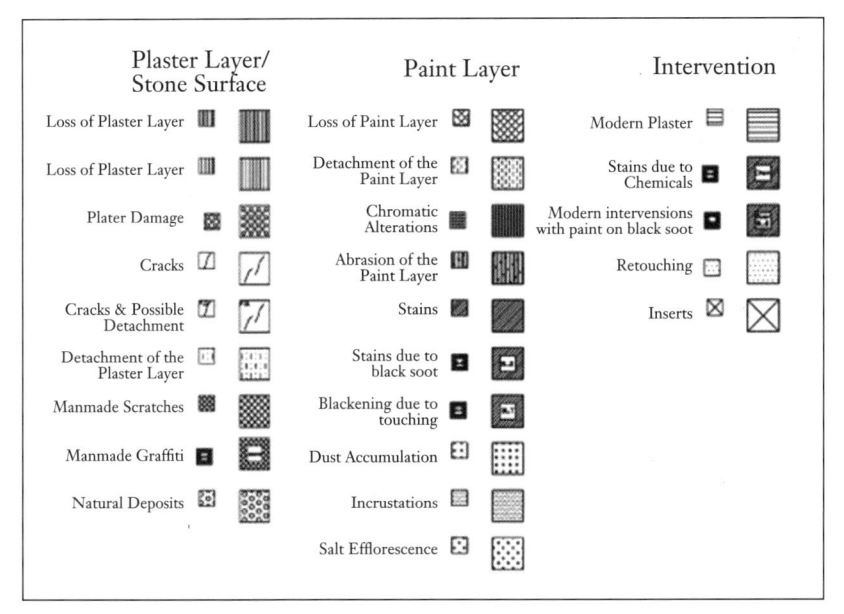

| Plaster Layer/ Stone Surface | Paint Layer | Intervention |
|---|---|---|
| Loss of Plaster Layer | Loss of Paint Layer | Modern Plaster |
| Loss of Plaster Layer | Detachment of the Paint Layer | Stains due to Chemicals |
| Plater Damage | Chromatic Alterations | Modern interventions with paint on black soot |
| Cracks | Abrasion of the Paint Layer | Retouching |
| Cracks & Possible Detachment | Stains | Inserts |
| Detachment of the Plaster Layer | Stains due to black soot | |
| Manmade Scratches | Blackening due to touching | |
| Manmade Graffiti | Dust Accumulation | |
| Natural Deposits | Incrustations | |
| | Salt Efflorescence | |

Fig. 46. Guide to conservation symbols. © Theban Mapping Project

## Photographic Survey Methodology

The TMP has undertaken a photo documentation project (compiled by Matjaž Kačičnik and Francis Dzikowski) for existing condition reports of tombs in the Valley of the Kings. The Theban Mapping Project, until the late 1980s, was focused on vertical aerial photographic coverage of sixty square kilometers of the Theban Necropolis. Then, in the 1990s, as excavation started in KV 5, the TMP shifted its focus underground and almost all decorated surfaces in KV 14 and KV 9 were photographed, from entryway to burial chamber. Parts of other tombs were also covered. For current condition reports, a complete record of tombs—each wall, each column, each ceiling—is needed. Since 2004, because of the scope of such a documentation project, limited time, and costs, the TMP decided to use digital cameras. For this work, our photographer, Matjaž Kačičnik, used a 6.1 Mega pixel digital SLR camera and a range of zoom lenses. Lighting the decorated surfaces of tomb walls was done with 1000-watt incandescent lights with umbrellas. Two to eight lights were used evenly to light the area being photographed.

The decision to use digital cameras meant that the TMP saved the expense of film, its processing, and scanning. But digital cameras require additional lenses, computer equipment, and computer image adjustment. We cannot avoid the dilemma of comparing film to digital images. Slide film still gives better quality than digital, but only if it is scanned with a top-quality scanner. Otherwise, 6.1 Mega pixel digital images are better. To get the best results, we shot in RAW format. To capture colors of painted walls accurately, the white balance of the digital camera had to be adjusted several times daily for each lighting setting.

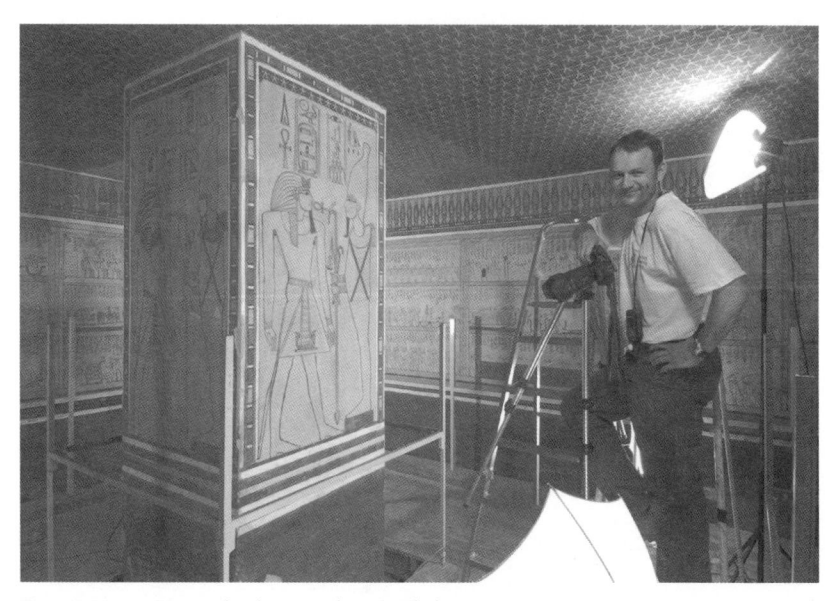

Fig. 47. Matjaž Kačičnik, photographer. © Theban Mapping Project

Dust has always been an issue with any photographic system, whether on lenses or slide negatives or in the camera chamber. Most digital SLRs eventually end up with dirt on the sensor (or, more accurately, on the low-pass filter protecting the camera's imaging sensor), resulting in smudges, blotches, and blobs on the final pictures. Today, dust is probably the biggest problem of digital SLR interchangeable-lens cameras, and there is much dust in tombs, on floors, on walls, and in the air. Therefore, photographic equipment has to be handled carefully. Equipment was cleaned on a daily basis, but we still got dust on the camera's sensor after a while. RAW format enables us to reduce the effects of any dust that might be present by means of computer programs, which compare RAW photographs with a reference image on which only dust is visible. (A reference image is created by capturing a bright, featureless white object from a short distance). When there is too much dust on the sensor, it has to be cleaned with special fluid and sensor swab. In this way, we were able to get the best quality images and an authentic copy of the area being photographed.

In the near future, we will have complete coverage of decorated surfaces in all tombs, from entryway to burial chamber, in high-quality digital format—easy to access and easy to work with—for future study, conservation, engineering, or environmental work.

## Tomb Environmental Monitoring

The condition of walls, plaster, and painted decoration in KV tombs can be seriously affected by changes in ambient temperature and humidity. It is therefore imperative that the temperature and humidity in KV tombs be constantly monitored and permanent records kept of the data. This is not currently the situation, and therefore we recommend that data sensors be installed on all open and potentially open tombs (table 57). Depending on the length and design of a tomb, monitoring may require from two to ten data sensors, installed at such features as ramps or staircases, changes in axis, narrow gates, or other architectural features that can affect airflow.

Sensors should not be placed at floor or ceiling level but as near the midpoint of a chamber or corridor as possible to record ambient room temperature. Attaching them to wooden handrails, for example, is a good option, provided they are discreetly positioned and securely mounted. Experience has taught that sensors that can be seen by visitors and easily removed are almost certain to be stolen.

The data sensors should be computer-compatible, and able to store at least sixty days' worth of data when taking readings at ten-minute intervals, twenty-four hours a day. Downloading should be a task assigned to specially trained members of the KV conservation staff.

The records generated by these sensors should be stored in multiple copies in the offices of the SCA and its conservation units and maintained as a permanent environmental record of the tomb. It should be kept in mind that "the role of microclimate can only be established if the processes involved are followed in situ simultaneously with accurate measurement of the microclimate. Sophisticated and extremely precise measurements of the microclimate do not explain anything unless they are related to the real processes occurring in situ."[3] Thus, accompanying notes should record any unusual activities in the tomb (cleaning, closure, heavy tourist traffic) so that these events can also be plotted in the environmental record. Unusually high or low readings should be monitored, and accompanying records of visitors and any activities that might help explain these readings should be noted. Correlations with visitor figures should be made, and the carrying capacity of a tomb may have to be changed if it appears that readings are too high or change too dramatically.

It has been clearly shown that the number of visitors in a tomb will affect temperature and humidity levels, but that effect is not immediate. There is a lag of two to three hours before visitors significantly raise temperature/humidity levels, and a lag of about one to two hours before their absence results in a decline. Thus, it is difficult to use changes in levels as a direct guide to controlling the number of visitors in a tomb. A warning system can, however, be installed in the most heavily visited tombs (such as KV 9 or KV 11), announcing that temperature/humidity levels have reached a predetermined critical level. At such a point, the tomb can be closed for an hour or two, until readings return to an acceptable level.

What is an "acceptable level"? It is believed that decorated tomb walls are not adversely affected by high or low temperature/humidity levels, as long as they remain in a range above 10° C or 20% and below 30° C or 65%. Within those ranges, any figures are acceptable, providing they do not change too rapidly or too dramatically. It is the changes in level, not the level itself, that poses problems. Ideally, then, an environmental monitoring system should be connected to an air-conditioning or air-exchange system that is turned on or off when certain temperature or humidity levels are reached. Such a system could maintain approximately constant levels, but only some of the time. An ideal temperature of 15° C ± 4° C, or an ideal humidity level of 50% ± 5%, for example, might be achieved 80% of the time, subject to the kind of equipment employed, the number of visitors, and the outside air quality. However, it would be expensive. (Because of the lag between tourist numbers and environmental changes, such a monitoring or warning system could not be effectively used to control visitor numbers. For that, we believe that a system based upon the ideal tomb carrying capacity should be used, as discussed below).

Furthermore, given that outside air temperature and humidity vary, that tourists have a significant effect on the temperature and humidity in a tomb, and that no long-term records of temperature and humidity levels in KV tombs exist, how do we maintain such constant environmental levels?

There are few previous studies, and the only reliable and detailed information available is from the study carried out by the GCI in the tomb of Nefertari in the Valley of the Queens (QV), and the more recent GCI study in KV 62, the tomb of Tutankhamun.

---

**Key Findings of the Getty Conservation Institute**
- Entrance of one person a causes rise in humidity.
- When tomb is closed, a stable temperature and humidity are recorded.
- Water vapor per person at 28° C is 0.013 gm/min.
- Plaster used in repairs can increase humidity.
- If air is changed twice/hr, the water vapor of 60 people and $CO_2$ of 43 people can be removed.

---

Therefore, to understand better the effect of visitors on the microenvironment of KV tombs, we selected one tomb in which to monitor temperature and humidity levels over a prolonged period. The tomb was KV 9, the tomb of Ramesses VI (fig. 50). One reason this tomb was selected was that it was due to reopen to the public after a period of restoration at the time of our study.

## Methodology

The data sensors we used are from the Ever Ready Thermometer Company, Inc. (ERTCO). The RHTEMP101 is a miniature, battery-powered, stand-alone temperature and humidity recorder (fig. 48). This device combines the latest in low-power technology with Windows-based software to provide a temperature and humidity recorder. Its real-time clock enables all data to be time- and date-stamped.

Fig. 48. ERTCO data sensor.
© Theban Mapping Project

Its reading rate is user-selectable and can range from one every two seconds to one per day. The start time and calibration are both programmable, and the device has the capability of alarming and real-time monitoring. Once activated, the device measures and records 4,096 humidity and 4,096 temperature measurements simultaneously. The storage medium is non-volatile solid-state memory, providing maximum data security even if the battery becomes discharged. It is small enough to be unobtrusive nearly anywhere. Once the data is collected, retrieval is simple. The software enables users to select reading rate, identify the device, and initiate the start of data collection within moments after hardware is connected.

ERTCO Data Sensor Technical Specifications
- Calibrated accuracy: ±0.5°C (0 to +50°C)
- Temperature resolution: 0.1°C
- Temperature range: -40°C to +80°C
- Humidity accuracy: 2% RH
- Humidity resolution: 0.5% RH
- Humidity range: 5% to 100% RH
- Operating environment: -40°C to 80°C, 5% to 95% RH

Fig. 49. Queues at KV 9. © Theban Mapping Project

As stated above, the tomb selected for our study was KV 9, the tomb of Ramesses VI. This tomb is centrally located and is considered by many to be one of the most beautiful tombs in KV. In addition, the tomb had just reopened after a period of restoration at the time of our study. Therefore, we knew we could expect high visitation figures during the study period.

We had six humidity- and temperature-recording devices available for use. These were positioned in KV 9 as in table 58 and figure 50. They were placed at regular intervals along the axis of the tomb and at positions where we knew groups of visitors would linger. The sensors were fixed at waist height to avoid dust from the floors and to utilize the readily available fixture point (the wooden handrail, positioned in the tomb about six inches away from the wall to discourage visitors from touching the reliefs). This height also made it easy to take readings (no need for a ladder or other more complicated methods). It also proved, however, to be a problem: we were concerned with the potential risk of vandalism and/or theft and, unfortunately, this turned out to be a reasonable fear.

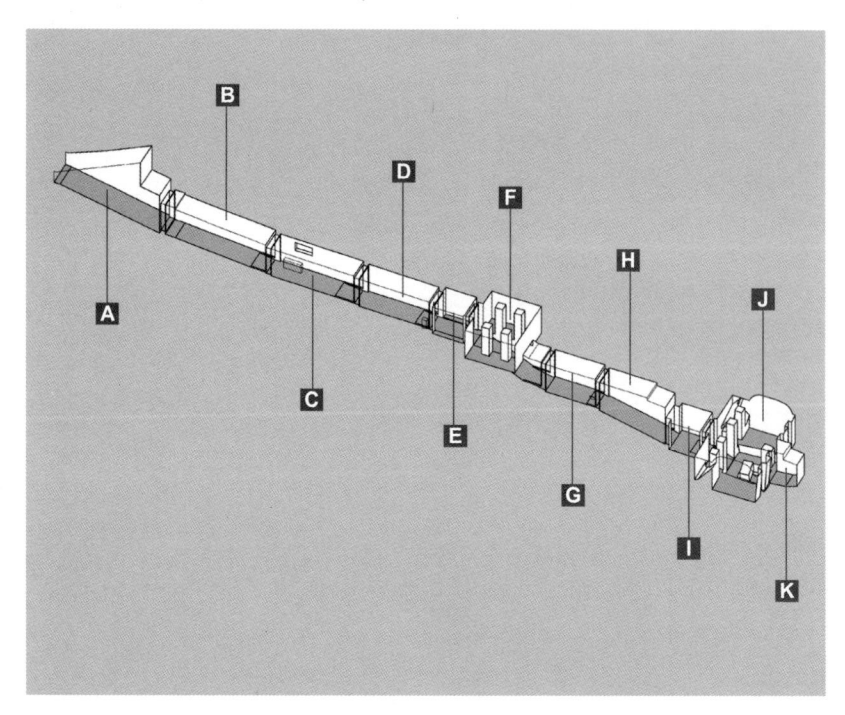

Fig. 50. Plan of KV 9, with chamber designations. © Theban Mapping Project

142 | Valley of the Kings Condition Survey

On the first day of use, we had one sensor stolen, and over the period of the study (less than twelve months), all but one were stolen. At a cost of US$100 per unit, this is a substantial loss. If the sensors are to be placed in all open tombs, a suitable way of securing them will have to be devised to avoid further losses.

| Serial No. | TMP No. | Postion |
|---|---|---|
| M17277 | 1 | Outside |
| M17278 | 2 | Chamber B |
| M17215 | 3 | Chamber D |
| M17264 | 4 | Chamber F |
| M17283 | 5 | Burial Chamber |
| M17296 | 6 | Burial Chamber |

Table 58. Data sensor positions

We recorded the data in three periods. These were:
1. 12 September 2004 to 27 November 2004
2. 31 January 2004 to 9 April 2005
3. 14 June 2005 to 28 August 2005

The tomb was closed to the public starting 15 April 2005.

## Data Results

Over a period of twelve months, temperature/humidity sensors were installed in KV 9, at locations shown in table 58. Their readings are shown in the accompanying charts.

| Position | Temp High C | Temp Low C | RH High % | RH Low % |
|---|---|---|---|---|
| **Exterior** | 54.6 | 7.8 | 67 | 5 |
| **Chamber B** | 33.1 | 11.7 | 60 | 14.5 |
| **Chamber F** | 33.1 | 21.2 | 71 | 18 |
| **BC-Front** | 33.6 | 23.7 | 74 | 19.5 |
| **BC-Rear** | 31.6 | 21.4 | 76 | 18 |

Table 59. Data sensor results KV 9, 12 Sept. 2004–27 Nov. 2004

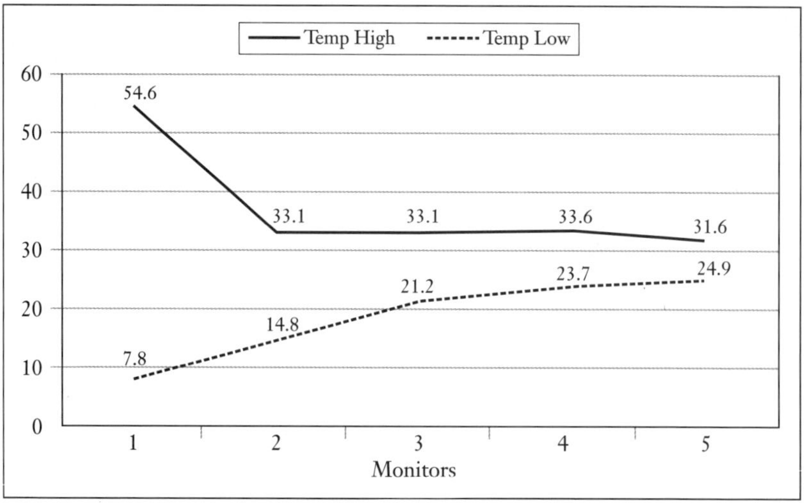
Temp High
Temp Low
60
50
40
30
20
10
0
54.6
33.1
33.1
33.6
31.6
7.8
14.8
21.2
23.7
24.9
1
2
3
4
5
Monitors

Table 60. Temperature highs and lows, KV 9, 12 Sept. 2004–27 Nov. 2004

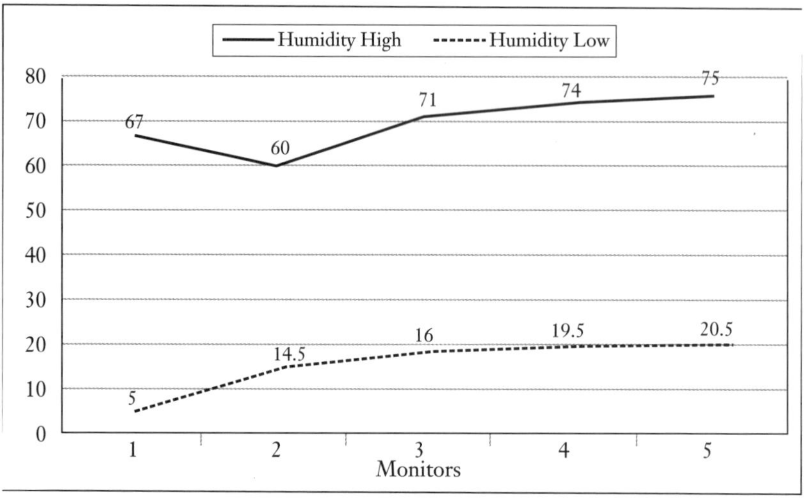
Humidity High
Humidity Low
80
70
60
50
40
30
20
10
0
67
60
71
74
75
5
14.5
16
19.5
20.5
1
2
3
4
5
Monitors

Table 61. Humidity highs and lows, KV 9, 12 Sept. 2004–27 Nov. 2004

| Position | Temp High C | Temp Low C | RH High % | RH Low % |
|---|---|---|---|---|
| Chamber B | 29.4 | 11.7 | 55.5 | 15.5 |
| BC-Rear | 29.3 | 21.4 | 71.5 | 18 |

Table 62. Data sensor results KV 9, 31 Jan.–9 April 2005

| Position | Temp High C | Temp Low C | RH High % | RH Low % |
|---|---|---|---|---|
| BC Rear | 27.8 | 27.2 | 34.5 | 26.5 |

Table 63. Data sensor results KV 9, 16 June–28 August 2005

The second and third sets of results are derived from two and then one monitor, respectively, due to the theft of the other monitors. The third set of readings was also taken when the tomb was closed to the public.

The difference between the lowest temperature readings, usually at 5:00 a.m., when the tomb had been closed for twelve hours, and the highest, at 5:00 p.m., when it had been open for twelve hours, is unacceptable from a conservation standpoint. To leave this changing environmental pattern unchecked will almost certainly mean that significant damage will occur to the tomb's decorated walls and ceilings. It was for this reason that the SCA decided to close KV 9 for an indefinite period starting 15 April 2005.

## 2010 Update

A brief survey was carried out in three tombs (KV 62, 47, and 2) by a member of the TMP staff on 5 October 2010 with a hand-held device.

In KV 62 from 11:44 a.m. until 12:00 noon, the internal temperature was 35.4°C –35.7°C with a range in humidity from 35%–40%, compared with the outside temperature that day of 36°C with humidity level of 26%. It should be noted that the tomb ventilation system was in operation during the inspection.

In KV 47 from 12:09 to 12:30 pm, the temperature ranged from 30.4°C to 34.4°C with a humidity range of 24%–37%. It should be pointed out that during our inspection a small group of seven visitors came in the tomb and engaged us in conversation in the burial chamber, and a noticeable spike in the readings was observed.

In KV2 from 1:05 p.m. to 1:15 p.m., the range of temperature was between 34.9°C and 37.8°C with a humidity level of 25%–34%.

## TMP Proposals

One possible solution to ensure the tomb's safety while maintaining access to the public is an air-exchange system that extracts air from the tomb and allows natural currents to replace it with air from outside.

Another is to use an air exchange system that treats the air that enters the tomb, either by chilling it or by lowering its level of humidity.

A third solution is to install air-conditioning equipment in the tombs. But many units are large, difficult to place without damaging the aesthetic of the Valley, use large amounts of electricity, are difficult to maintain, and depend on water for their chiller units. Many archaeologists do not want to pipe water into KV because the possibility of broken pipes and leakage could pose an unacceptable threat. But these problems can be mediated, and an example of such an installation is detailed below.

These are three possible actions: (1) set a maximum limit on the number of visitors allowed in the tomb at any one time, a figure to be determined by experimentation and careful monitoring of the environment or by setting arbitrary figures for carrying capacity; (2) install devices to control the environment and maintain temperature and humidity within a specified range no matter how many or how few visitors come into the tomb; or (3) actions 1 and 2 together.

In 2010, the GCI undertook plans to clean and conserve the walls of KV 62, the tomb of Tutankhamun, and that project is set to continue over the next several years. The GCI has also begun work in the Valley of the Queens, and their report (on work from 2006–2010, to continue through 2012) contains much valuable information on tourism and site management that is applicable to work in the Valley of the Kings. (See Getty Conservation Institute, *Valley of the Queens: Proposals for Conservation, Management and Presentation*, 2009.)

The complete conservation reports on principal KV tombs carried out by the Theban Mapping Project can be found online at www.thebanmappingproject.com.

# 6
# Valley of the Kings Infrastructure

As we have demonstrated in the preceding chapters, the greatest threats facing the Valley of the Kings today are a result of its popularity with visitors. To tackle the complex problems caused by such huge numbers of visitors, we have to identify the causes, and develop plans to manage the Valley in ways that will mitigate tourism's adverse effects. For example, we need to calculate how many people can safely visit the Valley in a single day; how many can visit in one hour; how tourists should be distributed within the Valley; what facilities must be provided for visitors; and how they should be provided so that they impose as little as possible upon the fabric of the Valley.

It is worth reiterating that the goal of the Valley of the Kings Masterplan is to secure the long-term future of the site. This has involved two large-scale stakeholder consultations on the future direction of any changes to KV, studies of the physical character of the Valley and its tombs, visitor behavior studies, planning with the SCA and the government of Japan regarding the construction and design of a Visitors Center for the Valley, and discussions with the government of Spain concerning implementation of a proposed management plan. These detailed surveys and analyses have helped us gain greater understanding of the day-to-day operations of the Valley, without which no management plan can be constructed.

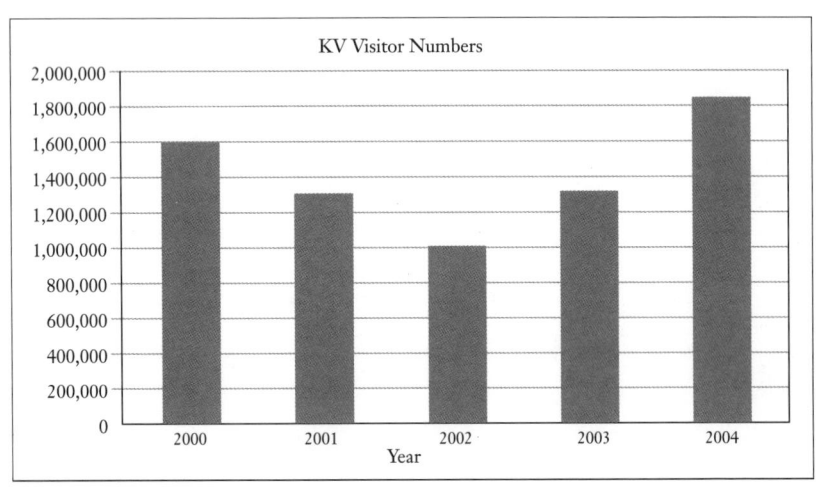

Table 64. Visitor numbers to KV, 2000–2004

This data will enable us to devise a visitor management strategy. It will consist of the following elements, discussed in more detail below:
- Access to the site
- Site facilities
- Security measures
- Carrying capacity of the site
- Visitor flow into and within the site
- Carrying capacity of the individual tombs
- Visitor access
- Site ticketing systems
- Site and tomb protection measures

To understand the present-day visitor experience, we will take the journey the visitor makes from the East Bank of the Nile (the main starting point for most visitors) to KV, through its tombs, and out again.

## The Visitor Experience and the Valley of the Kings

The majority of visitors travel to the West Bank on buses provided by their tour operators. Independent visitors usually travel by taxi or minibus, crossing over the Luxor Bridge to the Theban Necropolis, a trip of 15 km that takes approximately forty minutes. However, an increasing number of tourists, mainly independent travelers, now stay on the West

Fig. 51. Ferry on West Bank. © Theban Mapping Project

Bank of the Nile in any of a growing number of small hotels and self-catering flats. Their journey is normally made by taxi, local bus, or bicycle. A regular ferry system crosses the river, and some visitors still cross the Nile by local ferry or motorboat.

Once on the West Bank, the preferred route to the Valley is via the road beside the Colossi of Memnon (often the first monument visited, and one for which no ticket is required) to the central ticket office at Beit al-Medina (which, incidentally, no longer sells tickets to KV.)

From this point there are three routes to the Valley of the Kings. Two are poorly maintained footpaths that lead from Deir al-Bahari or Deir al-Medina over the hills to KV. They are used by only a handful of hikers or donkey riders. The third and most popular route is a paved road from Carter House to KV.

## Roads and Pathways to the Valley of the Kings

A visit to the Valley of the Kings begins well before one reaches the Valley proper, at the north end of the Theban Necropolis, near the house built eighty years ago by Howard Carter, the archaeologist who discovered the tomb of Tutankhamun, as his field headquarters. From Carter House, the road arcs over 4 km through a series of wadis. That road, which lies in part along the path used by ancient priests, was paved with asphalt about forty years ago. All vehicular traffic to KV travels this route. The entranceway is guarded by a small security detachment. This road should offer tourists fine examples of the Western Desert's natural beauty. Unfortunately, it does not.

For the past decade or so, despite regular protests by Egyptologists and occasional governmental prohibitions, people have used this well-traveled road as a dumping ground for rubbish. At first, excavation debris from projects working in KV tombs was dumped here. Then, seeing an opportunity to cut transport costs, local contractors began dumping construction waste, including broken tiles and old toilets. Villagers began to add household waste and garbage to the mix; a local septic pump-out service emptied tankers full of human waste; and local clinics began to discard used bandages, needles, scalpels, and vials of drugs.

Fig. 52a and b. Approach to KV. © Theban Mapping Project

Valley of the Kings Infrastructure

The result is that visitors to KV travel through an ugly, offensive, and often foul-smelling wadi. For local inhabitants, the garbage poses serious health problems. Raw sewage has migrated downhill toward a well that is a significant source of potable water at the north end of the necropolis. The well is already in danger of being severely polluted. The medical waste is a threat to the well-being of children who sometimes play here. Attempts to ban dumping have been only intermittently and marginally successful, largely because there is no on-site enforcement.

**TMP Proposals**
  A. The house built and occupied by Howard Carter at the north end of the Theban Necropolis, adjacent to the road leading to the Valley of the Kings, has been considered a possible site for a small museum. In fact, about ten years ago, The Arab Contractors, one of Egypt's largest construction companies, were hired to check the building structurally and prepare the surrounding area as a parking lot in anticipation of that use.
  B. We proposed making Carter House into a small museum devoted to the life of Howard Carter and his work in the Valley of the Kings, especially his discovery of the tomb of Tutankhamun. There are almost no objects currently known that could be installed in Carter House, although the SCA does have a series of photographic panels dealing with the Tutankhamun discovery, currently on display in the Egyptian Museum, Cairo. The SCA has agreed to remove these to Carter House to form the first set of exhibits. These panels could be expanded upon, and photographs of Carter working in the house and at the Valley of the Kings could gradually be added.

  Initially, Carter House would require only one guard to oversee the building during opening hours. Until more exhibits are installed and tour guides come to view the site as a useful tourist stop, we would recommend not charging an admission fee.

  Except for a small charge to transport and install the display panels, the only significant cost in preparing the house as a museum would be the installation of appropriate lighting. The preparation of additional panels in future would involve minor costs.

Fig. 53. Carter House. © Theban Mapping Project

2012 Update

A. In 2010, Carter House was opened as a museum, and a contract was let to a local hotel to operate a café at the site. To encourage guides to include "Carter's Café" in their itinerary, no admission fee was charged at first, but that has been changed. Visitors can now walk through Carter's kitchen, dining room, bedroom, office, and photography studio, which have been restored and filled with period artifacts, some belonging to Howard Carter. A twenty-minute film hosted by a holographic Carter transports the visitor back to the time of the discovery and recounts the excitement of the opening of the tomb of Tutankhamun. The number of visitors to the museum is small—a few dozen each day—and more interpretive signs are needed, but it is a useful addition to the West Bank's archaeological landscape.

B. Although most visitors are taken by tour companies to KV, clearer signage for independent travelers looking for KV would be an asset to the site. In addition, a welcome sign would be appropriate, with the name of the site and the SCA and World Heritage logos prominently displayed. Near Carter House, a map of the West Bank should be placed along with an indicator board notifying visitors

which tombs are open and the giving the current visitor status of the individual tombs (see below for more details).
C. The roadside area from Carter House to KV should be cleaned of rubbish, using front loaders and graders. The debris should be hauled farther into the desert, and there should be areas designated for archaeological excavation debris, construction waste, rubbish, and raw sewage. (Ideally, a waste treatment plant should be constructed on the West Bank and sewage lines laid in villages.) The area should be landscaped so that the roadway looks as much as possible like it did decades ago. Power, septic, and water lines to be laid from the Nile Valley to the entrance of KV should be installed underground in protective conduits. Intermediate pumping stations for incoming water and a holding tank at a midway pump-out station should be carefully sited to minimize problems of noise, smell, and visibility.

Plans are being discussed to build replicas of some KV tombs in the desert lowlands north of Carter House to help reduce pressures on the actual KV tombs. Serious planning must be undertaken before such construction begins, and care must be taken not to damage the several archaeological sites—quarries, tombs, and hermitages—scattered around the proposed construction area. Still, the use of replica tombs for tourism is probably an idea whose time has come. The use of replicas has been discussed for over a decade now, but no final plans have been made. A constraining factor is the likely cost of the work, and the problems posed by accurately replicating tombs over a hundred meters in length that slope steeply downward from entrance to burial chamber.

D. The grading of the wadi leading from Carter House to KV should be carefully planned so that its slope can help control the direction and the speed of any floodwaters that pour along here whenever there is a rainstorm in KV. Northwest of Carter House, the city has already dug a trench to divert such floodwaters away from archaeological sites and modern villages. However, five years after work began, the city-built flood-control system is not yet complete: the slope of the ditch must be recalculated to ensure that it proceeds downhill (in some places, it does not). In addition, channels, covered with steel gratings, must be cut across the paved road so that floodwaters flowing along its southern side can be channeled into the diversionary ditch on its north. Several cross-road channels should be cut at hundred-meter intervals across the road, and an additional two or three should be dug, perhaps ten to fifteen meters apart, northwest of the ditch's starting point.

E. A program of regular inspection of the roadway should be undertaken by the antiquities inspector responsible for KV. He or she must ensure that no further dumping occurs and that violators are punished. Flood-control measures must be regularly inspected and cleaned so that they remain in good condition. Maintenance staff should patrol the roadway at weekly intervals to collect windblown papers and rubbish tossed from vehicles. They should also empty rest-stop waste receptacles.

F. The road from Carter House to the KV bus parking lot is paved with asphalt and at present is in good condition. The curbing, however, has been removed in places (presumably by the drivers) to permit trucks to dump excavation debris illegally alongside it. The curbing should be replaced and future dumping prevented.

G. Footpaths from KV to Deir al-Bahari and Deir al-Medina should be cleaned and steps cut into the bedrock where needed to prevent injuries to tourists. A panoramic photo of the Nile Valley at Thebes should be installed low to the ground at the top of the footpath, near the so-called Village de Repos, labeled to identify the monuments in the Theban landscape. Three years ago, the Security Office erected a sign that says tourists are prohibited from walking this footpath. The SCA objected and a compromise was reached: any tourists who choose to walk on the footpath will not be stopped by police, but the sign will remain.

## Types of Transport

The vast majority of visitors to KV come by bus. These range in size from ten-passenger minivans to large fifty-passenger models. The latter are more common, although few of them arrive more than 50 percent to 70 percent full (i.e., with 25–35 passengers). Most of the buses bring tourists from hotels and cruise boats moored on Luxor's East Bank, or drive from Hurghada and other towns on the Red Sea, arriving at about 8:00 a.m. and returning to the Red Sea at 5:00 p.m. Several times each year, these are joined by dozens of buses bringing Egyptian school and university students to KV.

Taxis and private cars are the second most common means of transport. On average, these vehicles carry only two passengers each. About forty to sixty arrive at KV daily.

Other vehicles making the journey to KV include utility vehicles such as septic pump-out tankers, SCA trucks, security cars and vans, and tractors with trailers that carry excavation debris from KV or water to KV toilet facilities. These vehicles, although few in number (perhaps fifteen to twenty per day), cause further congestion because of their slow progress and frequent stops.

A few tourists come to KV by donkey. These are usually young travelers who have come in small groups of ten to fifteen persons, and who contract with a guide or stable manager to hire donkeys for a morning. In past years, only two or three such groups came to KV each day. Recently, however, the donkey trip has become increasingly popular, and as many as fifty to a hundred riders can be seen each morning. They set out from the west bank of the Nile with a guide and a couple of donkey drivers at about 7:00 a.m. and proceed west to the traffic checkpoint, then turn north to al-Tarif, then west again along the paved road to KV. Since donkeys are not permitted in the Valley itself, the riders dismount at the entrance to the parking area, buy their admission tickets, and visit KV. Meanwhile, their donkeys are taken over the hills around KV to await their riders on the path leading to Deir al-Medina or to Deir al-Bahari.

A few riders come to KV by donkey from Deir al-Medina or Deir al-Bahari, riding up the hill and leaving their animals on the hillside above KV. They must then walk through KV to the ticket office (and only then go through a security check) before returning to KV for a visit to the tombs. When finished in KV, they climb the hill, remount, and return to their point of origin.

Horse carriages are rare—seldom more than two or three per week. They bring tourists from the East Bank via the new bridge or from the Nile to KV. Most passengers are unaware that a carriage ride to the Valley is a very long one—it takes several hours—or that the long, uphill, and waterless trip is extremely hard on the horses. The carriages wait outside the parking area for an hour or two before returning to the Nile. Such trips, in fact, are prohibited, and usually the carriage drivers are not the carriage owners but men who rent the carriage from the owner (who remains ignorant of its itinerary, and who receives little of the money paid out by the tourist). The Brooke Animal Hospital in Luxor has posted signs in several hotels urging tourists not to make the trip to KV by carriage, but a few carriages arrive at the valley each week.

Bicyclists, usually young backpackers traveling in pairs, ride from the Nile to KV along the main road. About ten riders a day make the trip. They park their bicycles just outside the parking area.

A few visitors come on foot, some along the main road, but most, perhaps ten daily, hike over the hill from Deir al-Medina or Deir al-Bahari. The hikers must then walk through the Valley of the Kings to the parking lot in order to purchase tickets for the tombs. On their return to the Valley, they must check their video cameras at the main gate. After their visit, having retrieved their cameras, they must then either walk out of KV along the main road, or sneak around the security post since video cameras are not permitted in KV.

**TMP Proposals**

    A. As stated above, an increasing number of tourists travel to KV by donkey, bicycle, or foot. Few realize that the road they must take is long and uphill. Three simple, shaded roadside rest stops should be constructed at appropriate intervals along the road. At the moment there is only one, which is awkwardly situated, in poor condition, and has little shade. Waste receptacles should also be provided there.

    B. With construction of the new Visitors Center (see chapter 6), the donkeys will have to change their route around KV. Moreover, when a fixed-line water supply is provided at KV, it would be very useful to construct a small watering place for the donkeys near the newly proposed car park.

    C. Prohibited vehicles, such as horse carriages and trucks carrying waste, should be stopped at the start of the main KV road near Carter House by security services.

Fig. 54. Current parking lot. © Theban Mapping Project

## Vehicle Parking

The road from Carter House leads to a small, irregularly shaped parking area at the juncture of the roads to the East and West Valleys of the Kings. The parking lot can accommodate as many as seventy-five large tour buses, but any number above thirty-five or so results in congestion that is dangerous to pedestrians and results in delays when buses leave. It is not unusual for buses to fill the KV parking area and have to park in the approach road, and traffic can be so bad that it can take a departing bus twenty minutes to navigate its way out of the 150-meter length of the parking lot. Since the bombing of a hotel in Taba in 2004, taxis and private vehicles have been prohibited from stopping in the KV parking area, and must instead park alongside the road before its entrance, causing significant congestion. At present, large buses are charged LE 5.00 to park in the KV lot; smaller vans pay LE 1.00. This money goes to the Luxor City Council, not to the SCA.

| Vehicle Type | No | % |
| --- | --- | --- |
| Coach | 414 | 58.39 |
| Mini bus | 164 | 23.13 |
| Taxi | 115 | 16.22 |
| Private car | 16 | 2.26 |
| Total | 709 | 100.00 |

Table 65. Vehicle numbers in KV, 6am–5pm, 6 February 2005

## TMP Proposals

The existing parking area is currently used only by tour buses, since passenger cars are prohibited from entering and must park outside along the road leading from Carter House to KV. We have proposed redesigning the current parking area as part of a broader plan for a new Visitors Center. According to that plan, the present car park would become a load/unload zone. Once a bus had dropped off its passengers, it would return down the road to the new parking area in the next wadi to the east, where it would wait until the tour guide telephoned to inform the driver that the group was ready to be picked up. The bus would then return to the load/unload zone. This procedure means that each tour bus would make two trips into the load/unload zone, but by designing that area properly we do not believe this doubling of traffic would pose safety problems or create delays. The advantage of having a new parking area is that it would lie in a wadi that permits almost unlimited expansion of parking facilities (fig. 55).

*2012 Update*

The area previously recommended by the TMP as an additional or alternative parking area is now the site of the new electrical tram charging station.

Fig. 55. Proposed new parking area. © Theban Mapping Project

It is occasionally used by private cars and some buses if the main KV parking area is congested. Another area, between the Visitors Center and the West Valley of the Kings guard house (to the west of the paved parking lot), has now also become an unpaved parking area, dedicated to minivans. It is unclear how or why this came to be. Since the paved parking lot is used for just that, instead of as a drop-off/loading area only, it has become more crowded than we had anticipated, and the additional parking area we had established is considered too far away for drivers to gather together and smoke a cigarette while waiting for the return of their passengers.

## Vendors' Area

Before a bus enters the parking area, it stops at the parking area entrance where its passengers disembark. This is done so that tourists must walk past a row of thirty-eight kiosks in which local merchants sell postcards, hats, costumes, film, and replica antiquities, before reaching the tram that will take them to KV.

Our stakeholders consultation indicates that many tourists, especially the elderly and handicapped inexperienced travelers, found this an unpleasant experience. After visiting KV, tourists will again walk past the

Fig. 56. Vendors' area. © Theban Mapping Project

sales kiosks into the parking lot where they locate and board their bus and depart the Valley. (Buses going to the Tomb of Ay drive through the parking lot directly into the West Valley.)

The parking and vendor area is also flanked by a first-aid station and ambulance garage, and a cafeteria that has been closed for the past six years. Behind the cafeteria, small diesel tractors pull passenger carriages that serve as a tram line carrying tourists the 350 meters farther south to the entrance of the Valley of the Kings.

## TMP Proposals

With the construction of the new Visitors Center and the redesign of the adjacent parking area and vendors' stalls, this area will be significantly changed.

- A. A maximum of forty kiosks should be built in front of the entrance to the new KV Visitors Center. These would replace the thirty-eight kiosks currently operating. A plan showing their possible location has been prepared by the Architectural Office of the SCA.
- B. One kiosk should be dedicated to the sale of SCA publications and SCA-approved videos, CDs, DVDs, films, posters, and copies of Egyptian artifacts. The SCA kiosk should be given pride of place, nearest the entrance to the Visitors Center and directly on the path of tourists entering and leaving the site. Proceeds from its sales should go directly to the newly created SCA Holding Company that will fund various SCA conservation and restoration activities at archaeological sites.
- C. The remaining kiosks should be rented to the current leaseholders of kiosks east of the KV parking lot, if those leaseholders agree to newly established rent levels and certain conditions of operation. (A smaller number of kiosks, perhaps each operated by a consortium of current leaseholders, could also be considered.) We suggest that the kiosks on the west side of the Visitors Center—the side along which arriving tourists will walk—should concentrate on selling items that visitors might use during their KV visit: hats, film, camera batteries (even though cameras are banned), guidebooks, and maps, for example. Those on the east side, along the path departing tourists will use to reach the bus pickup point, can sell

other, "take-away," merchandise: posters, copies of artifacts, clothing, and books. According to the TMP Stakeholder Survey, kiosk leaseholders are amenable to the idea of having kiosks specialize in the sale of various items—one selling film, another statuettes, for example—and of having the SCA set general standards for the quality of merchandise offered. A decision on this, on the order in which kiosks are placed, on the kinds and quality of goods to be sold, on prices, and on rental fees to be charged, should be made by a committee of kiosk operators, representatives of the SCA, and other relevant parties. The size and layout of each kiosk should also be discussed, as should questions of lighting and electrical wiring, painting, security, and the types of merchandise displays to be allowed. A kiosk-operators' representative should be chosen to represent their interests in future ongoing discussions.

D. One or two kiosks should sell food and drink. To minimize litter, the kinds of food to be sold should be strictly limited to small packages of chips or biscuits, the drinks to water and soft drinks. Hot food should not be made available, nor should foods or drinks in large containers. Tables with umbrellas and immovable seats can be set out in front of the Visitors Center, near the bus departure area. Appropriate trash receptacles should be located throughout this area and in all of KV.

E. Kiosks should be open throughout the day, observing the same hours as the Visitors Center and KV itself. To this end, electricity will have to be installed and metered and its cost factored in when determining kiosk rental rates.

2012 Update

In the last few years, a new vendors' area has been opened to visitors to the Valley, adjacent to the Visitors Center proper. Unlike the previous arrangement, visitors now enter and leave the valley through the vendors' area. Some tourists still complain about the vendors, although their interaction with visitors has improved as more vendors find that hassling produces fewer sales than maintaining a quiet presence. Improvements still need to be made. As of 2012, the SCA plans to build its own large sales area through which tourists will pass before exiting the valley through the vendor area. This building, covering about eight hundred square meters, will offer SCA publications. The cafeteria, which proved unsuccessful, has closed, but is to be remodeled and reopened in 2012 on a smaller scale, serving only soft drinks and chips. As of January 2013, neither the SCA shop nor a new cafeteria has yet been opened.

## Visitors Center

At this point in the visit to KV, visitors would previously have encountered the now closed cafeteria and proceeded by diesel train to the security and camera check. However, this building has now been demolished and the site is to be the location of a Visitors Center. Here we will discuss the likely impact of such a development.

> Often conservation or management plans omit recommendations for making the significant values of a site understood: interpretation. If this somewhat elitist view is pursued, the ongoing destruction of archaeological sites of significance is assured.
> —G. Grimwade and B. Carter, 2000[1]

Interpretation of heritage sites is primarily about explaining significance and meaning; this is the planned role of the Visitors Center in KV. It requires research, planning, and strategic consideration of the best media forms to use and the principal messages to be conveyed to the targeted audiences. It must present the meaning behind the site, which creates value and significance.

### The Commissioning of the Visitors Center

In 2004, the SCA signed an agreement with the government of Japan under which the Japanese International Cooperation Agency (JICA) will build a Visitors Center at the Valley of the Kings, on the site of the old and abandoned cafeteria and rest house. It was agreed that JICA would provide the building, but the SCA would be responsible for water, septic, and electrical connections, and for all surrounding facilities (including parking, vendors' stalls, tramlines, cafeteria, first-aid station, and security posts). JICA was also to provide a 3 m x 3 m plastic model of the Valley

Fig. 57. Demolition of old cafeteria. © Theban Mapping Project

of the Kings for installation in the Center. The Theban Mapping Project agreed to design the exhibits, mainly a series of wall-mounted display panels (in Arabic, Japanese, and English) in the Visitors Center, to develop continuously running films to be shown on TV monitors, and to install computer programs to be made available on interactive computer stations. The Center was to be completed early in 2006.

It is planned to include 620 square meters of exhibition space. The building itself has already been designed, and its plan, including fixed internal features (walls, computer terminals, 3-D model displays, TV monitors, toilets, check points, sales and information desks), have been approved by the SCA and contractually agreed to. If 1,400 tourists are to pass through this space each hour, then twenty-four visitors will enter the building every minute. We estimate that the average time tourists will spend in the Visitors Center is ten minutes. This is the amount of time needed for a cursory examination of the displays, and also the amount of time, under the current ticketing system, that tourists will have to wait while their guide buys KV admission tickets at the ticket kiosk (to be a part of the Visitors Center). It is unlikely that tour groups, most of them on very tight schedules, will ordinarily stay longer than ten minutes in the Center. The exhibits in the Visitors Center must be designed in such a way that they can be viewed by about a thousand persons per hour—about two hundred people every ten minutes. They should lead tourists along a clear path from entrance to exit.

In February 2005, Dr. Holeil Ghaly and Dr. Kent Weeks submitted a proposal to the SCA describing the purpose of such a Visitors Center and offered suggestions as to what that Center and its adjacent buildings should contain. The Visitors Center now being constructed conforms in general to those suggestions. Three principal concerns were emphasized in that proposal:

1. Planning and construction had to take into account the anticipated increases in tourist numbers in KV, and facilities built in 2005 must accommodate a twofold increase in tourist numbers over the next decade.
2. Proper water mains and septic systems should be installed that rely on pipes running from al-Tarif to the site, not on storage tanks, pump-out vehicles, and water carriers. Only in this way can noise and odor pollution be controlled and health standards be maintained.
3. New electrical lines must be installed, replacing the existing wires, which are not adequate to power the Visitors Center, the Valley, and the proposed new outdoor lighting.

If these cannot be installed immediately, then any temporary measures must ensure that septic tanks are well away from the Visitors Center, out of sight and hearing; water tanks must also be placed away from the Center and pumps be installed to ensure adequate water pressure in toilets and sinks; and back-up generators must be installed, again out of sight and hearing, that are adequate to supply all facilities.

**Designing the Visitors Center Complex**
It was our view that a Visitors Center complex must include the following:
- An interpretative center explaining the history and character of the Valley (this requires training and job descriptions for staff)
- An area in which two brief films on the Valley can be shown; one is being prepared by National Geographic and will not exceed five minutes in length; the other is footage from 1920 taken in KV by

Harry Burton, the photographer of the Tutankhamun excavation, and donated by the Metropolitan Museum of Art in New York
- A cafeteria serving water, other drinks, and minimal food, in environmentally friendly packaging
- A 'bazaar' where existing vendors can relocate their shops and where the SCA can sell its publications and merchandise (CDs, DVDs, posters, cards, stationery, t-shirts, pencils, etc.)
- A first-aid station and ambulance parking facility
- An office for the antiquities inspectors
- A ticket office
- An office for the security police
- Parking for buses, taxis, security, and VIP vehicles
- A tramline from the Center to KV and a recharging station for the trams
- A large toilet facility with handicapped facilities
- A septic line running five hundred meters east to a pump-out station; a regular pump-out system with proper tankers is needed, and a clearly marked place in the desert to dump sewage must be identified and used, unless some kind of septic cleaning system can be installed in the pump-out station. It should also be connected to a smaller toilet facility at the entrance to KV, and it should be designed eventually to be connected to a West Bank sewage system
- A water tank and tanker vehicles to provide a regular water supply, suitable for later connection to a water main
- Electricity supplied by lines from the West Bank, supplemented by the use of solar panels installed on the roof of the Center
- The Visitors Center should be able to accommodate eight thousand tourists per day, with peaks of one thousand tourists per hour.

**Construction of the Visitors Center**

One of the most important plans to consider was where the Visitors Center should be built. The Center had been built away from any archaeological monuments, down the slope from KV to protect accidental leakage of water or sewage into the site in an area large enough to accommodate the component parts in an aesthetically acceptable manner. We believe the site of the present (abandoned) cafeteria and parking lot is an acceptable building site.

A topographic map of the area of the new Visitors Center has been made. The area covered extends from the current entrance to the bus parking lot south to the entrance to KV and to the hills and cliffs on either side of the wadi.

An architect, chosen in conjunction with the Japanese government (which has played a leading role in the design and construction of the Visitors Center), will oversee the entire project. Using the topographic and geological maps, the architect has now drawn up a general site plan showing the location of the various component parts of the Center, the layout of the parking lot, and the route of the tramline, keeping in mind comments of the various stakeholders.

The other components of the Center—the cafeteria, vendors' area, etc.—will be designed following the completion of the interpretive center. The cafeteria should be no more than a place to buy water. Snack foods can be sold, but we do not want to encourage people to spend a long time there. The cafeteria must be able to handle up to a thousand people per hour. Seating should be minimal—about fifty seats. Packaging of food and drink should be environmentally friendly. A system of trash disposal and removal must be designed for the cafeteria and the entire KV area. The vendors' area should be designed after discussions with the relevant stakeholders. An SCA shop should be considered.

The sewage line should be laid and a holding pump-out tank installed at least five hundred meters down the road from the Center. The tank should be designed to handle waste from eight thousand persons a day and the tank size and pump-out schedule should be planned accordingly. An environmentally sound waste disposal system should be chosen.

The entire area should be cleaned of debris and rubbish and landscaped simply. An environmentalist or landscape architect should be subcontracted by the architect to design and oversee these activities.

**Installations in the Visitors Center**

Design and production of the displays in the Visitors Center are to be undertaken by the TMP. Content is to be approved by the SCA; Japanese text is to be approved by JICA. Panel labels are to be in Japanese, Arabic, and English. Material on the ten computers will be in English only. The subjects to be treated are listed below. They are deliberately selected so as

Fig. 58. KV Visitors Center.
© Theban Mapping Project

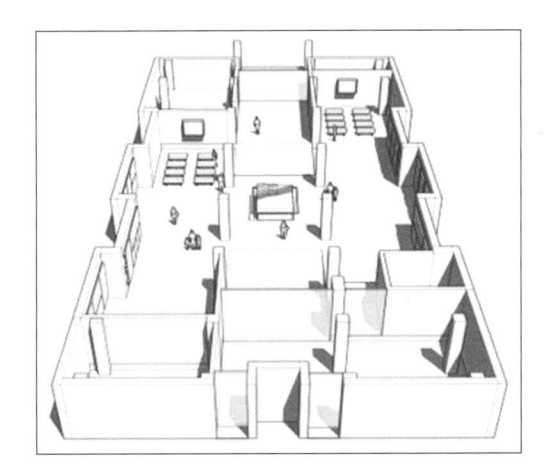

Fig. 59. KV Visitors Center.
© Theban Mapping Project

Fig. 60. KV Visitors Center.
© Theban Mapping Project

Visitors Center | 167

not to duplicate information available on the already existing signage in KV. Each of the following 'panel subjects' will occupy one or more panels in the Visitors Center. The design of the panels will emphasize graphics instead of lengthy text.

*Panels*

1. **Timeline.** A chart covering the whole of Egyptian history, from the Neolithic to the early modern period, with expanded emphasis on the New Kingdom.
2. **The Valley.** The location of KV and the likely reasons for choosing it as a burial place, as well as the relationship between royal tombs and memorial temples and its evolution in the New Kingdom.

Fig. 61. "The Valley" panel in Visitors Center. © Theban Mapping Project

3. **Hieroglyphs.** An introduction to the way in which royal names were written and to the hieroglyphs used to write them. Two royal cartouches are shown, along with an explanation of how they are to be read.
4. **The Gods.** Images of major deities in KV scenes are depicted and their functions described. These include Hathor, Isis, Osiris, Horus, Anubis, Amun, Thoth, and Ra.
5. **Royal Tombs.** Based on artwork supplied by the National

Geographic Society (NGS), the process of cutting a royal tomb is explained. Close-up thumbnails illustrate the stages of work, from rough quarrying to final painting.

6. **Tomb Scenes.** A painting of a tomb scene is accompanied by an explanation of its symbolism and function.

7. **Mummies.** The purpose and process of mummification are explained. Tomb robberies and the priests' desire to protect the bodies of the pharaohs, which resulted in caches of mummies in the Valley of the Kings and Deir al-Bahari, are discussed.

8. **Explorers.** Exploration and tourism of KV from Greco-Roman times to the present is presented. Important archaeological figures in these activities are noted. KV numbering is explained.

9. **Protecting KV.** Problems of heat and humidity are explained and visitors are encouraged to exercise care when visiting the tombs. The SCA's proposals for tomb protection are discussed.

10. **Grave Goods.** Some of the more common items found in tombs, including canopic jars, *shabti*s, statuettes, boat models, furniture, clothing, and jewelry are described.

11. **Map of the West Bank.**

*Other Exhibits*

1. **Model of KV.** A 3-D model of the Valley has been prepared and installed by JICA. This shows the tombs' relative geographic positions and provides a sense of scale for visitors.

2. **Video Monitor 1.** A four- to five-minute film on KV, prepared by the National Geographic Society, will be shown on a loop, approximately every seven to eight minutes.

3. **Video Monitor 2.** Four minutes of black-and-white silent film, shot by Harry Burton, of the opening of the tomb of Tutankhamun and Howard Carter's excavations in KV in the 1920s. The footage, which is owned by the Metropolitan Museum of Art, will be shown continuously.

4. **Computer Information Screens.** A simplified version of the TMP website will be available on eight terminals in the Visitors Center. They will provide information on each tomb in KV.

## TMP Proposals

The effect of the Visitor Center on the movement and flow of visitors into KV needs careful study. We propose that for a period of six months from the Center's opening a study should monitor:

- The time taken to enter the VC
- The number of visitors entering the VC
- The time spent by visitors in the VC
- Numbers trying to reenter the Center
- Flag any potential problem areas

### 2012 Update

The Visitors Center is now complete and open to the public. All visitors to KV leave their vehicles, enter the Center through one door, and go through one of two security channels before entering the main hall of the Center. Guides use the time to purchase tickets from the ticket office at the exit of the Center. A few guides will provide an overview of the Valley using the model exhibited in the middle of the main hall. However, the air conditioning in the center was out of operation for over a year (2010), and few tourists spent any time inside. That problem has recently been corrected.

The computers provided by JICA are unsuitable for the role they are meant to play. No measures have been taken to prevent visitors tampering with the computers, and on every visit by our team we have found them out of service. A simple maintenance program would prevent this, but does not alter the fact that they are unsuited to heavy, unsupervised use.

The two video monitors are often left off by the center manager, for no apparent reason. When they do operate, they are the most-watched displays in the building. Of the two monitors, the most popular shows the 1920s footage of Howard Carter's work in Tutankhamun's tomb, supplied by the Metropolitan Museum of Art. The other is a film of poor quality with barely intelligible audio featuring a welcome to KV by Dr. Zahi Hawass.

The toilets are heavily used, and the cleaning staff make their living selling toilet paper to the tourists who use them. This is the system that has been carried over from toilet facilities at other SCA-managed archaeological sites.

No landscaping or regular cleaning of the road to KV or of the Visitors Center area has yet been undertaken.

# Tramline and Road from Visitors Center to Valley of the Kings

Between the parking area and the KV entrance gate, diesel-powered trams (fig. 62a and b) now serve as the principal transport (the 'tuf-tuf'). They run along a path currently paved with asphalt, and that paving extends into the Valley, nearly to the entrance of KV 6.

The tramline in KV is environmentally unfriendly, unattractive, and inefficient. The present 'tuf-tuf' system is operated under contract issued by the Luxor City Council to a private company. Tourists pay LE 1 for the round trip. Approximately 4,000 to 6,000

Fig. 62a and b. Tramline. © Theban Mapping Project

tickets are sold each day (about 98 percent of all visitors use the service). Tickets are sold at the parking area and an honor system is employed for those using the tram when returning from the Valley. It is the responsibility of the contractor to maintain the vehicles and to pay a percentage of the revenue to the City Council (for the support of the Luxor Youth Clubs, it is said). Its engines burn diesel fuel, belch smoke, leak oil, and make noise. In addition, advertising posters (sold by the contractor to various companies) cover their sides and their painted decorations are embarrassingly bad. There are five two-car units, each pulled by a tractor. The tramline employs about ten people.

**TMP Proposals**

A. We propose replacing the 'tuf-tuf' with a new tramline, powered by rechargeable batteries, that is attractive, quiet, non-polluting, and efficient. The tram will travel from the south entrance of the Visitors Center to the turn-around point at the current entrance to the Valley of the Kings and back again, a loop approximately 1 kilometer in total length.

We should plan now for a tramline that can carry about ten to twelve thousand passengers daily. Assuming we are successful in distributing tourists more or less evenly throughout the day, that means that trams must be able to carry about fourteen hundred people per hour to the Valley, and the same number back to the Visitors Center. The German-built "Still" trams now in operation at Deir al-Bahari (fig. 63) each consist of two passenger cars pulled by a battery-powered electric engine. Each passenger car can carry a maximum of twenty-four persons, and each unit therefore can transport forty-eight persons per one-way trip. The units we propose for the Valley of the Kings would be similar in design and carrying capacity. The color and design of the carriages and engines of the new units should be similar to those of the Still models— plain, tan earth colors—with no decorative touches or advertising.

Assume that each tram consists of one engine and two passenger cars; that each two-car unit will carry forty-eight passengers per one-way trip; that each trip, including loading and unloading time, will take ten minutes; and that each unit will make five one-way

Fig. 63. Hatshepsut Tramline. © Theban Mapping Project

trips per hour. That is two hundred persons per hour per train. To carry two thousand persons per hour (a thousand each way) will therefore require ten tram units, or, allowing for maintenance, down time, and delays, and a branch line into the West Valley, a total of fourteen engines and twenty-six passenger cars.

To service the trams, a recharging unit and maintenance garage must be built. These should lie away from the Valley of the Kings and the Visitors Center, in the next wadi down where plans call for a new and enlarged parking lot to be constructed.

Tickets generate about LE 6,000 per day, LE 42,000 per week, and LE 2,280,000 per year. We estimate operating expenses to be less than LE 200,000 per year. Whether this plan should be maintained, or whether the SCA should take control of the tram service and contract it out to a (high bidder) private operator, must be decided by the SCA and the Luxor City Council. Alternatively, the costs of the tramline can be factored into KV admission ticket charges.

B. The road between the Visitors Center and KV is currently paved with asphalt, and that paving extends into the Valley, nearly to the entrance of KV 6. We suggest that this asphalt be removed and the road between the Center and the Valley be left as a natural surface. Beyond the Visitors Center, the idea is to have KV look as much as possible as it looked a century ago, with minimal modern intrusions. To eliminate problems with blowing dust, wear, and flood damage, the roadway, and also the footpaths throughout KV, should be sprayed with a liquid copolymer soil stabilizer such as Soiltac. We tested Soiltac on the dirt road running north to south immediately west of Carter House and have found that ten months later, in spite of regular use by trucks and tractors, the track remains dust-free and undamaged. Soiltac should also be used on the footpaths in KV itself, both to reduce dust and to create a waterproof surface that, by careful grading, can be used to safely deflect flood water from tomb entrances and direct it out of KV, around the Visitors Center and bus park, and into the desert.

C. In addition to regular tram service between the Visitors Center and the East Valley of the Kings, a less frequent tramline should run between the Center and the Tomb of Ay in the West Valley. This track, too, should be sprayed with Soiltac or the equivalent. The tramline could provide an on-demand service, ferrying people into the West Valley, waiting for them to visit the site (about fifteen minutes), and then returning them to the Visitors Center. They can then ferry another group into the Valley. Initially, units should consist of an engine and a single twenty-four-passenger carriage. If demand increases, two two-carriage trams could be operated, with the service running every thirty to forty-five minutes. Making the Tomb of Ay (and eventually that of Amenhotep III) more accessible to tourists will help reduce the number of tourists visiting tombs in the East Valley, and/or reduce the amount of time they spend there.

2012 Update

Since 2006, the existing 'tuf-tuf' train has been replaced by an electric tram system with a charging station adjacent to the Visitors Center (rather than in the overspill parking area, as originally planned). The tram drops visitors at the KV gate near the tomb of KV 1. From that point on, the asphalt paving has been removed from KV, from the entrance rest stop into the Valley, the idea being to maintain the Valley's ancient appearance and avoid "modernizing" its landscape. A cut-stone, meter-wide sidewalk has been laid from the entrance to near KV 7 to make wheelchair access easier. But the dust from the unpaved road is a major problem, especially during windstorms and when trucks drive into the Valley to cart away excavation debris. The use of a surface treatment such as Soiltac would easily solve this problem.

## Security Entrance and Camera Rules

The 'tuf-tuf' drops its passengers at a gate that marks the official entrance to KV. (It lies about twenty meters south of what was probably the ancient entrance, a narrow place in the wadi originally blocked by a three-meter-high face of bedrock.) The road is barely wide enough for the 'tuf-tuf' to turn around, and the area where passengers wait before returning to the parking lot is covered with leaked oil and tourist refuse. Buses and automobiles for VIPs and security vans also park here, creating severe congestion when tourists arrive. The gate into KV has a single entrance on its left and a single exit on its right; a gate for vehicles lies between them, open only when security officers allow traffic to enter or leave the Valley. Beside the entrance is a ticket office where tickets can be purchased for the tomb of Tutankhamun (previously LE 70, in addition to the LE 55 KV admission; as of 2010, the price has been raised to LE 100). Tickets are checked and torn by an SCA employee as tourists pass through the gate.

Like all major archaeological sites and museums in Egypt, KV has security guards posted at its entrance. These guards are part of the Tourism and Antiquities Police, which itself is part of the Ministry of the Interior, over which the SCA has little direct authority. At the Valley of the Kings entrance, the security officers man a metal detector through which each visitor must pass. (Tourists coming to KV over the hill from Deir al-Bahari or Deir al-Medina do not pass through such a checkpoint until they walk through KV to its entrance and purchase tickets to the tombs. Then they return to the Valley through the entrance checkpoint.) The amount of time spent passing through this checkpoint is generally minimal, although a large number of arriving tourists can create congestion and a significant delay.

A major part of the delay is due to the rule that visitors must check any video cameras at a booth at the entrance. In 2010, the SCA imposed a total ban on cameras and camera-equipped cell phones in the Valley of the Kings. No photos are permitted inside KV tombs or outside the tombs anywhere in the Valley, and cameras and cell phones are now banned from the valley. The official reason given is to prevent flash photography from damaging paintings inside the tombs. However, the ban on cameras in KV generally, not just in the tombs, is understandably a major irritant to tourists and serves no serious purpose.

Video cameras are not allowed inside KV, either. (Video filming by professional videographers is sometimes allowed, but this requires advance permission from the SCA in Cairo and the purchase of a special ticket.) Several reasons have been given to explain this rule: video cameras could be used by filmmakers who want to produce films without paying a fee to the SCA; video users would try to film inside tombs (where all cameras are banned); video users would create congestion in the Valley. None of these explanations are valid. Professional filmmakers cannot use small hand-held videos to produce acceptable commercial footage; the rule banning any photography inside the tombs is already in effect, but still-camera users are allowed to photograph outside tombs. Owners of video cameras are annoyed by the nuisance of having to check their camera and then retrieve it when they leave. It is especially annoying to tourists who want to walk over the hill after visiting KV because they cannot retrieve their video cameras and then reenter the Valley. Today, most mobile phones can take video clips, and the ban is becoming increasingly unenforceable. Our survey of visitors to KV found that tourists find this ban the most annoying part of a visit to KV.

Security checks of tourists made by Tourist Police and ticket collecting by the SCA currently require a minimum of six seconds per tourist to perform, or ten tourists per minute. In the proposed new Visitors Center, there are three security lanes. These three lanes can handle thirty tourists per minute (10 x 3), an hourly total (30 x 60) of 1,800 tourists. If the number of security lanes is increased to four, then the hourly total (40 x 60) rises to 2,440 tourists. Five lanes could accommodate 50 x 60, or three thousand per hour. But these numbers are significantly reduced, perhaps even halved, if one must factor in the checking of video cameras at the KV entrance.

Fig. 64a and b. Security and camera check. © Theban Mapping Project

Security rules in KV seem arbitrary and sometimes appear to be arbitrarily enforced or needlessly changed. Two years ago, security briefly forbade workmen from entering the Valley if they carried picks, trowels, or shovels, arguing these could be used as lethal weapons. Three years ago, workmen in the Valley had to provide four copies of their identity

Security Entrance and Camera Rules | 177

card at the gate. Last year, only foreigners were forced to pass through the metal detector; local workmen walked around it. Each rule was enforced for two or three days, then ignored. After the hotel bombing in Taba in 2004, security forces banned taxis and private vehicles from the KV parking lot. Now, taxis are again allowed. The result of such inconsistency is that security personnel are ignored, their rules laughed at, and repeat visitors to KV take pleasure in becoming scofflaws.

Security is considered essential by the Egyptian government, as indeed it must be. But rules must be regularly applied, demonstrably logical and fair, and, to the extent possible, unobtrusive and efficient. The existing security entrance will move to the new VC building.

## TMP Proposals

A review of security procedures in KV has been carried out by DEFEX (a Spanish security firm) under the auspices of the SCA and funded by the Spanish government. Their key recommendations are the installation of:

- A. A perimeter detection system, which can consist of one of the following: a microwave barrier, an infrared barrier, a fiber-optic intrusion detection system, or a buried electromagnetic cable.
- B. An access control system, which should consist of a road barrier to control vehicle access and a tripod turnstile (card swipe and ticket swipe) to control visitor access.
- C. Security inspection equipment, consisting of an X-ray system for luggage, a metal detector, and/or a hand-held metal detector.
- D. A video surveillance system, consisting of cameras with color capability, indoor and outdoor cameras, thermal cameras, digital motion detectors, and a recording system to store images.
- E. A digital mobile radio communications network.
- F. A control center to monitor all of the above.

### 2012 Update

The main change in the security rules for the Valley is that not only video cameras but all cameras and cell phones are now banned from the site. Signs exist at the entrance to the Visitor Center and at the entrance to the Valley and guides are instructed to inform their visitors to leave their cameras and cell phones in the vehicles they arrived in. This is a source of considerable unhappiness among tourists. Ticket prices have been increased for KV tombs: Tutankamun's extra ticket is now LE 100; that for Ramesses VI is LE 70.

## Toilets

The toilets in KV that are currently in use are unacceptable. Since the closing of the rest house over five years ago, the only toilets are four women's units and three men's units in a Porta-loo parked on the pathway into KV just before KV 5. The number of units is hopelessly inadequate for the number of visitors each day. There is no piped water available; therefore, it is brought three times weekly by a tractor and tank carriage. The water always runs out before a new supply becomes available, and the holding tanks, which are pumped out by a pumping truck about once a week, overflow. The results are toilets that are unclean, unsanitary, and produce foul odors, noise, and air pollution, and an ugly building sits in the middle of what should be an impressive panorama of KV.

The toilets are currently operated by local individuals who, in exchange for the tips they receive from visitors, are required to keep the toilets clean and supplied with paper and water. We estimate that on an average day, the toilet attendants receive over LE 1,000 from tourists, making them

Fig. 65. Current toilet facilities. © Theban Mapping Project

among the best-paid individuals in KV. However, the system does not work, largely because the facilities themselves are unsuitable, and because there is inadequate water and infrequent pump-out. There are also no toilet facilities for the staff of KV, who are barred from using the visitor toilets. This results in nearby wadis being used as makeshift latrines, and in some cases, closed-tomb doorways are used for the same purpose. This is clearly unacceptable both from a point of view of conservation of the site and the welfare of KV employees.

**TMP Proposals**
   A. The new Visitors Center will have toilets in it: four stalls and four urinals for men, six stalls for women. This is not adequate for the number of tourists, and an additional toilet facility will have to be built somewhere in the parking area with at least six more units each for men and women. Another facility for bus and taxi drivers should be attached to the tramline garage and recharging center, to be constructed in the large wadi east of the current parking lot. In addition, there must be a further toilet facility closer to KV. A significant number of tourists to Egypt suffer from minor intestinal problems during their visit, and a mad dash to reach a facility ten to fifteen minutes away is unacceptable. We propose building a third toilet facility near the entrance to KV, downhill and away from any archaeological features. The building can be semi-subterranean so as not to spoil the landscape, with four units each for men and women. Two possible locations are: at the entrance to the side wadi beside the current tramline parking area, beside the KV entrance gate; or at the start of the pathway to KV. We have surveyed these areas and are confident that there are no archaeological features there. They lie far enough from any tomb, and far enough downhill, that any accidental spillage will be deflected away from KV, not into it.
   B. To replace the unacceptable water tanker and pump-out truck, all toilets will have to be connected to water and sewage lines. The water line should start from near Carter House and run 5 km along the road to the KV Visitors Center and parking area, cafeteria, first-aid station, and tram maintenance shop. A smaller

spur line should extend to the toilet near the KV entrance. Two or three booster pumps will be needed en route to maintain water flow. The sewage line should run from the KV toilet, connect to those in the Visitors Center and the parking area, and then extend down the road to a holding tank 1 to 1.5 kilometers away, where pump-out trucks can perform their work out of sight, hearing, and smell of tourists and others. These two lines, for water and sewage, will cost about LE 500,000 to install, but that is a small price to ensure better site protection and visitor comfort. Provisions should also be made to connect water and septic lines to Davis House, at the entrance to the West Valley.

2012 Update

The Porta-loo has been moved from its previous location to a new position off the main valley floor on the path to the tomb of Ramesses VII, KV 1. It is unsightly, visible from some distance, and would prominently appear in general photographs of al-Qurna (if cameras were allowed in KV's entrance). Again in 2011, orders were given by the SCA to create a subterranean toilet facility in the area where the Porta-loo now stands, but there is argument among the inspectors as to how it should be sited. Some want the entrance to face away from the entrance to KV, others want it to face away from the path to KV 1. This concern can easily be dealt with. Some want the septic holding tank moved down the road; others want it to remain where it is. The former idea is easily implemented; the latter, because of its elevation, is not feasible. Wherever they are finally located, the toilet facilities need to double in size. In 2011, on any day of heavy tourism (usually Sundays, Mondays, Tuesdays, and Fridays), as many as thirty men and an even larger number of women can be seen standing in line waiting up to fifteen minutes to use the facilities.

## Shelters and Rest Stops

The SCA has built small, wooden shaded areas near several tombs in which tourists can find relief from the sun while listening to their tour guides. In many cases, signs describing the adjacent tomb or showing a map of KV have been installed within them. Their locations are as follows:

Fig. 66. KV shelter used for guiding. © Theban Mapping Project

- At the entrance to KV (enlarged in 2011)
- Beside the entrance of KV 1
- Beside the entrance of KV 2
- In the central part of KV, serving KV 6, 9, 62, and 11
- Above the central part of KV, serving KV 16
- Beside the entrance of KV 8
- Near the entrance of KV 35 and KV 57
- Between KV 14, 15, and 47

Benches also can be found at the base of cliffs (which provide adequate shade) beside KV 34 and KV 43.

## TMP Proposals

The number and location of these shelters seem adequate and no more need to be built. Additional shelters would also add to the visual pollution in KV. The main shelter, across from KV 62 in the center of KV, was converted to a cafeteria in 2011. (Such a cafeteria existed here twenty years ago, but was removed because it was deemed too offensive.) In late 2011, the head of the SCA ordered that the cafeteria be removed (the contract with

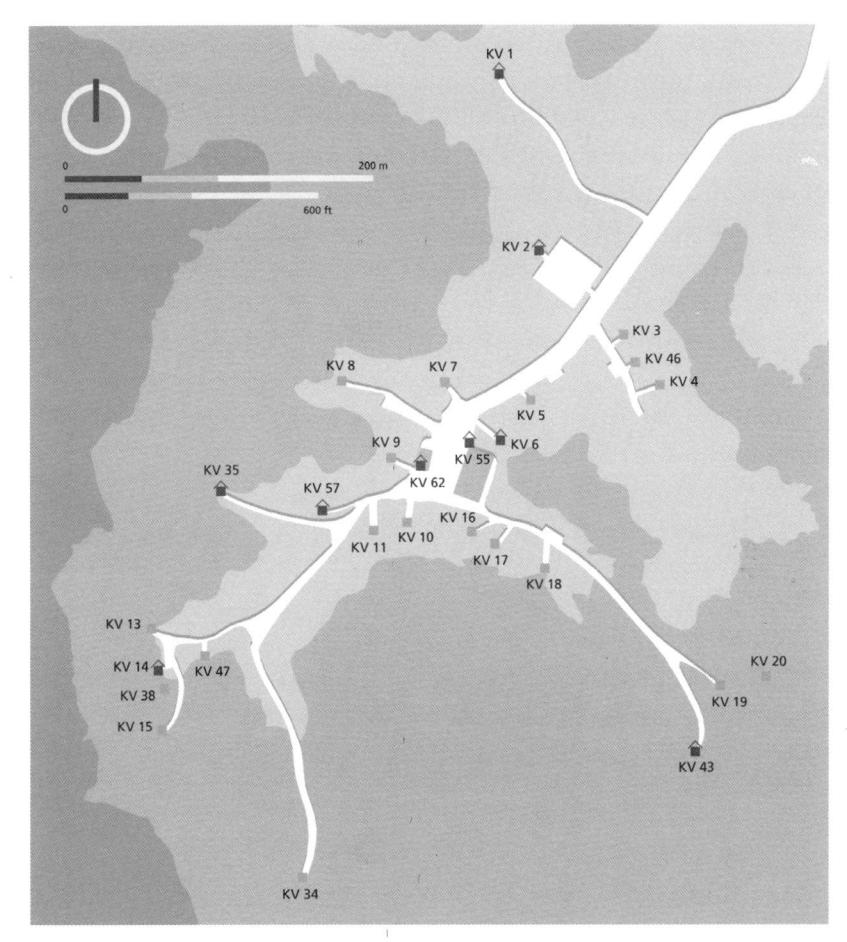

Fig. 67. Location of shelters. © Theban Mapping Project

the SCA allowed a kiosk selling bottled water only, not a full-service coffee shop). The coffee shop was removed in 2012; the kiosk has not appeared.

## Tomb Interiors
### Tomb Interior Protection
KV tomb interiors are protected in a variety of ways. Traditionally, wooden floors, handrails, and central balustrades (fig. 68) were installed in open KV tombs. These, however, afford little protection to the walls and reliefs; for example, visitors with backpacks could still lean against the walls or accidentally damage the walls if the tomb was crowded. Therefore, large glass panels

(fig. 69), some 1.5 meters wide and 3.5 meters high, were installed several decades ago, twenty centimeters in front of the walls of some of the tombs, in an attempt to deter visitors from touching the reliefs. The panels, however, have caused damage because the brackets needed to support their weight were sometimes plastered directly into the very walls they were supposed to protect. Worse, because the glass is permanently fixed and cannot be moved easily, workers armed with a bottle of Windex and a cloth must slide between the wall and the glass panel in order to clean it. They rub against the painted relief and spray chemicals that raise the humidity and stick to the painted walls. The damage done is greater than any tourists might have inflicted.

In this report, we have identified several problems in the protection and care of KV tombs. These include:
- Infrequent and improper cleaning of tomb floors;
- The lack of a program for cleaning and checking the condition of decorated walls;
- Irregular replacement of burned-out fluorescent tubes;
- Continued use of inappropriate and dangerously heavy glass panels in front of decorated walls;
- The performance of work inside tombs (such as sanding wood floors and varnishing their surfaces) that should be done outside.

Fig. 68. Protective walkway.
© Theban Mapping Project

Fig. 69. Full-size glass panels.
© Theban Mapping Project

*TMP Proposals*

The present system is ineffective at preventing damage to the interiors of KV tombs and in some cases exacerbates the situation. New designs of protective barriers should be considered, and before they are installed throughout the Valley they should be beta-tested in one or two tombs.

A. As noted in chapter 8 below, a schedule should be developed to ensure that tombs are regularly vacuumed to prevent a buildup of dust that damages decorated walls, creates an unpleasant environment, and covers the glass panels through which wall decoration must be viewed. The TMP has donated an industrial vacuum to the SCA, but it has yet to be used. Its use should be restricted to qualified conservation personnel, not untrained site guards, and vacuuming should only be done of the floor, not wall surfaces, and only after a careful inspection of the floor at the base of walls has been made to ensure that there are no fragments of decoration that have flaked off the walls. The wooden walkways that have been installed in many tombs to provide a safer, less slippery surface for tourists serve to trap dust. In the future, they should be designed so that sections of them can be raised and the floor beneath them can be vacuumed.

B. Walls, too, should be cleaned by specially trained conservators at the same time that a regular program of conservation inspection is undertaken.

C. It is essential that environmental monitors be installed at several places in each tomb in order to monitor changes in temperature and humidity.

D. The glass panels that have been installed in many tombs are a serious problem. They are very heavy (supports have been drilled into some walls to keep them from falling over); they are highly reflective, making them difficult to see through; and they collect dust, making viewing of tomb decoration even more difficult. They are a special-order glass that can no longer be bought in Egypt and when they break (several of them have), they cannot be replaced. Some of them (in KV 1, for example) are so large and fragile that they cannot be removed from their iron mounts. When they are cleaned, only the front surface can be easily accessed. Cleaning the back requires that someone slide into the twenty-centimeter space between the glass and the decorated wall the glass is meant to protect. The cleaner cannot help but rub against the wall, causing damage, and the Windex that he often uses splashes onto the paint and causes further damage. This is not acceptable. We have proposed a new combined system of walkway and protective panels that calls for a forty- to fifty-centimeter tall Plexiglas barrier installed by a handrail at elbow level, creating a barrier against accidentally touching walls, but otherwise leaving nothing between viewers and the decoration they have come to admire. A kick plate at floor level will also prevent accidental contact.

E. It must be emphasized that sanding, cutting, or varnishing wooden floor boards for installation in a tomb should be done outside. This was not the case recently in KV 8, when a new walkway was installed, and sawdust and varnish stains can still be found on walls and floor.

Individual Tomb Recommendations
1. KV 1: Ramesses VII
   - Install new lighting
   - Install HVAC system
   - Replace flooring, glass panels
   - Install temperature and humidity (T & H) controls in chambers B and K
2. KV 2: Ramesses IV
   - Install new lighting
   - Install HVAC system
   - Replace flooring
   - Install T & H controls in chambers B, C, and K
3. KV 6: Ramesses IX
   - Add rope lines outside and in chamber A for crowd control
   - Install new lighting
   - Install HVAC system
   - Replace flooring, glass panels
   - Install T & H controls in chambers B, E, and J
4. KV 8: Merenptah
   - Install new lighting
   - Install HVAC system

- Replace flooring, glass panels
- Install T & H controls in chambers B, F, H, J, and K

5. KV 9: Ramesses VI
    - Add rope lines outside and in chamber A for crowd control
    - Install new lighting
    - Install HVAC system
    - Replace flooring
    - Move sarcophagus pieces in chambers J and Ja to permit walkway room
    - Install T & H controls in chambers B, E, G, J, and K
6. KV 11: Ramesses III
    - Install new lighting
    - Install HVAC system
    - Replace flooring, glass panels
    - Install T & H controls in chambers B, D1, Fa, H, and J
7. KV 14: Tawosret/Setnakht
    - Add threshold for flood control at entrance
    - Install new lighting
    - Install HVAC system
    - Replace flooring
    - Install T & H controls in chambers C, F, J1, and J2
8. KV 15: Seti II
    - Add threshold for flood control at entrance
    - Install new lighting
    - Install HVAC system
    - Replace flooring
    - Install T & H controls in chambers B, E, and J
9. KV 16: Ramesses I
    - Install new lighting
    - Install HVAC system
    - Install T & H controls in chambers A, B, and J
10. KV 17: Seti I
    - Install new lighting
    - Install HVAC system
    - Install new flooring
    - Install T & H controls in chambers B, F, G, and J

11. KV 19: Mentuherkhepeshef
    - Install new lighting
    - Install HVAC system
    - Replace flooring, glass panels
    - Install T & H controls in chamber C
12. KV 34: Thutmose III
    - Install new lighting
    - Install HVAC system
    - Install T & H controls in chambers B, D, F, and J
13. KV 35: Amenhotep II
    - Install new lighting
    - Install HVAC system
    - Install T & H controls in chambers B, D, F, and J
14. KV 43: Thutmose IV
    - Install new lighting
    - Install HVAC system
    - Install T & H controls in chambers B, D, F, G, and J
15. KV 47: Siptah
    - Install new lighting
    - Install HVAC system
    - Replace flooring, glass panels
    - Install T & H controls in chambers B, F, I, and J2
16. KV 57: Horemheb
    - Install new lighting
    - Install HVAC system
    - Install T & H controls in chambers B, D, I, J, and Jc
17. KV 62: Tutankhamun
    - Install new lighting
    - Install HVAC system
    - Install T & H controls in chambers B, J, Ja, and Ia
18. WV 23: Ay
    - Add threshold for flood control at entrance
    - Install new lighting
    - Install HVAC system
    - Install T & H controls in chambers B, D, and J

## Tomb Lighting

The current system of lighting in KV tombs is unsatisfactory. Forty-watt fluorescent tubes sit on the tomb floor along the wall, some exposed, some covered by a wood and plastic box. These tubes produce an inappropriate and uneven light, electrostatically attract large quantities of dust, and generate heat. In the tomb of Ramesses VI (KV 9), for example, 196 fluorescent tubes generate not only 8,000 watts of light, but 8,000 watts of heat, raising the ambient temperature significantly. The wiring in many tombs is a potential source of electrical fire and electrocution.

*TMP Proposals*

    A. Until such time as LED lighting can be installed in the KV tombs, fluorescent bulbs should be replaced when they burn out, and the Plexiglas boxes in which they sit should be dusted on a regular basis.

    B. We suggest that a test of LED lighting be conducted in KV 9 for a period of one year. The tomb should be closed to tourists for half that time, open to tourists the other half. Temperature and humidity should be monitored throughout the period. LED lighting has

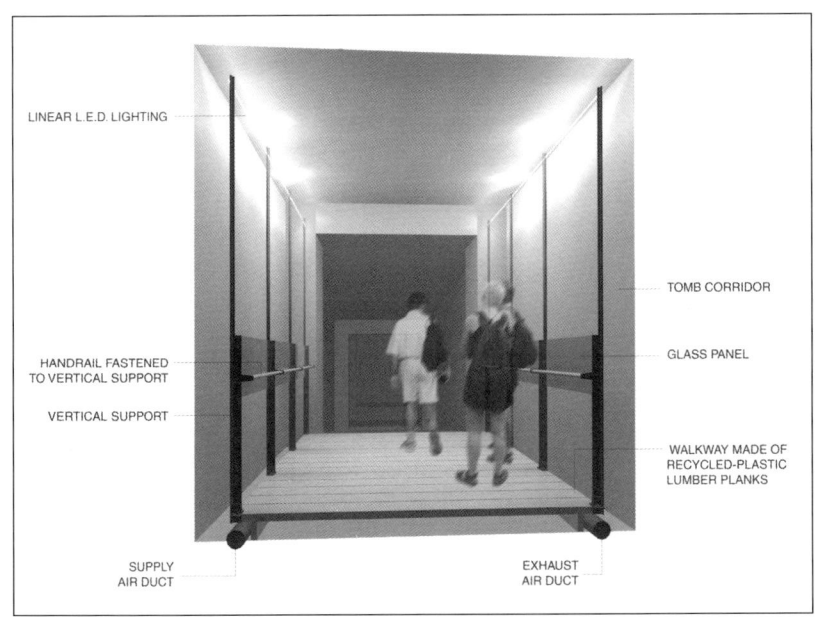

Fig. 70. One type of proposed walkway and lighting. © Theban Mapping Project

many advantages: it provides an excellent source of adjustable and appropriate light, it does not attract dust, it does not generate heat, it is relatively inexpensive, and it is long lasting. If the one-year test proves satisfactory, LED lighting should be installed in all tombs open to the public.

2012 Update

As yet, nothing has been done about tomb lighting, although the SCA continues to claim that the project will be undertaken "soon." It is crucial that new lighting, temperature and humidity controls, and especially tourist management plans be implemented as soon as possible. The wear and tear the current system imposes on tomb conditions cannot continue without serious damage, destroying the fabric of the monuments.

## Site Utilities

By contractual agreement with the SCA, JICA has built a Valley of the Kings Visitors Center and is providing its necessary internal electrical and plumbing fixtures. The Theban Mapping Project has designed its display panels. It is the responsibility of the SCA to connect the building's water and electrical lines to external sources, and to deal with the disposal of sewage. Unfortunately, the SCA has decided not to upgrade either water or electrical systems, and to rely on pump-out trucks to remove waste. Sewage from the toilets will go to a holding tank immediately beneath the Visitors Center's exit path and will have to be pumped out while tourists are present. Water will be delivered by tanker, as is being done now, not by piping fresh water from the Nile Valley. Electricity will continue to depend upon existing power lines, the size and condition of which may not be adequate to supply the needs of the Visitors Center air conditioning and lighting, as well as power for the recharging of tram line batteries, lights in KV tombs, and other fixtures. However, the SCA says it intends to upgrade these systems within one year. That upgrade should also include new telephone lines.

The electrical system in KV is over sixty years old. To accommodate a new lighting system, the proposed area-wide lighting of KV hillsides, the air conditioning units in the new Visitors Center, and the recharging units for the new tram line, new cable should be run underground from the Nile

Fig. 71. Existing backup generator. © Theban Mapping Project

Valley to KV, and new wiring installed in all KV tombs. In addition, the existing old, unreliable emergency generator should be replaced by a new, on-demand generator to ensure that tourists are not stranded in total darkness at the bottom of KV tombs. The possible use of solar panels to provide at least a part of KV's electrical needs should be seriously examined. Such panels would have to be installed in an environmentally friendly, aesthetically pleasing manner, of course. They probably could not satisfy all KV's needs (temperature and humidity controls have high energy demands), but they might provide adequate power for all tomb lighting.

**TMP Proposals**
Any new electrical lines should be laid below ground from the Nile Valley to the Visitors Center, parking lot, KV, and West Valley, as opposed to the current overhead power lines and street lighting. Water should be piped to KV from the Nile Valley, and a sewage line installed to carry sewage to a holding tank at least half a kilometer downhill from the Visitors Center as soon as possible. Failure to upgrade these installations will result in poor service to tourists and regular power failures.

If the planned nighttime opening of the site takes place, then the lighting system installed should be discreet, eco-friendly, and low-maintenance.

Solar energy may provide a useful and cost-effective source of power for KV tomb lighting. It could be a supplement, but not a replacement, for electricity carried to the Valley by new cables. Any installation of solar panels, however, must be done in such a way that it does not alter or adversely affect the Theban landscape.

2012 Update

A new housing for the old generator has been built. However, a new generator is needed. Power outages in KV continue to occur two or three times every day, leaving tourists stuck in pitch-dark tombs for several minutes before power can be restored.

## Site Fabric

The existing geological, topographical, and meteorological conditions in KV are covered in some detail in chapter 2. However, it should be noted that previous hydrological surveys have now been invalidated because of significant changes to KV's morphology (because of recent excavations that have greatly altered the topography).

## TMP Proposals

Detailed studies of topography and hydrology should be commissioned and take into account any further changes in flood protection measures or debris clearance. In addition, a weather station in the Valley of the Kings (along with at least one other elsewhere on the West Bank), is essential if temperature and humidity control in KV tombs is to be successful.

There are three types of hillside debris in KV: debris left by the ancient excavators of tombs, debris left by archaeologists, and debris borne by floodwaters from the hillsides above the Valley. It has been suggested that all of this debris be removed in order to better explore the Valley. This was done several years ago in the Valley of the Queens. It should be noted that any excavation must be carefully done, for it is known that much of this debris contains artifacts. (Clearance around the entrance of KV 17 in 2004–2005 yielded several hundred potsherds, dozens of ostraca, and two mummified human heads.) Such clearing will require preparation of a new hydrological survey because it will dramatically alter the character of the existing KV watershed.

Geological fractures on KV hillsides should be filled. During rainstorms, these fractures serve as pathways through which water can pour into tombs. Several years ago, the fractures in the hillside above KV 5 were cleaned and filled with sand, stone, and cement. A similar project should be conducted on other KV hillsides

## Summary of Proposals and Status as of 2012

- Carter House to become a museum by 2011: completed
- Signage to be installed at road near Carter House: not done
- Road from Carter House to KV to be landscaped and graded for flood control by 2011: begun but improperly executed; not corrected as of 2012
- Maintenance and cleaning schedule of roadway to be established: not done
- Water mains and electrical cable to be installed: not done
- Footpaths from Deir al-Bahari and Deir al-Medina to KV to be improved: not done
- Rest stops for visitors and watering trough for donkeys on approach to KV: not done
- Illegal vehicles (such as horse carriages) to be stopped at Carter House: not done
- New parking lot to be constructed in 2011: two built, one informal; partially completed
- New vendors' kiosks to be built in 2011: completed
- SCA sales desk to be constructed by 2011: not done
- Tramline from Visitors Center to KV and WV, and its support facilities, to be installed: completed
- Asphalt road from Visitors Center to KV to be removed and replaced with Soiltac: completed
- Update KV security installations: begun
- Install additional toilets for visitors and staff in parking area and at KV entrance: not done
- Implement programs for regular tomb cleaning and conservation monitoring: not done
- Replace walkways and remove glass panels in tombs: not done

- Install new lighting system within tombs while maintaining existing system: not done
- Conduct trial lighting, temperature, and humidity control schemes within tombs: tested in 2007, project reexamined in 2013
- Install exterior KV lighting: not done
- Upgrade KV utilities: partially completed
- Explore possible use of solar power: not done
- Conduct new hydrological studies: not done
- Clear hillside debris and repair hillside fractures: partially done
- Install weather stations on West Bank: done in 2004, removed in 2005

# 7 Visitor Management in the Valley of the Kings

Certain fixed entities and capacities—vehicle parking, security, Visitors Center, and tramline—all suggest that a thousand visitors per hour is the maximum number that can enter the Valley of the Kings without significant changes being made to the system's infrastructure. The question we must now ask is: can the Valley of the Kings deal with this number of people without damaging its fabric?

## Carrying Capacity

Carrying capacity is a term used to describe the optimum visitor level at an attraction or location. Above this level, the quality of visitor experience declines and the fabric of the site may be adversely affected. Once the carrying capacity is calculated, a management plan is needed to maintain visitor numbers at or below that level. The use of carrying capacity as a management tool is normally achieved by restricting access, increasing the resource capacity, or a combination of the two.

Often, the calculation of carrying capacity is simply a 'guesstimate' of the number of visitors that would cause crowding or other problems at a site. These physical capacity measurements, along with methods of control, such as pricing and ticketing, are often the only considerations taken into account. However, one should also consider the 'social carrying capacity' of a site, because it helps determine the quality of visitor

Fig. 72. KV 9 overcrowding. © Theban Mapping Project

experience. Social factors affecting carrying capacity are more difficult to quantify and are therefore often ignored, but visitor experience and opinion must be considered. One should try to determine, for example, at what point a site is perceived by the visitor to be overcrowded, and when the number of visitors begins to adversely affect individual visitor experience. There are also factors that determine the number of tourists who can even reach a site, and these numbers will play a role in setting the parameters of carrying capacity by setting the practical limits of visitor capacity. The practical limit of visitor capacity in the Valley of the Kings can be defined in several ways, but all definitions are affected by the physical limitations of transportation, space, site administration, education, and environment.

The carrying capacity of site facilities such as toilets, catering venues, and parking lots, because they have well-defined holding capacities, are easier to quantify than the actual heritage attractions of which they are a part. When visitors to these facilities exceed the permitted numbers, sometimes they can be directed to other facilities. The heritage attraction does not have this option: people have come to see *it*. As GCI director Miguel Angel Corzo said in 1992: "You can't have unlimited access, unlimited hours, and unlimited numbers. You can't because the tourism reality of the 1990s is not the reality of the 1940s and 1950s. If we fail to apply sensible limitations in the visiting of cultural sites, many sites will not last another generation."[1]

## Defining the Valley of the Kings' Carrying Capacity

One method of defining a site's carrying capacity is to begin with the various elements of its physical structure. For example, the present KV tour-bus parking area can hold no more than seventy buses at a time. Assuming an average load of thirty passengers per bus (buses vary in size—from twelve to fifty passengers—but thirty is the average size of a tour group), a total of 2,100 persons (70 x 30) can be delivered into the KV parking area before some buses must leave to make way for others. Since the average tour group spends ninety minutes in KV (and an additional thirty minutes leaving and returning to the bus, making a total of 120 minutes), that means that buses can bring no more than 1,050 visitors per hour to the site. Add to this figure the visitors who come by taxi, private car, bicycle, donkey, or on foot, and we reach about 1,200 tourists per hour. That number can be increased only if bus parking spaces are increased, tour groups become larger, more tourists use other means of transportation, or changes are made to the parking system.

However, the carrying capacity of KV is a number that can only be determined by subjective observation. Does KV appear too full? Does it *feel* too crowded? Is the movement of individuals and groups being hindered? Are lines forming at the entrances of tombs? Are rest areas fully occupied? Are there long lines at the toilets? Are crowds blocking the gate at KV's entrance? If the answer to any of these questions is "yes," then the optimum carrying capacity has probably been exceeded. Observations of KV on the busiest days of the week suggest that these adverse conditions appear when there are more than a thousand visitors in the East Valley of the Kings. Unfortunately, this figure is now being greatly exceeded on at least three days every week (Friday, Saturday, Sunday), when KV regularly hosts 1,700 visitors per hour between 7:00 a.m. and 11:00 a.m. (The carrying capacity of the West Valley has not been tested, but, since its main attractions are silence, solitude, and natural beauty, subjective observation suggests that approximately thirty people—one busload—would be the maximum desirable.)

Barring major shifts in tourist management or changes that are forced upon travel operators by the SCA, it seems likely that there will continue to be an unequal distribution of tourists to KV throughout the day, with the heaviest crowds in early and mid-morning, the lightest in the late afternoon. Most visitors arrive on Friday, Saturday, and Sunday.

### Controlling Visitor Flow into and within the Valley of the Kings

Visitor movement through a site is controlled at some level in nearly all cultural heritage sites, and is referred to as visitor flow management. This can be as simple a process as directing visitors through a site using signage or stewards, or it can be more sophisticated, involving the planning of visitor access routes and the use of computer ticketing systems.

To understand visitor behavior in KV, the TMP carried out various studies looking at the numbers of visitors entering the site within one hour, the number entering the site in one day, the duration of their visit, the time spent in individual tombs, and the numbers of visitors entering these tombs.

At present, KV tombs are open from 6:30 a.m. to 5:00 p.m., a total of ten and a half hours a day. Recent TMP surveys show that the number of

| Time Slot | Sat. 23 October 2004 | | Sun. 24 October 2004 | |
|---|---|---|---|---|
| | No. | % day total | No. | % day total |
| 08.00–08.10 | 413 | 7.37 | 282 | 3.47 |
| 08.10–08.20 | 275 | 4.91 | 401 | 4.93 |
| 08.20–08.30 | 159 | 2.84 | 198 | 2.44 |
| 08.30–08.40 | 103 | 1.84 | 237 | 2.92 |
| 08.40–08.50 | 61 | 1.09 | 245 | 3.01 |
| 08.50–09.00 | 91 | 1.62 | 169 | 2.08 |
| 09.00–09.10 | 131 | 2.34 | 218 | 2.68 |
| 09.10–09.20 | 151 | 2.70 | 276 | 3.40 |
| 09.20–09.30 | 182 | 3.25 | 368 | 4.53 |
| 09.30–09.40 | 127 | 2.27 | 188 | 2.31 |
| 09.40–09.50 | 84 | 1.50 | 102 | 1.26 |
| 09.50–10.00 | 77 | 1.37 | 103 | 1.27 |
| 10.00–10.10 | 160 | 2.86 | 123 | 1.51 |
| 10.10–10.20 | 55 | 0.98 | 70 | 0.86 |
| 10.20–10.30 | 57 | 1.02 | 203 | 2.50 |
| 10.30–10.40 | 105 | 1.87 | 101 | 1.24 |
| 10.40–10.50 | 16 | 0.29 | 74 | 0.91 |
| 10.50–11.00 | 65 | 1.16 | 35 | 0.43 |
| 11.00–11.10 | 1 | 0.02 | 72 | 0.89 |
| 11.10–11.20 | 134 | 2.39 | 22 | 0.27 |
| 11.20–11.30 | 372 | 6.64 | 248 | 3.05 |
| 11.30–11.40 | 389 | 6.94 | 426 | 5.24 |
| 11.40–11.50 | 301 | 5.37 | 299 | 3.68 |
| 11.50–12.00 | 110 | 1.96 | 221 | 2.72 |
| 12.00–12.10 | 4 | 0.07 | 14 | 0.17 |
| 12.10–12.20 | 57 | 1.02 | 9 | 0.11 |
| 12.20–12.30 | 0 | 0.00 | 131 | 1.61 |
| 12.30–12.40 | 6 | 0.11 | | |
| Sample Totals | 3686 | 65.80% | 4835 | 59.49% |
| Total Admissions | | 5602 | | 8127 |

Table 66. KV visitor numbers by time slot

tourists per hour in KV varies by hour and by day of the week. A survey we conducted in October 2004 gave the figures shown in tables 66 and 67.

As we can see from these results, visitation to KV is not evenly spaced. There are peak periods during the day when visitor numbers become dangerously high. These occurred at approximately the same time each day, between 8:00 and 8:30 a.m. and again from 11:20 to 11:50 a.m. On 23 October, 34 percent of the total visitor admissions for that day entered within these peak periods, and on 24 October, 22 percent of the total visitor admissions for that day entered within these two thirty-minute time slots. These results show the urgent need for a crowd-control system to be implemented within KV.

Carrying Capacity | 199

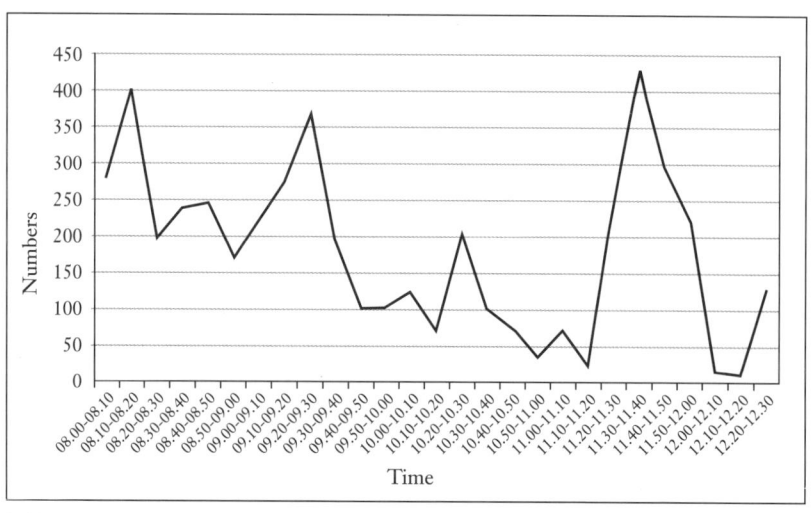

Table 67. KV visitor numbers, 23 October 2004

As discussed above, fluctuations in the temperature and humidity within KV tombs are affected by a rise in visitor numbers. The data collected in KV 9 on 23 and 24 October 2004 shows quite clearly how these peaks in visitor numbers affect the tombs' microclimate. Table 68 illustrates this danger. However, understanding how visitors use the site and how different groups move throughout the site is essential.

As stated previously, almost all visitors to KV come as part of organized tours led by government-licensed tour guides. These groups vary in size from one or two persons to as many as forty to fifty. Informal surveys indicate that the average group size is about twenty-three people. The tour guide buys the tickets for his or her group and usually delivers a brief introductory lecture about KV somewhere near the entrance to the Valley, or in the shaded visitor rest area at its center. The guide then takes the group to two tombs, in front of which he delivers a brief talk using the tomb's sign as a backdrop. The guide remarks on features of interest in the tomb, then waits outside while the group walks through it. This is repeated at a second tomb of the guide's choosing. Normally, the two tombs chosen are near the center of KV: KV 6, 9, or 11; less frequently, KV 1 or 2; still less frequently, KV 14, 15, 34, or 43. The guide then gives the group thirty minutes on their own, to visit a third tomb of their choice. Most tourists, not knowing the Valley, will opt for a tomb whose entrance is visible from where they are standing at that moment. Few wander

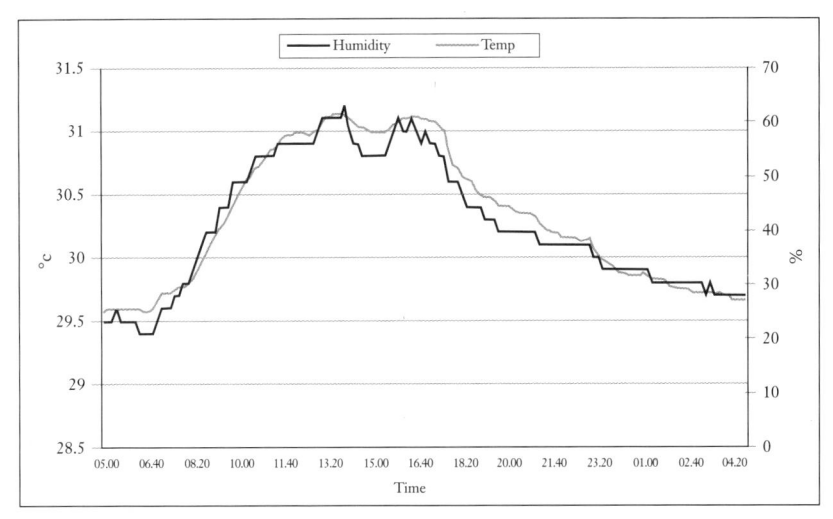

Table 68. Temperature and humidity, KV 9, 24 October 2004

into the Valley's recesses. Some will have paid the extra money for a ticket to the tomb of Tutankhamun and will visit there instead of selecting a third tomb that is permitted on their general admission ticket. A few will choose to do nothing, and will sit in the visitors' rest area until the group returns to their bus.

Guides usually choose the tombs they visit based on three criteria: (1) the tomb must be close by, to minimize the time it takes to get to its entrance; (2) the tomb must be one they can talk about comfortably (and not one about which they know little or nothing); (3) the tomb must be easily accessible, with few staircases, if any, and with a large amount of painted decoration. Large, level tombs are preferred over small or deep ones. In addition, time constraints notwithstanding, the fact that a tomb meeting these criteria is already crowded with tourists seems not to be a major concern. For instance, tourists often will stand in line in front of KV 9 for fifteen to twenty minutes waiting to enter because their guide has told them that it is especially beautiful.

## TMP Proposals: Visitor Flow into the Valley of the Kings

Our surveys have shown that visitor numbers in KV need to be managed to protect the fragile environment and to enhance visitor experience. Therefore, we need to address how to manage the number of visitors entering KV at any one time.

There are two points at which it is possible physically to control the number of visitors to KV.

1. Before driving to KV, tour leaders can be informed even before their vehicle turns at Carter House toward the Valley of the Kings that the valley is near full capacity and that buses continuing into the Valley at this time will be forced to wait in the parking area before offloading their passengers.
2. Tourists can be informed at the Visitors Center that the Valley is full and there will be a delay of (however many) minutes before they will be permitted to board the tram. Visitors can occupy themselves while they wait by shopping in the vendors' bazaar, sitting at tables in the cafeteria, or spending more time in the Visitors Center, viewing its exhibits and using its computers.

Methods used at other heritage attractions to control and regulate visitor numbers include the following. After each method, the effectiveness of the application to KV is considered.

A. **Restrictions on physical numbers allowed on site or component parts:** Visitor numbers can be controlled at the entrance to each tomb, with electronic counters or guards keeping a record of the number of tourists in the tomb at any point in time and temporarily stopping more visitors from entering if the carrying capacity has been reached. This was informally tried in the tomb of Ramesses VI (KV 9) over a period of one month, with a single guard tallying visitor numbers. It worked well and met with no complaints from tourists or their guides. If electronic counters replace the guard, the counters selected should be aesthetically appropriate and able to withstand the harsh KV environment.

B. **Restrictions on group sizes:** If no more than, say, thirty tourists were allowed to be in the hands of a single guide, the size of groups standing in KV for lectures or waiting in line to enter a tomb could be reduced. In fact, this is probably the case now, except for visitors arriving from the Red Sea, who arrive in very large groups under the control of only a few guides.

**C. Extended opening hours:** One way to reduce the number of tourists in KV at any one time is to extend visiting hours in the Valley and encourage tourist guides to go there at off-peak hours. At present, KV is open roughly from sunrise to sunset. That could be extended from 6:00 a.m. to 9:00 p.m., since tomb interiors depend entirely on artificial light, and plans are now being made to illuminate the Valley exterior after sunset. This time extension must be coordinated with the Security Police, since it was they who imposed the 5:00 p.m. closing time and they who also enforce a rule prohibiting foreigners from crossing the Luxor Nile Bridge after sunset. This extension would increase opening time in KV from eleven hours to fifteen hours daily and, theoretically, it could mean that fewer tourists would visit during peak hours, 7:00 a.m. to 11:00 a.m. If we assumed a constant maximum of a thousand tourists per hour, this extension would allow fifteen thousand visitors each day, a figure unlikely to be reached for at least a decade.

Alternative visiting times would require the cooperation of tour guides and operators. They would have to be convinced that it is in their best interest to visit the West Bank in the evening, for example, not in the morning. Such a change in itinerary might entail extra costs for the tour operator: it might require additional bus-rental time, a rearrangement of well-established tourist itineraries, or changes in dining schedules on tour boats. Indeed, perhaps only independent travelers and those staying in Luxor on cruise boats or in hotels for two- or three-day tours might have the flexibility to adjust their itineraries. However, the possibility of visiting uncrowded tombs in a more leisurely fashion might in itself be sufficient incentive for such changes to standard schedules. Offering discounted tickets to monuments in off-peak hours would also be a possible way to encourage change, but this is not acceptable to the current SCA administration, which fears any loss of revenue. (Perhaps one should offer not a discount for off-hours, but charge a premium for peak hours.)

Such scheduling changes might not be acceptable or even possible for day-trippers coming from Hurghada. These groups depart the Red Sea at about 4:30 a.m., arriving in Luxor at 9:00 a.m. They spend three hours on the West Bank before driving to Luxor for a visit to Karnak Temple and lunch. They leave for Hurghada at about 4:30 p.m. So brief a visit leaves little room for schedule adjustments. This sector of the West Bank visitor pool is growing rapidly, especially among the thousands of Russian and Eastern Europeans who visit the Red Sea. As many as a hundred buses, filled with about three to four thousand tourists, have been known to make the trip to Luxor in a single morning. On a few occasions in 2004, they constituted over 50 percent of the total number of visitors to KV.

Reversing their schedule so that day-trippers would visit Karnak in the morning and the West Bank in the afternoon might alleviate some of the crowding in the Valley of the Kings, but it would only exacerbate the already intolerable early-morning crowds in Karnak. Perhaps, since time constraints on these day-trippers is so great, they could purchase a special KV ticket that allows a visit to only two tombs instead of the current three, thereby reducing their impact on the tombs and reducing their time in KV from 120 minutes to ninety minutes. Our surveys suggest that this would be an acceptable alternative for many tour groups.

There is a similar problem for tourists who arrive or depart Luxor by Nile cruiser. Because of the scheduling of charter flights to and from Europe, most Nile cruises depart Luxor for Aswan on Saturday or Wednesday and most return to Luxor on Sunday or Thursday. This means that Mondays and Fridays are two of the busiest days in KV, as these tourists make it the first stop on their Luxor tour. Again, it would require complex negotiations with tour operators to change these schedules. It is unlikely that European operators would be willing to switch to mid-week flights instead of flights that take advantage of their customers' weekends. (A holiday package that extends from Friday evening of Week One to Sunday evening of Week Two allows for a ten-day holiday with only five working days being missed.)

Group tourists and independent travelers who stay in Luxor hotels for several days or longer have the greatest flexibility in their schedules, and it is they who might be encouraged to visit KV at off-peak hours. This could be done by posting notices in hotel lobbies, notifying travel agencies and publishers of guidebooks, and urging local guides to suggest alternate visiting times. We are not yet able to determine what percentage of visitors to KV fall into the Luxor hotel-resident category; it is likely to be only about 40 percent of the total number of visitors. But even this number could make a difference to conditions in the KV tombs.

D. **Restrictions on parking:** Signs on the West Bank might indicate by means of flashing lights or a number board that the parking area at KV was full. Currently, that would mean there were over fifty buses in the area. If the parking area is moved down the road and enlarged, it might mean a hundred buses. Drivers and guides would know that they will be forced to wait several minutes before being allowed into the parking area to offload passengers and should visit other, less crowded, West Bank sites before proceeding to KV.

E. **Economic restrictions through pricing:** Some KV tombs are more popular with guides and visitors than others. Probably the most visited are KV 8, 9, and 11. An extra charge could be made to visit these tombs, thereby reducing visitor numbers without reducing income. Another option is to arrange KV tombs into three groups, based on their popularity and ease of access. Visitors would be allowed to visit only one tomb in each of these three categories on a single three-tomb ticket. The tombs might include KV 9 (Ramesses VI, most popular); KV 1 (Ramesses VII, moderately popular); and KV 19 (Mentuherkhepeshef, less popular).

F. **Closure of part or all of site at specific times:** Tombs could be temporarily closed when carrying capacity has been reached. Tomb openings could rotate, with, for example, KV 9 being open M/W/F 6:00–11:00 a.m. and T/Th/S/S 11:00 a.m.–5:00 p.m., and KV 8 being open M/W/F 11:00 a.m.–5:00 p.m. and T/Th/S/S 6:00–11:00 a.m. Guides would be informed of this schedule in advance so they could plan their timing and visits accordingly.

G. **Provision of replicas:** Preparation of full-size replica tombs has often been discussed, either making them from full-color photographs or carved and painted plaster or plastic. Most proposals have not been cost effective. And where can one put a full-size model of a large tomb without doing serious aesthetic damage to the landscape? Making the floors of replicas level, instead of steeply sloping as the original might do, could alleviate some of the problems. Adding a rear exit would also help reduce congestion. For some visitors, the lower price charged to visit a replica might be an attractive option if it were emphasized that the experience is little different from viewing the original. Replicas could easily be made of the tomb of Tutankhamun and the QV tomb of Nefertari since complete photos of both are available. The TMP has now acquired comprehensive photographic coverage of most decorated KV tombs, and these images could also be used to create replicas. The desert south of Malqata on the West Bank might be a suitable location for their exhibition.

H. **Diversion to nearby sites or other parts of KV:** Signs at the approach road, at the entrance to KV, and at junctions of pathways inside it could indicate the status of tomb carrying capacity within KV, letting visitors and guides know in advance whether a tomb has exceeded its carrying capacity and is temporarily closed. The levels of congestion can be given a color code:

> Green: operating normally, visitors free to enter site
> Amber: Levels rising, may be some congestion, suggest alternative options
> Red: Site temporarily full, please go elsewhere and try again later

Therefore, a visitor counting system would need to be installed and a record kept of the number of visitors in KV at any time, as well as within individual tombs.

## TMP Proposals: Visitor Flow within the Valley of the Kings

Managed visitor flow within KV is essential if congestion and overcrowding within certain areas and tombs are to be avoided. Current visitor and guide behavior patterns make the central area of KV very overcrowded while other areas are deserted.

Some examples of crowd control options include:
- Information on open tombs
- Signage

- Pathways
- Physical barriers
- Ticketing systems

*Information on Open Tombs*

If the three-tomb-per-ticket ticketing system is retained, tourists ideally would see a tomb from each of the three New Kingdom dynasties (table 69). Tombs varied over time in plan and content in this era, and their evolution is important for an understanding of Egyptian religion and religious architecture. This would mean that tourists would choose one tomb from each of these three dynastic lists. However, because of the unequal number of tombs from the three dynasties, the fact that several tombs are closed, and their scattered locations, variable size, and relatively difficult access (because of stairs and ramps), such an archaeologically informative itinerary is rarely possible.

| Dynasty 18 | |
|---|---|
| KV 35 | Amenhotep II |
| KV 34 | Thutmose III |
| KV 43 | Thutmose IV |
| KV 62 | Tutankhamun |
| KV 57 | Horemheb |
| WV 23 | Ay |
| Dynasty 19 | |
| KV 8 | Merenptah |
| KV 16 | Ramesses I |
| KV 17 | Seti I |
| Dynasty 20 | |
| KV 1 | Ramesses VII |
| KV 2 | Ramesses IV |
| KV 6 | Ramesses IX |
| KV 9 | Ramesses VI |
| KV 11 | Ramesses III |
| KV 14 | Tawosret/Setnakht |
| KV 15 | Seti II |
| KV 19 | Mentuherkhepeshef |
| KV 47 | Siptah |

Table 69. KV accessible tombs, by dynasty

An alternative would be to have tourists visit one of each of three different groups of tombs based on geographical location and tomb popularity. If one considers the central zone to be the area adjacent to the main rest house, then the farther two outlying zones would go out in concentric circles from that area. Under this plan, visitors would only be able to visit one tomb from each zone (table 70).

| Zone One | |
|---|---|
| KV 2 | Ramesses IV |
| KV 6 | Ramesses IX |
| KV 8 | Merenptah |
| KV 9 | Ramesses V and Ramesses VI |
| KV 11 | Ramesses III |
| KV 16 | Ramesses I |
| KV 17 | Seti I |
| Zone Two | |
| KV 1 | Ramesses VII |
| KV 14 | Tawosret/Setnakht |
| KV 15 | Seti II |
| KV 47 | Siptah |
| KV 57 | Horemheb |
| Zone Three | |
| KV 19 | Mentuherkhepeshef |
| KV 34 | Thutmose III |
| KV 35 | Amenhotep II |
| KV 43 | Thutmose IV |

Table 70. KV accessible tombs, by zoning

*Signage*

The TMP installed new signage in KV in 2000. The previous signs were inadequate, with poor information, and could not withstand the harsh environment (figs. 74a and 74b). TMP obtained the permission of the Egyptian government to design, produce, and install new signs in the Valley. Our goal was to make accurate information available to tourists and to help ensure that tourist guides make their presentations outside the tombs, not inside. We believed that this would help alleviate the dangerous overcrowding in tombs that threatens their decorated walls. It also made the visitors' experience more meaningful. The signs we installed are laser-printed on aluminum sheets,

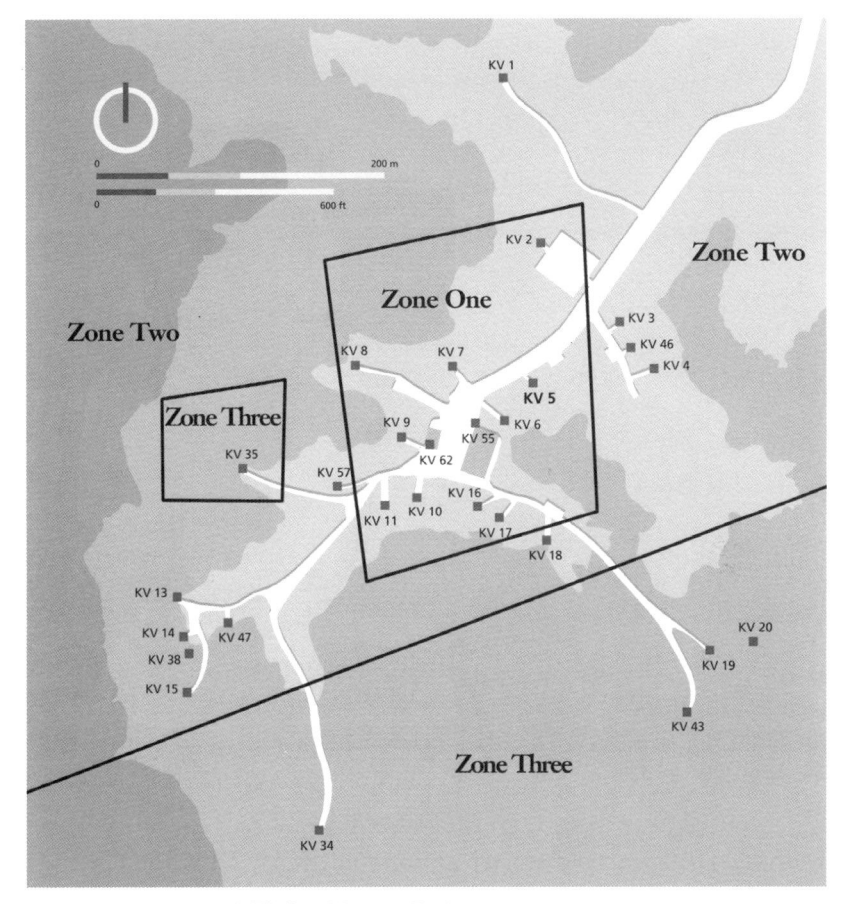

Fig. 73. KV zone map. © Theban Mapping Project

guaranteed to last at least forty years, even in the Valley's harsh conditions. They were designed to a high aesthetic standard and produced by a firm in Switzerland.

The TMP installed twenty signs—general interpretive signs, signs specific to each of the eleven tombs that are now open to the public, and six others for tombs scheduled to be open during the next few years. They were installed in purpose-built, shaded pavilions erected by the SCA beside each tomb entrance. They also include seven maps that show the topography of KV and the location and plans of its tombs. The signs were installed at the KV entrance and at the intersections of footpaths. The signs list the tombs currently open to the public, those that are wheelchair accessible, and those that have steep stairways. Signs describing individual tombs were placed in front of each open tomb and they give an axonometric plan of the tomb; information about its date, discovery, and significant features; and photographs of its principal scenes and texts. The signs are designed to serve as a backdrop to the lectures of tour guides, and to provide basic information to independent travelers.

When the signs were installed, the SCA announced that guides would henceforth be banned from lecturing inside the tombs. Although at first opposed to the signs, guides quickly came to approve of them when they discovered that tourists liked the quieter, less hectic time in the tombs encouraged by the absence of lecturing. Guides also like being able to remain outside the tomb, smoking and talking to colleagues. Tourists, too, approve of the signs, and often photograph them to be used as *aides-mémoires* when they return home. The signs are in English only (at the request of the SCA), and the TMP therefore published a thirty-six-page, illustrated pamphlet in Arabic intended for the use of school groups and teachers who visit KV. An initial printing of 7,500 quickly sold out (at LE 1 per copy), and additional printings are planned. The booklet is sold at SCA sales desks at various Theban sites but, unfortunately, it is not yet available in KV itself. An English-language version of the guide is also planned.

There are three different kinds of maps now posted in the Valley, each giving different information. All are drawn to scale (shown on each map) and oriented so that the direction in which you look when facing the sign is always at the top of the sign. Thus, if you are facing east when looking at the map, then east is at the top of the map. Some maps show the elevation of the surrounding hills by means of contour lines that give a general impression of the terrain. Others include plans of principal tombs, drawn as if one could see them through the bedrock. Some maps show only tomb entrances; tombs are identified by their number and, on some maps, also by the name of their owner. These map signs are installed at several places in the Valley to help direct tourists to the tombs.

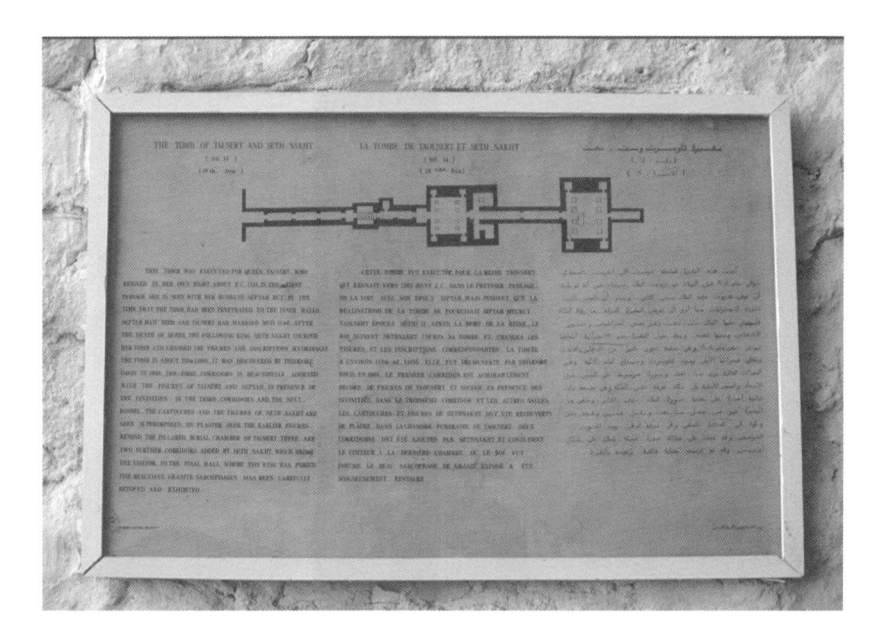

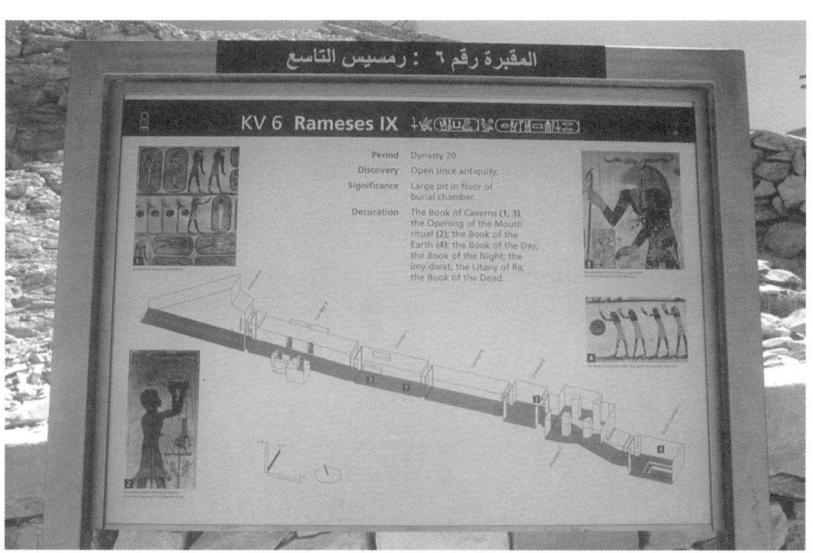

Fig. 74a and b. KV 6 signs, before and after. © Theban Mapping Project

Carrying Capacity | 211

## Valley of the Kings

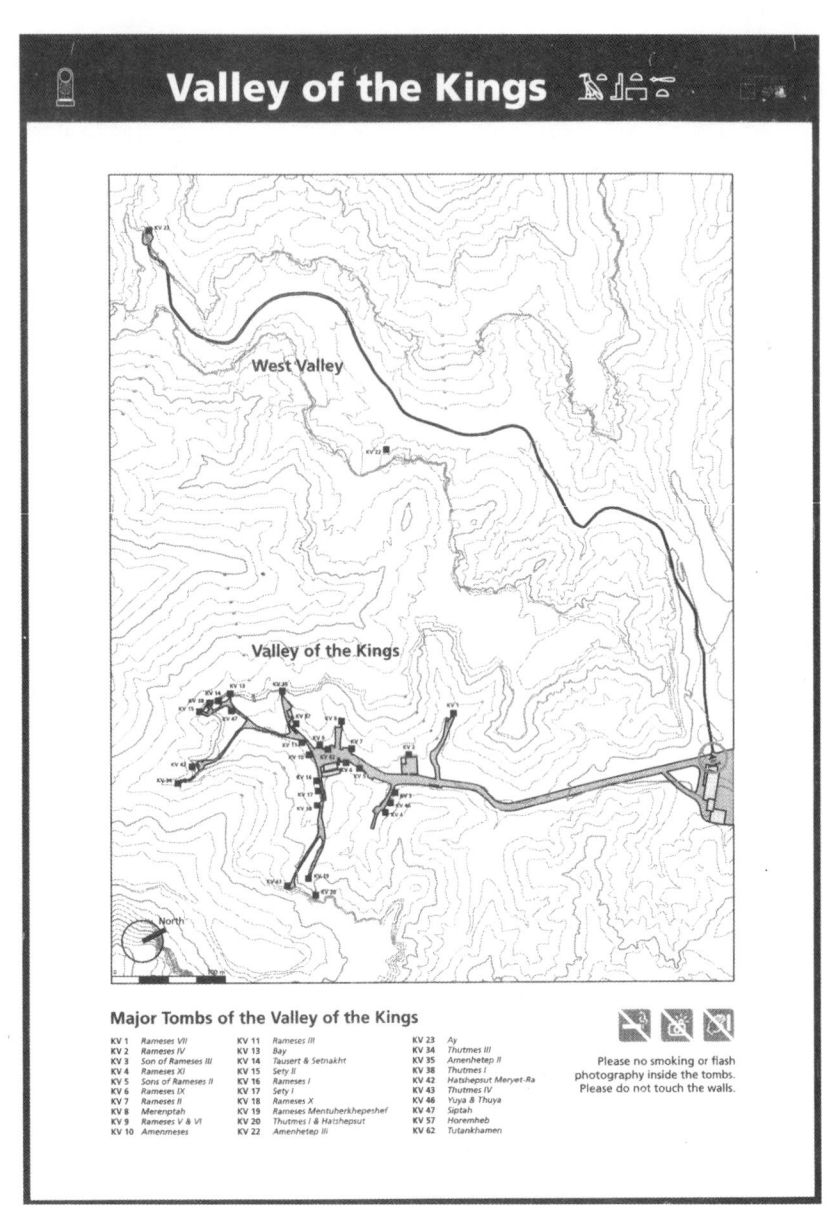

**Major Tombs of the Valley of the Kings**

| | | | | | | |
|---|---|---|---|---|---|---|
| KV 1 | Rameses VII | KV 11 | Rameses III | KV 23 | Ay | |
| KV 2 | Rameses IV | KV 13 | Bay | KV 34 | Thutmes III | |
| KV 3 | Son of Rameses III | KV 14 | Tausert & Setnakht | KV 35 | Amenhetep II | |
| KV 4 | Rameses XI | KV 15 | Sety II | KV 38 | Thutmes I | |
| KV 5 | Sons of Rameses II | KV 16 | Rameses I | KV 42 | Hatshepsut Meryet-Ra | |
| KV 6 | Rameses IX | KV 17 | Sety I | KV 43 | Thutmes IV | |
| KV 7 | Rameses II | KV 18 | Rameses X | KV 46 | Yuya & Thuya | |
| KV 8 | Merenptah | KV 19 | Rameses Mentuherkhepeshef | KV 47 | Siptah | |
| KV 9 | Rameses V & VI | KV 20 | Thutmes I & Hatshepsut | KV 57 | Horemheb | |
| KV 10 | Amenmeses | KV 22 | Amenhetep III | KV 62 | Tutankhamen | |

Please no smoking or flash photography inside the tombs. Please do not touch the walls.

- Figure 75a is a general map that shows both the East and West Valleys. It is posted in the parking area west of the cafeteria, where the dirt road into the West Valley begins. This map shows the location of tombs on a topographic map of the area. It also shows roads

212 | Visitor Management in the Valley of the Kings

and principal pathways. Contour lines indicate the shape and elevation of the hills surrounding the two valleys. When facing the map, one is looking toward the west, and west is at the top of this map.

- Figure 75b is a topographic map of the East Valley, showing not only the entrance of each tomb, but also the plan of each tomb. Pathways are shown and contour lines indicate the shape and elevation of the hills around the Valley. Tombs are identified by number and there is a list giving both the numbers and the names of the owners of the principal tombs. East is at the top of these signs, and east is the direction one is looking when facing them. A copy of this map has been installed in the shaded sitting area behind the ticket office at the entrance to the Valley, and two others are mounted in the rest area in the center of the Valley.

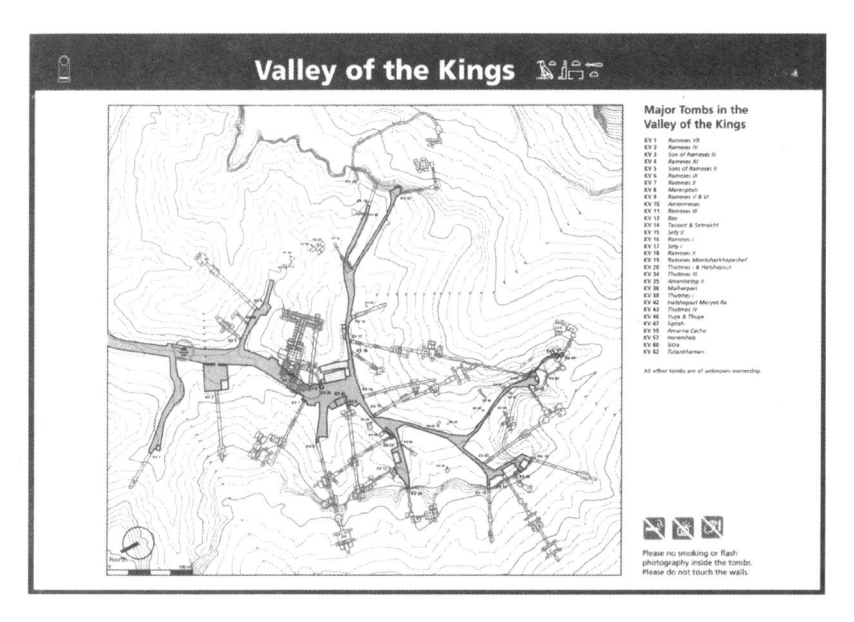

- Figure 75c is a simpler version of the East Valley map showing paths and tomb entrances, but not topographic features or tomb plans. The principal tombs are indicated by tomb number and owner's name. Each tomb is dated to the Eighteenth, Nineteenth, or Twentieth Dynasty. Tombs with steep stairways are noted to warn infirm

Carrying Capacity | 213

travelers, and tombs accessible to wheelchairs are also marked. Copies of this sign are installed in several places within the East Valley. Depending on its location and orientation, either south or east will be at the top of the map. Dotted lines indicate the paths over the *gebel* (mountain or hill) to Deir al-Bahari and Deir al-Medina. The sign also has a list of the principal tombs in the Valley, indicating which tombs are currently open to tourists and which are not.

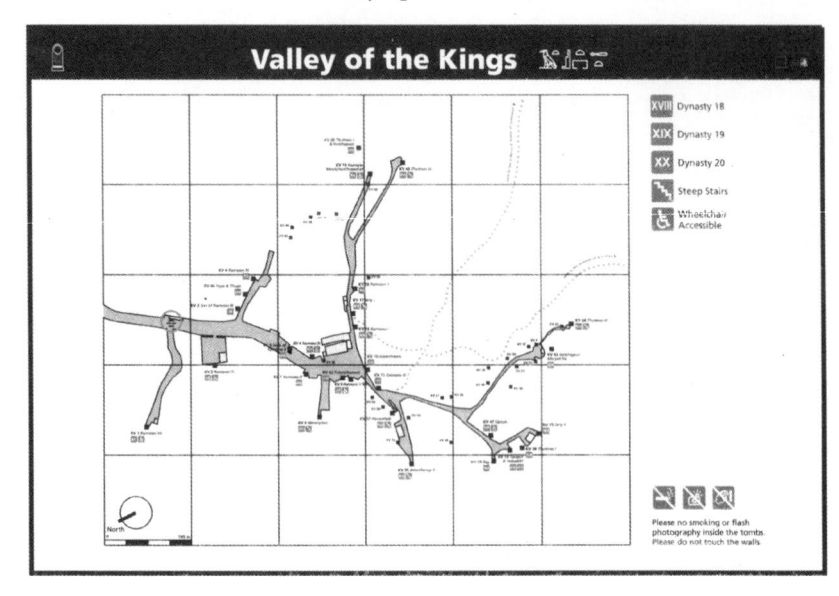

*Pathways*

The management of crowds of tourists in KV can only be done effectively if some of the Valley's pathways are widened. This is particularly true of the path between KV 11 and KV 57, where a traffic bottleneck occurs nearly every day. The newly opened path from KV 3, 46, and 4 to KV 21 has helped alleviate some congestion. Now that a steep and awkward staircase has been installed in the pathway immediately east of KV 18, the new pathway should be made wheelchair accessible and a sign should be installed near KV 3 indicating that the path leads to several open tombs.

*Physical Barriers*

Crowd control in front of KV 6, 9, and 11 is a serious problem because these tombs draw large audiences. Ropes and posts could be used to

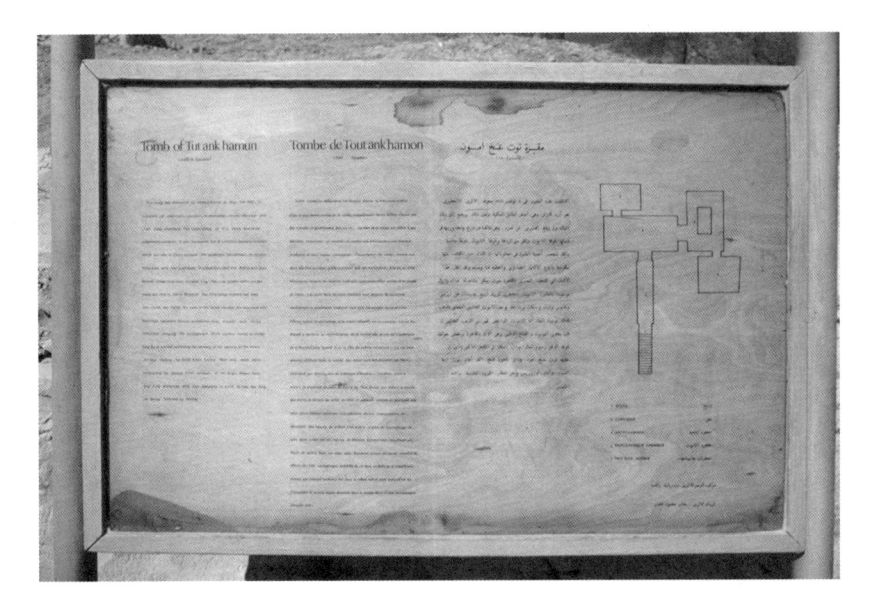

Fig. 76a and b. General KV signage. © Theban Mapping Project

create aisles similar to those used at airport check-in counters to ensure that long lines of tourists do not snake out into the Valley, posing serious problems of congestion.

Carrying Capacity | 215

*Ticketing Systems*
Discussed in the section "Ticketing Systems," below.

Fig. 77. Visitors hiking from KV to Deir al-Medina. © Theban Mapping Project

## Carrying Capacity of Tombs in the Valley of the Kings

Tombs in the Valley of the Kings vary considerably in size and plan. Of the tombs open to the public, the smallest is KV 16: Ramesses I, which occupies 254 square meters. The largest is KV 8: Merenptah, which is 2,742 meters. Tomb plans vary from steeply sloping Eighteenth Dynasty tombs with curving axes (e.g., KV 34: Thutmose IV) to nearly level, single-axis tombs (e.g., KV 1: Ramesses VII). Tombs can accommodate different numbers of tourists depending on size and plan, and it is important to determine the optimum carrying capacity of each tomb. Exceeding this capacity is likely to damage the fabric of the tomb, exacerbating environmental and tourism problems.

By carrying capacity, we mean the maximum number of persons who can occupy a tomb at any point in time without causing unacceptable changes in the physical environment or a decline in the quality of visitor experience. Too many persons in a tomb can result in unacceptably high ambient temperatures and humidity, uncomfortable feelings of crowding for the visitor, and damage to decorated walls.

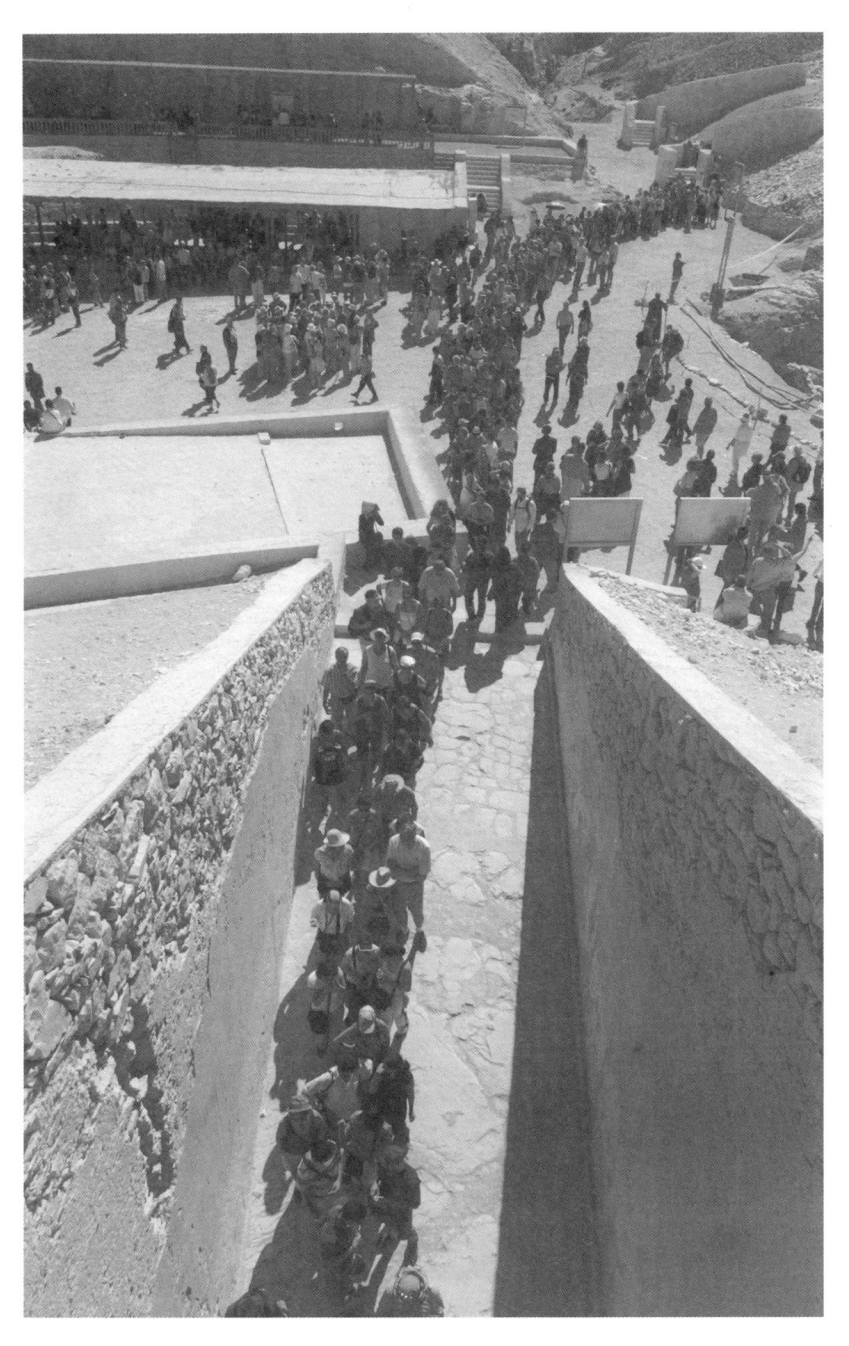

Fig. 78. Overcrowding in tombs. © Theban Mapping Project

How is carrying capacity to be determined? One could monitor a tomb's temperature and humidity and temporarily close the tomb when those measures reach unacceptable levels. However, this assumes a close and almost immediate correlation between occupancy levels and environmental factors, and this has been shown not to be the case.

Another method is to allocate to each visitor one linear meter of space as they walk through a tomb. This may appear to be an arbitrary number, but on-site observations suggest that it is meaningful. We have observed that people walking in queues feel uncomfortable with less separation than this, and will naturally try to establish at least this spacing if other factors do not intervene. Thus, we could argue that a tomb with a visitor-accessible corridor 80 meters long can accommodate eighty persons walking single file into the tomb and another eighty walking out, giving it a maximum carrying capacity of 160 persons. Some architectural features require that adjustments be made to this 'one-meter rule.' For example, if a tomb has steep staircases (as in KV 57, Horemheb), visitors move more slowly and require greater linear space, and the number of visitors should therefore be reduced. (Tombs with wide corridors could conceivably accommodate

| Tomb | Length (m) | CC (Persons) | Adjusted Figure | Notes |
| --- | --- | --- | --- | --- |
| KV1 | 30 | 60 | 60 | |
| KV2 | 56 | 112 | 112 | |
| KV6 | 58 | 116 | 116 | |
| KV8 | 83 | 166 | 133 | Sloping Corridors / Steps |
| KV9 | 82 | 164 | 132 | Steps / Crowded Chamber |
| KV11 | 56 | 112 | 101 | Narrow Corridor |
| KV14 | 84 | 168 | 168 | |
| KV15 | 65 | 130 | 130 | |
| KV16 | 22 | 44 | 36 | Steps |
| KV19 | 16 | 32 | 32 | |
| KV23 | 43 | 86 | 77 | Steps |
| KV34 | 35 | 70 | 50 | Steps |
| KV35 | 25 | 50 | 40 | Steps |
| KV43 | 65 | 130 | 91 | Steps / Axes |
| KV47 | 26 | 52 | 52 | |
| KV57 | 80 | 160 | 128 | Steps |
| KV62 | 15 | 30 | 24 | Steps |

Table 71. TMP proposed KV tomb carrying capacity

visitors walking in pairs, but we have not allowed this because our studies show that it will result in congestion as tourists walking into a tomb block tourists trying to leave.)

Calculations based on this 'one-meter rule' provide the figures shown in table 71 for each of the open tombs in KV. Tombs with steep stairs, unusually narrow corridors, or other mitigating features are given adjusted figures.

The next stage of the process is to measure the actual number of visitors to KV tombs. In fact, in several tombs currently, the number of visitors greatly exceeds the ideal carrying capacity, in some cases to a dangerous degree. Figures are available for the Valley as a whole, but the numbers of people entering individual tombs has not been previously recorded. In an attempt to quantify this and address the scale of the overcrowding, the TMP monitored the numbers of visitors in three tombs on two consecutive days. Tables 72 and 73 show the numbers of visitors to tombs KV 6, 9, and 11, counted at ten-minute intervals between the hours of 7:00 a.m. and 1:00 p.m. on Tuesday 21 September 2004, by the TMP survey team.

| Time Slot | Number | | |
|---|---|---|---|
| 07.30–07.40 | 152 | 10.30–10.40 | 81 |
| 07.40–07.50 | 227 | 10.40–10.50 | 62 |
| 07.50–08.00 | 246 | 10.50–11.00 | 67 |
| 08.00–08.10 | 293 | 11.00–11.10 | 106 |
| 08.10–08.20 | 237 | 11.10–11.20 | 55 |
| 08.20–08.30 | 193 | 11.20–11.30 | 51 |
| 08.30–08.40 | 174 | 11.30–11.40 | 86 |
| 08.40–08.50 | 136 | 11.40–11.50 | 57 |
| 08.50–09.00 | 180 | 11.50–12.00 | 74 |
| 09.00–09.10 | 144 | 12.00–12.10 | 52 |
| 09.10–09.20 | 148 | 12.10–12.20 | 58 |
| 09.20–09.30 | 87 | 12.20–12.30 | 50 |
| 09.30–09.40 | 85 | 12.30–12.40 | 106 |
| 09.40–09.50 | 95 | 12.40–12.50 | 29 |
| 09.50–10.00 | 87 | 12.50–13.00 | 36 |
| 10.00–10.10 | 52 | | |
| 10.10–10.20 | 67 | Total | 3649 |
| 10.20–10.30 | 76 | Average | 114.03 |

Table 72. KV 6 visitor numbers, 21 September 2004

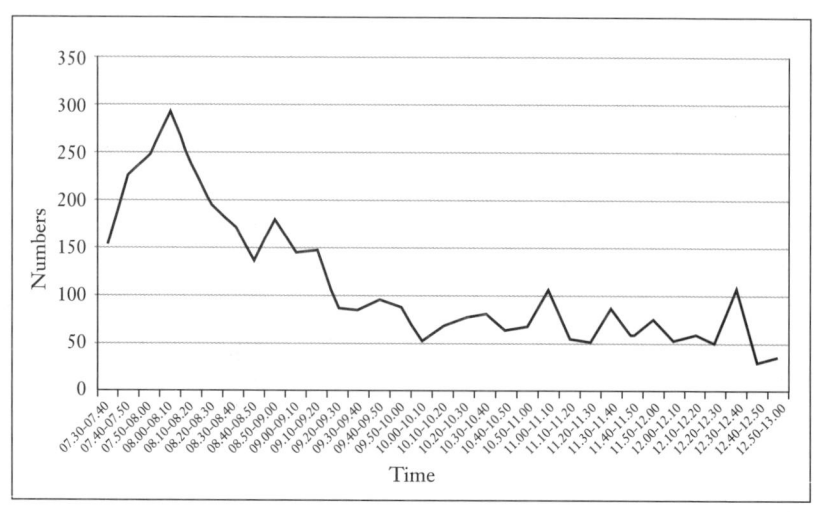

Table 73. KV 6 visitor numbers, 21 September 2004

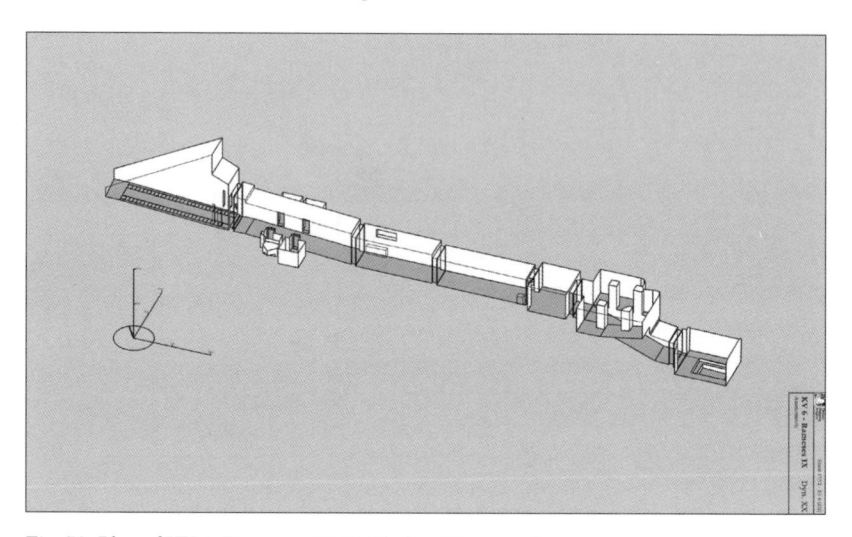

Fig. 79. Plan of KV 6, Ramesses IX. © Theban Mapping Project

## Tomb Visitor Numbers
*KV 6 Survey*

Tables 72 and 73 clearly illustrate that from 7:40 to 9:30 a.m. numbers in KV 6 exceeded our recommended carrying capacity of 116 visitors present at any particular time within the tomb. At their peak, the numbers exceeded recommended levels almost threefold.

KV6 (Ramesses IX) is a popular tomb with visitors due to its convenient location adjacent to the central rest house and its excellent state of preservation with many fine reliefs on its walls. The simple layout of the tomb, without many levels and stairs, makes it accessible for a wide range of visitors.

*KV 9 Survey*

During the peak periods of occupancy, numbers within KV 9 (Ramesses V/VI) exceeded the recommended carrying capacity of 132 persons by over 250 percent (table 74). Throughout both mornings visitor numbers rose until a peak of 307 was reached at 9:40–9:50 a.m. on 20 September, and a peak of 303 at 9:20–9:30 a.m. on 21 September, almost immediately resulting in a large increase in the temperature and humidity levels (tables 75 and 76).

| Time Slot | Mon. 20 September 2004 Number | Tues. 21 September 2004 Number |
|---|---|---|
| 07.30–07.40 | 68 | 165 |
| 07.40–07.50 | 56 | 154 |
| 07.50–08.00 | 102 | 167 |
| 08.00–08.10 | 109 | 163 |
| 08.10–08.20 | 125 | 160 |
| 08.20–08.30 | 168 | 154 |
| 08.30–08.40 | 217 | 176 |
| 08.40–08.50 | 191 | 186 |
| 08.50–09.00 | 258 | 215 |
| 09.00–09.10 | 286 | 217 |
| 09.10–09.20 | 258 | 236 |
| 09.20–09.30 | 301 | 303 |
| 09.30–09.40 | 274 | 280 |
| 09.40–09.50 | 307 | 244 |
| 09.50–10.00 | 283 | 242 |
| 10.00–10.10 | 255 | 217 |
| 10.10–10.20 | 263 | 208 |
| 10.20–10.30 | 287 | 184 |
| 10.30–10.40 | 290 | 83 |
| 10.40–10.50 | 221 | 57 |
| 10.50–11.00 | 139 | 19 |
| Total | 4458 | 3830 |
| Average | 212 | 182 |

Table 74. KV 9, number of visitors in ten-minute intervals, 7:30–11:00 a.m., 20–21 September 2004.

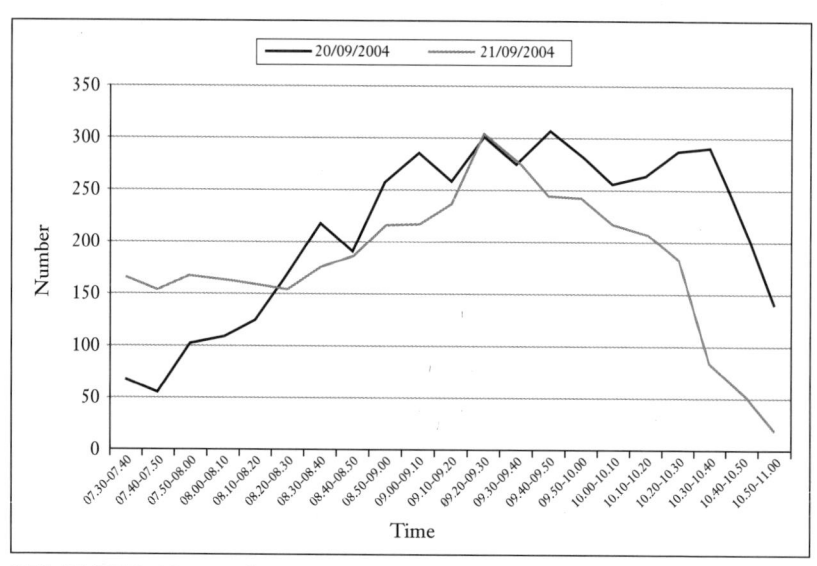

Table 75. KV 9 visitor numbers

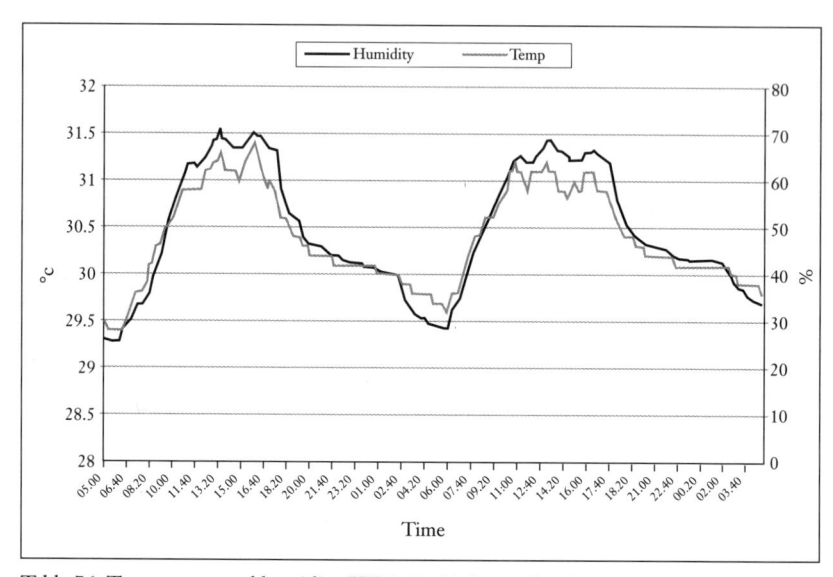

Table 76. Temperature and humidity, KV 9, 20–21 September 2004

KV 9's popularity with visitors (not unlike KV 6) stems from the nature of the tomb's layout, its fine reliefs, and its position in the central zone of the Valley. This was one of the main reasons the TMP selected the tomb for environmental monitoring.

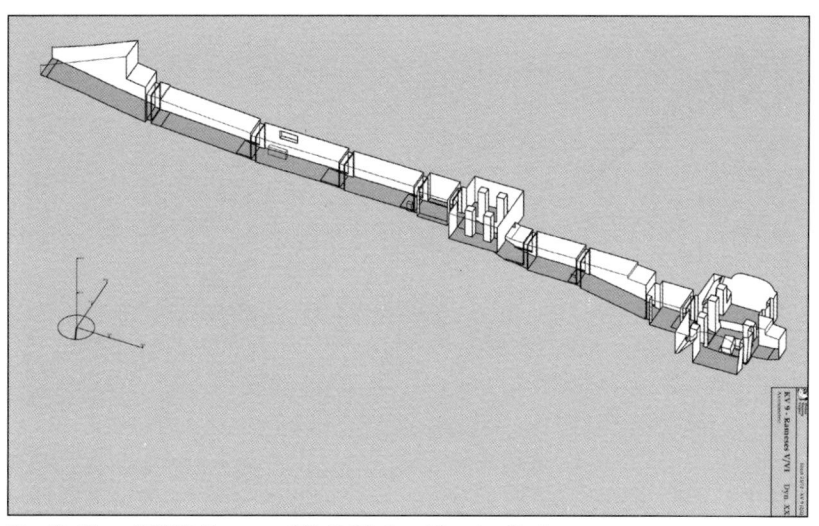

Fig. 80. Plan of KV 9, Ramesses VI. © Theban Mapping Project

## KV 11 Survey

| Time Slot | Number | | |
|---|---|---|---|
| 07.30–07.40 | 54 | 10.50–11.00 | 120 |
| 07.40–07.50 | 35 | 11.00–11.10 | 99 |
| 07.50–08.00 | 131 | 11.10–11.20 | 56 |
| 08.00–08.10 | 154 | 11.20–11.30 | 96 |
| 08.10–08.20 | 115 | 11.30–11.40 | 66 |
| 08.20–08.30 | 85 | 11.40–11.50 | 126 |
| 08.30–08.40 | 117 | 11.50–12.00 | 99 |
| 08.40–08.50 | 138 | 12.00–12.10 | 158 |
| 08.50–09.00 | 138 | 12.10–12.20 | 165 |
| 09.00–09.10 | 151 | 12.20–12.30 | 182 |
| 09.10–09.20 | 81 | 12.30–12.40 | 180 |
| 09.20–09.30 | 128 | 12.40–12.50 | 133 |
| 09.30–09.40 | 111 | 12.50–13.00 | 94 |
| 09.40–09.50 | 114 | 13.00–13.10 | 44 |
| 09.50–10.00 | 171 | 13.10–13.20 | 116 |
| 10.00–10.10 | 168 | 13.20–13.30 | 170 |
| 10.10–10.20 | 92 | 13.30–13.40 | 147 |
| 10.20–10.30 | 105 | 13.40–13.50 | 161 |
| 10.30–10.40 | 86 | 13.50–14.00 | 151 |
| 10.40–10.50 | 109 | **Average** | **145.19** |

Table 77. KV 11 visitor numbers, 21 September 2004

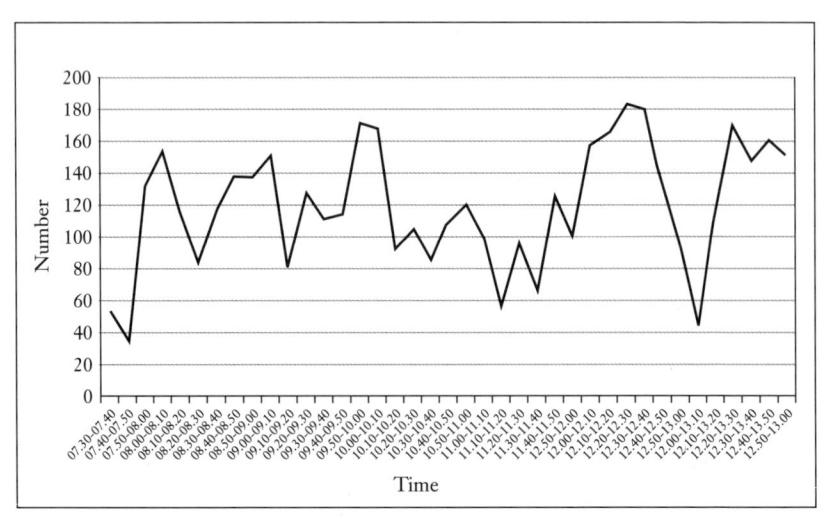

Table 78. KV 11 visitor numbers, 21 September 2004

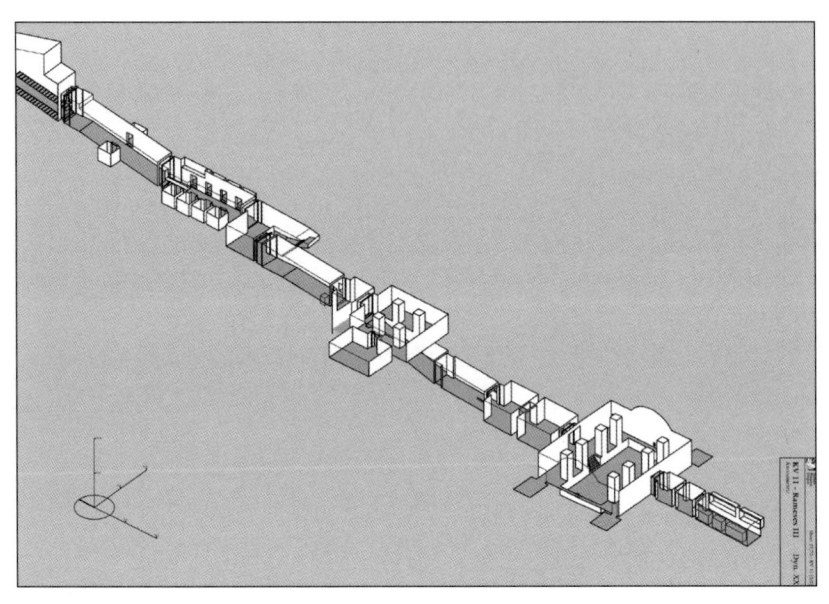

Fig. 81. Plan of KV 11, Ramesses III. © Theban Mapping Project

The recommended carrying capacity of KV 11, Ramesses III (101 persons) was exceeded in almost two-thirds of the time slots recorded by the TMP. At the peak time slot, occupancy exceeded recommended levels by 80 percent. This tomb, like KV 6 and 9, is situated in the central zone of KV.

## Tomb Visit Duration

How long does the average tourist spend in a tomb? This is an important consideration because it allows us to determine the maximum number of tourists who can comfortably visit a tomb per hour and per day. The following figures are based on TMP surveys undertaken in September 2004. We tallied the duration of visits in three tombs, KV 6, 9, and 11 (monitored above for carrying capacity). Every tenth visitor to the tomb was handed a card as they entered the tomb; the time of day was written on the card. The card asked (in five languages) that the visitor return the card upon exit. When it was returned, the time was noted and the duration of the visit then calculated. Times were arranged in ten-minute intervals, so that the duration of visits could be tabulated for the periods 7:00 to 7:10 a.m., 7:10 to 7:20 a.m., 07:20 to 7:30 a.m., and so on. The duration of visits to each of the three tombs is shown in the following tables (tables 79–82, and 84–88).

Fig. 82. TMP surveying. © Theban Mapping Project

## KV 6 Visit Duration Survey

| Time Slot | Average Duration (minutes) | | |
|---|---|---|---|
| 07.40–07.50 | 8 | 10.10–10.20 | 6 |
| 07.50–08.00 | 6 | 10.20–10.30 | 3 |
| 08.10–08.20 | 8 | 10.30–10.40 | 7 |
| 08.20–08.30 | 5 | 10.40–10.50 | 6 |
| 08.30–08.40 | 9 | 10.50–11.00 | 6 |
| 08.40–08.50 | 7 | 11.00–11.10 | 7 |
| 08.50–09.00 | 11 | 11.10–11.20 | 5 |
| 09.00–09.10 | 8 | 11.30–11.40 | 4 |
| 09.10–09.20 | 5 | 12.00–12.10 | 4 |
| 09.20–09.30 | 7 | 12.10–12.20 | 3 |
| 09.30–09.40 | 6 | 12.20–12.30 | 4 |
| 09.40–09.50 | 9 | 12.30–12.40 | 5 |

Table 79. KV 6 visit duration, 21 September 2004

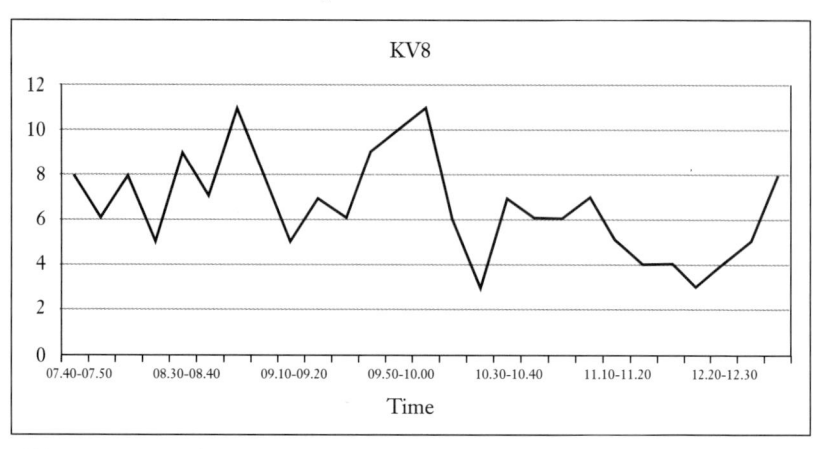

Table 80. KV 6 visit duration, 21 September 2004

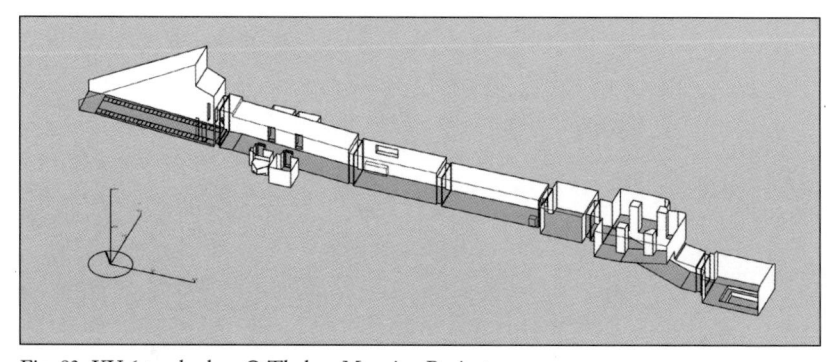

Fig. 83. KV 6 tomb plan. © Theban Mapping Project

## KV 9 Visit Duration Survey

| Time Slot | Average Duration (minutes) | Time Slot | Average Duration (minutes) |
|---|---|---|---|
| 07.30–07.40 | 9 | 10.40–10.50 | 14 |
| 07.40–07.50 | 12 | 10.50–11.00 | 11 |
| 07.50–08.00 | 12 | 11.00–11.10 | 10 |
| 08.00–08.10 | 12 | 11.10–11.20 | 7 |
| 08.10–08.20 | 13 | 11.20–11.30 | 9 |
| 08.30–08.40 | 20 | 11.30–11.40 | 10 |
| 08.50–09.00 | 24 | 11.40–11.50 | 8 |
| 09.00–09.10 | 11 | 11.50–12.00 | 11 |
| 09.10–09.20 | 16 | 12.00–12.10 | 13 |
| 09.20–09.30 | 15 | 12.10–12.20 | 10 |
| 09.30–09.40 | 18 | 12.20–12.30 | 6 |
| 09.40–09.50 | 17 | 12.30–12.40 | 8 |
| 09.50–10.00 | 14 | 12.40–12.50 | 8 |
| 10.00–10.10 | 10 | 12.50–13.00 | 7 |
| 10.10–10.20 | 15 | 13.00–13.10 | 10 |
| 10.20–10.30 | 15 | | |
| 10.30–10.40 | 17 | **Average Duration** | **12.25 minutes** |

Table 81. KV 9 visit duration, 20 September 2004

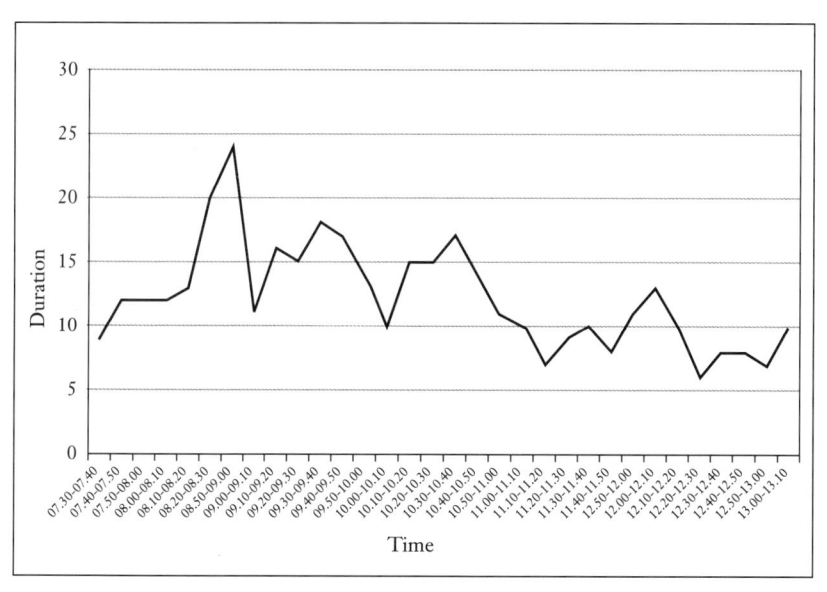

Table 82. KV 9 visit duration, 20 September 2004

Carrying Capacity of Tombs in the Valley of the Kings | 227

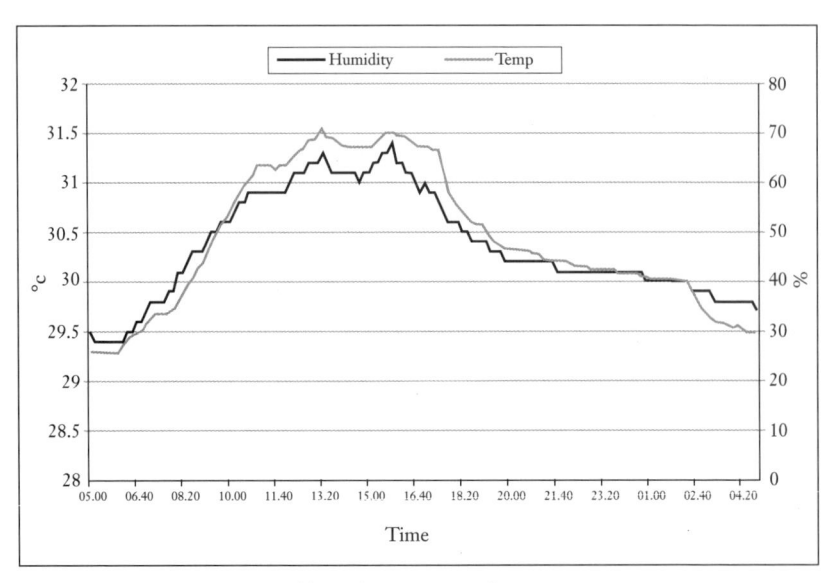

Table 83. KV 9 temperature and humidity, 20 September 2004

| Time Slot | Average Duration (minutes) | | |
|---|---|---|---|
| 07.30–07.40 | 8 | 10.20–10.30 | 10 |
| 07.40–07.50 | 13 | 10.30–10.40 | 15 |
| 07.50–08.00 | 12 | 10.50–11.00 | 9 |
| 08.00–08.10 | 14 | 11.00–11.10 | 9 |
| 08.10–08.20 | 14 | 11.10–11.20 | 9 |
| 08.20–08.30 | 9 | 11.20–11.30 | 9 |
| 08.30–08.40 | 13 | 11.30–11.40 | 9 |
| 08.40–08.50 | 11 | 11.40–11.50 | 11 |
| 08.50–09.00 | 13 | 11.50–12.00 | 8 |
| 09.00–09.10 | 11 | 12.00–12.10 | 9 |
| 09.10–09.20 | 14 | 12.10–12.20 | 6 |
| 09.20–09.30 | 14 | 12.20–12.30 | 7 |
| 09.30–09.40 | 14 | 12.30–12.40 | 7 |
| 09.40–09.50 | 9 | 12.40–12.50 | 9 |
| 09.50–10.00 | 10 | 12.50–13.00 | 6 |
| 10.00–10.10 | 10 | | |
| 10.10–10.20 | 10 | **Average Duration** | **10.38 minutes** |

Table 84. KV 9 visit duration, 21 September 2004

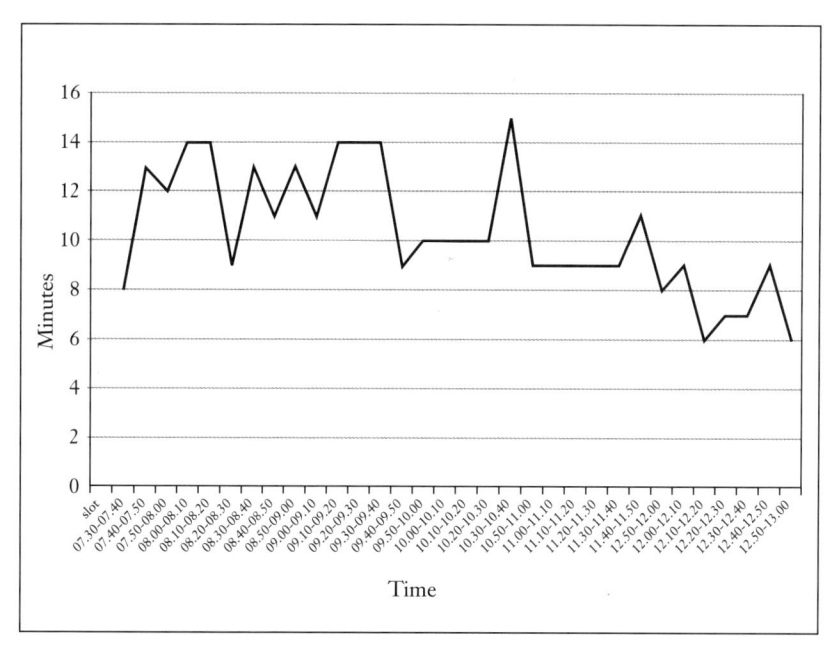

Table 85. KV 9 visit duration, 21 September 2004

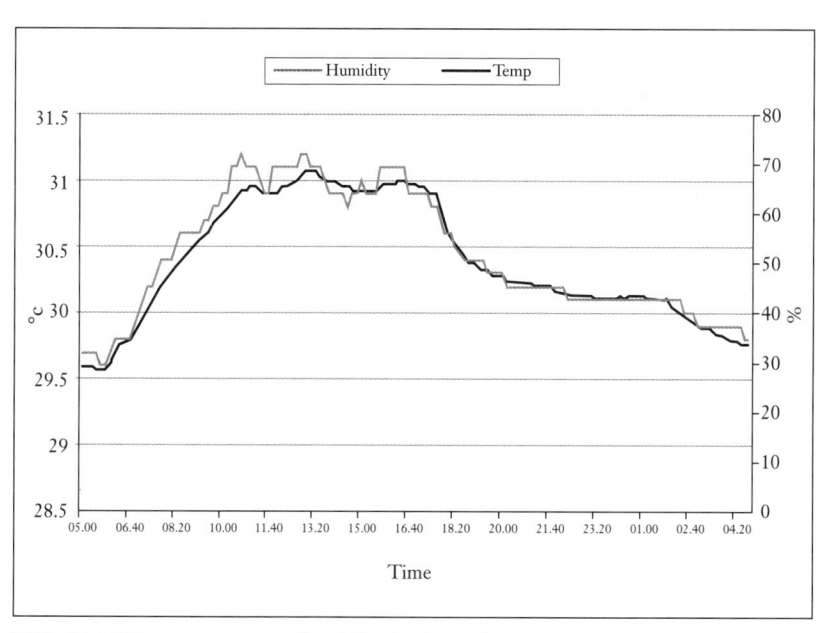

Table 86. KV 9 temperature and humidity, 21 September 2004

Carrying Capacity of Tombs in the Valley of the Kings | 229

## KV 11 Visit Duration Survey

| Time Slot | Average Duration (minutes) | | |
|---|---|---|---|
| 07.40–07.50 | 9 | 10.50–11.00 | 11 |
| 07.50–08.00 | 14 | 11.00–11.10 | 10 |
| 08.00–08.10 | 11 | 11.20–11.30 | 11 |
| 08.10–08.20 | 13 | 11.30–11.40 | 8 |
| 08.20–08.30 | 10 | 11.40–11.50 | 9 |
| 08.30–08.40 | 17 | 11.50–12.00 | 8 |
| 08.40–08.50 | 12 | 12.00–12.10 | 8 |
| 08.50–09.00 | 10 | 12.10–12.20 | 8 |
| 09.00–09.10 | 11 | 12.20–12.30 | 8 |
| 09.20–09.30 | 11 | 12.30–12.40 | 6 |
| 09.40–09.50 | 8 | 12.40–12.50 | 6 |
| 09.50–10.00 | 10 | 12.50–13.00 | 6 |
| 10.00–10.10 | 10 | 13.00–13.10 | 7 |
| 10.10–10.20 | 9 | 13.10–13.20 | 9 |
| 10.20–10.30 | 9 | 13.20–13.30 | 6 |
| 10.30–10.40 | 14 | 13.40–13.50 | 7 |
| 10.40–10.50 | 9 | **Average Duration** | **9.56 minutes** |

Table 87. KV 11 visit duration, 20 September 2004

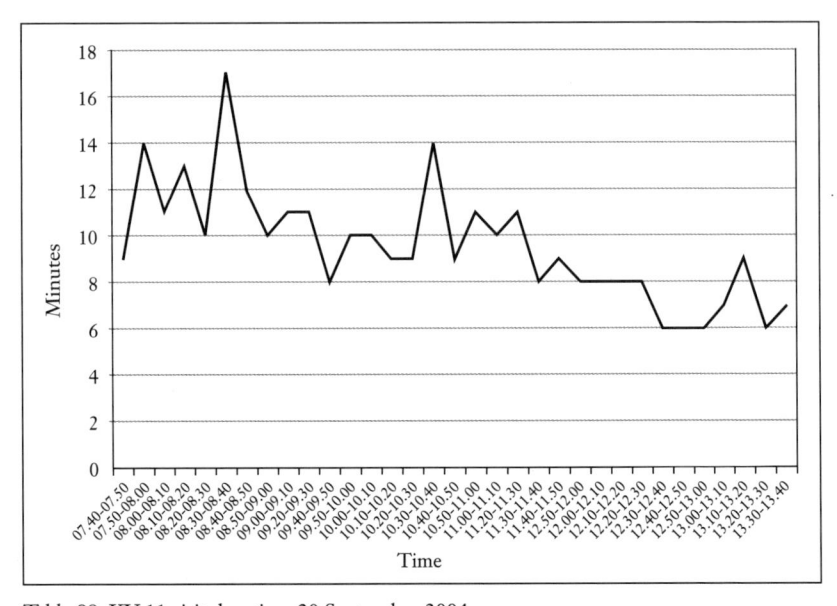

Table 88. KV 11 visit duration, 20 September 2004

Visitor Management in the Valley of the Kings

Unsurprisingly, we found that the more crowded a tomb was, the longer the tourist's visit. This is because visitors are forced to move more slowly along corridors that are packed with people. Longer visits also occur early in the morning, when tourist numbers are relatively low, and people are able to move leisurely through the corridors.

We have not been able to determine if there is a correlation between the duration of visits and types of visitors. Perhaps group tourists spend less time in tombs than independent tourists; perhaps returning visitors spend more time than first-timers. Perhaps less-visited tombs receive longer visits than more popular ones. These possibilities were not investigated.

**TMP Proposals**

From the work conducted above, the TMP was able to suggest a manageable carrying capacity for every open KV tomb. We have shown, however, that this safe level is being exceeded on a daily basis. In addition, overcrowding tends to occur mainly in the peak morning hours. However, the picture is not entirely bleak: many tombs receive few visitors, mainly due to their location. The central zone of the Valley around the main rest house is massively overcrowded during the peak period, yet other parts can be relatively quiet. The main problem therefore appears to be one of visitor flow management.

A system to control and manage the numbers of visitors to the tombs in the Valley of the Kings is an essential part of the site management masterplan. The system needs to be fully integrated into any tomb protection plans, the ticketing system, and infrastructure plans. This system could be relatively low tech, using KV personnel as stewards and marshals and using a zone system, as described above, to regulate the flow of visitors around the site and its tombs.

High-tech solutions could be linked to the ticketing system (discussed more fully below) and display information on the level of overcrowding from a central operations room to information panels in the Visitors Center and rest houses. Tourists can be informed at the Valley entrance and at the entrance to each tomb how many visitors are inside and the expected waiting time, if applicable. Thus, if KV 9 is full and there is a line already waiting to enter, red lights and, possibly, an indication of the length of the wait will be posted. In the meantime, visitors can wander through the Valley or visit another tomb.

Other options to be considered regarding restricting or diverting entry to KV tombs include:
- Groups to be assigned tombs on arrival by the SCA
- Restriction of entry to popular tombs
- Rotation of tombs on a daily/weekly basis
- Human intervention: guard controlling access
- Temperature/humidity alarms
- Rest days

2012 Update

Of the TMP proposals outlined above, only a few have been put into effect. Additional tickets are now needed (in addition to the standard KV entry ticket) to visit KV 64 (Tutankhamun) and KV 9 (Ramesses V/VI). Under discussion is an additional ticket for KV 8 (Merenptah). This has cut down dramatically on the number of visitors to these tombs, but has resulted in an increase in other tombs. Particularly adversely affected by increasing numbers are KV 1, 2, 6, and 11—tombs that are close to the entrance, easy to access, and well decorated, making them popular with tour guides.

Only eleven tombs are currently open to the public, making crowding even more troublesome. No Eighteenth Dynasty tombs are currently available to the public. No changes have been made in the scheduling of visitors to KV or to individual tombs, nor has any system of monitoring carrying capacity been put into effect.

Since the 2011 Revolution, visitor numbers have declined in KV by about 40 to 50 percent, but this still means that significant numbers of tourists are visiting the site. Serious thought should be given to building replicas of the more popular tombs (KV 64, KV 11, perhaps even KV 17) and making them available to large groups making one-day or half-day visits to Luxor.

## Ticketing Procedures

Tickets for admission to KV are purchased at the Visitors Center. Entrance tickets for groups are purchased by their tour guide while the groups navigate through the retail sales area. However, independent travelers purchase their own tickets. The current pricing structure consists of four levels of general entry: one for foreigners, another for foreign students, one for Egyptians, and finally one for Egyptian students (table 89).

This general admission ticket allows entry to three tombs in the East Valley. A further ticket is required for the Tomb of Ay in the West Valley. Another ticket is needed for the Tomb of Tutankhamun, again in four different price categories.

|  | Foreigner | Student | Egyptian | Student |
|---|---|---|---|---|
| General Valley (3 tombs) | 55 | 30 | 4 | 2 |
| Tomb of Tutankhamun | 70 | 30 | 20 | 10 |
| West Valley | 20 | 10 | 2 | 1 |
| All prices in LE, as of January 2006 | | | | |

Table 89. Ticket prices in the Valley of the Kings

Admission tickets are checked once at the main security gate and again at the entrance of each tomb, where a corner is torn off by the guardian to indicate one tomb has been visited. This system is inadequate. Some guards tear very small corners from the tickets, some rip the tickets in certain places. There is no common system. Therefore, there is often confusion over how many tombs have been entered, and disputes can arise. During our stakeholder consultation, visitors also expressed unease over this practice, and of particular concern was the fact that the ticket stub, which was to be retained as a memento, had been damaged.

## TMP Proposals

Any new ticketing design must take into account the desire of the visitor for a record of their visit and the fact that over seven thousand tickets are currently handled at least four times in each visit by site personnel. What is needed is something that can easily be checked by the guards and can be retained by the tourist as a souvenir.

Alongside general ticketing issues discussed below, we feel that to build in capacity for the future, any ticketing system should be part of a larger management information system. The issue of cash handling must be also addressed; it would benefit the SCA if facilities accepting payment in dollars and credit cards were installed in the new Visitors Center. This would be particularly beneficial if in the future the SCA decides to sell merchandise, such as guides, maps, and souvenirs. However, the handling of foreign currency is strictly regulated by the Ministry of Finance; therefore, this may prove difficult to implement.

Fig. 84. Visitors Center ticket window.
© Theban Mapping Project

One of the easiest ways to tally and control visitor numbers in KV and its tombs is by varying ticketing procedures. The possibilities range from simple to complex, from cheap to costly, and all offer both positive and negative features.

A new ticketing scheme should be implemented in KV. This plan should utilize coded tickets and automatic ticketing machines to dispense tickets at various points of sale (East Bank of Luxor, West Bank ticket office, the entrance to KV, and a central location within KV). A general ticket for KV will be purchased from a teller using an automatic barcode ticket machine, allowing any specifications to be made at the time of purchase. (This is a viable option only if it is possible for guides to purchase large quantities of tickets in advance, and for day-trippers from the Red Sea to be able to buy tickets on the day of their arrival without fear of tickets being sold out for a certain visit time.) After the tickets are collected, the tourist will visit a specific number of tombs, passing through turnstiles at the entrance to KV and in the entryway of each selected tomb. This will allow an accurate count of visitors in the Valley as a whole and in each individual tomb. The turnstiles can be connected to a larger network that will broadcast how many visitors the Valley is supporting at one time, allowing guides and individual travelers the opportunity to go elsewhere until the crowding has subsided. A downside to the turnstiles, however, would be the maintenance infrastructure that would have to be implemented in order to keep them operating in the harsh desert environment, as well as their cumbersome appearance.

Other possibilities include the following (it is important to keep in mind that more than one of the following options may be implemented at one time):

A. **Individual tomb tickets.** Instead of selling a single ticket that offers admission to several tombs, one could sell tickets to individual tombs. It would be up to the tourist or his tour guide to decide which tombs should be visited and how many should be included. It is likely that some groups, such as day-trippers coming from the Red Sea, would probably visit only two tombs; amateur Egyptologists might want to visit eight or nine. Individual tickets could each be for any one tomb or for a specific tomb, to be specified at the time of purchase.

Different prices could be charged for individual tombs depending on their popularity. KV 9 (Ramesses VI), for example, is consistently one of the Valley's most visited tombs because of its well-preserved decoration. More could be charged for its ticket than for KV 19 (Mentuherkhepeshef), a small, out-of-the way, and seldom-visited tomb. KV 62 (Tutankhamun) could continue to have its own specially priced ticket.

B. **Multiple tomb tickets.** At present, visitors buy one ticket that allows access to any three tombs except Tutankhamun and Ay, both of which require separate, specially priced tickets. There are several possible variations, all of which would probably assume the continuance of the separate tickets for Tutankhamun and Ay.
  1. One ticket could allow access to any two tombs. This might appeal to day-trippers from the Red Sea who are traveling on very tight schedules.
  2. One ticket could allow access to more than three tombs.
  3. One ticket could allow entry to all KV tombs. This would appeal to that small number of amateur Egyptologists determined to see everything, and to tour guides who want the great flexibility in itinerary it would offer. But, obviously, the price of such tickets would have to reflect these different numbers of tombs, and their cost might be a negative factor.
  4. As discussed above, one ticket could allow access to one tomb in each of three different groups of tombs. For instance, the tombs could be grouped into three categories depending on their popularity, thereby taking some of the strain off the more visited tombs and encouraging tourists to see some of the

out-of-the-way tombs, spreading out the crowds. These groups could be: KV 1, 2, 6, 8, 9, 11 (the most popular); KV 14, 15, 34, 43, 47 (the middle range); and KV 16 and 19 (the least visited). Another possibility would be to have one ticket allow access to one tomb from each dynasty represented in the Valley.

C. **Timed tickets.** Whether they were for one, two, three, or more tomb visits, timed tickets would allow the visitor access to KV at predetermined times during the day. By allocating a fixed number of tickets to each time slot (7:00–8:00, 8:00–9:00, 9:00–10:00, for example), the number of visitors in KV at any one time can be controlled. The tickets would have to be purchased in advance, of course, and therefore a ticket sales office would have to be established on the East Bank (perhaps at the Luxor Museum, Luxor Temples, or the Museum of Mummification), where guides and tourists could purchase tickets up to twenty-four or forty-eight hours in advance of their visit. Such tickets would not be exchangeable or refundable. For day-trippers from the Red Sea, such timed tickets might prove difficult, since their schedules are so tight and their stay in Luxor so short. For those who cannot purchase timed tickets in advance, the SCA could set aside a number of 'open' tickets that permit the user to visit KV at any time of a specified day—for the payment of an additional charge.

D. **Passes for some tourists.** Especially for amateur Egyptologists whose stay in Luxor is for longer than one or two days, a special pass could be sold that offers access to all Theban monuments for a fixed period of three or four days or one week. These could be sold in Luxor and would have a photo ID affixed to them.

E. **VIP tickets.** Some individuals will visit KV without paying for a ticket. These might include VIPs, dignitaries, and scholars. In order to maintain accurate records of the number of persons in a tomb at any one time, they should be given a free ticket that would be tallied with all other tickets when statistics are compiled.

F. **Electronic tickets.** Any consideration of new ticketing methods must consider the introduction of bar-coded tickets. These will assist in crowd control, site management, and financial management.

Ticket sales points should be located in the Visitors Center at KV, at a centralized sales office on the West Bank (at Beit al-Medina, for example), and in an office on the East Bank in Luxor. Tickets should be available up to twenty-four to forty-eight hours in advance of visiting, if a system of timed tickets is used. Tickets should be non-refundable and non-exchangeable. Payment for tickets should be possible in Egyptian pounds or by credit card. Ticket prices should be agreed upon by the SCA and any changes announced publicly at least nine months in advance of the change, to allow travel companies to adjust their fees accordingly.

Therefore in summary, the decisions to be made regarding the ticketing system are:
- The cost of tickets
- Timed ticketing
- How many tombs are accessible on one ticket
- One-tomb-only tickets
- One ticket for all KV tombs
- Variable ticket prices for popular/less popular tombs
- Site zoning
- Site scheduling
- How many ticket options will be available
- Off-peak tickets
- Place of purchase
- Credit-card processing
- Longer opening hours
- Management of ticketing system
- Investment in ticketing system

## Visitor Experience in the Valley of the Kings

The overall visitor experience of KV is affected by many factors: time of visit (both seasonally and by time of day), method of transport, climate conditions both external and within tombs, first impressions of site, level of customer service, traveling companions, level of interpretation available, and others. The management of KV can try to affect some of these factors in a positive way and, in doing so, manage the visitor experience; other factors, however, are outside their control.

Fig. 85. Visitors harassed by illegal vendors. © Theban Mapping Project

Fig. 86a, b, and c. Some visitor experiences in KV. © Theban Mapping Project

Visitor Experience in the Valley of the Kings | 239

From the stakeholder surveys carried out by the TMP in KV we received numerous responses from the visitors regarding positive and negative aspects of their visit. Without repeating here what is covered in chapter 4, we can summarize some of the main factors that influence the overall experience of KV:

**Positive aspects:**
- Overwhelmed at being there
- Tombs and their decoration
- Visiting Tutankhamun
- Natural environment of KV
- Guides who explain the history of KV

**Negative aspects:**
- Numbers of visitors and feeling of being overcrowded
- Noise and irreverent atmosphere in tombs
- Lack of site personnel able to provide information
- Lack of visitor control
- Harassment by guards, traders, and hawkers
- Lack of interpretive material, such as guidebooks and leaflets

**TMP Proposals**

There are so many factors affecting visitor experience that each of the TMP proposals in this report, if implemented, would have a positive effect on visitor experience.

## Summary of Proposals

- Visitor numbers in KV and in individual tombs should be monitored
- Display panels in KV and its approaches should inform guides of current capacity
- New systems for ticketing should be studied and tested
- Multiple locations for ticket sales should be explored
- Crowd control should be implemented
- KV opening times should be extended

# 8 Site Management at the Valley of the Kings

The implementation of any future proposals, and the acceptance of the proposals contained in this report by the stakeholders responsible for the management of KV, is essential. The institutional stakeholders include:
- Office of the President
- Ministry of Culture
- Supreme Council of Antiquities (SCA) (now Ministry of State for Antiquities)
- Ministry of Tourism
- Ministry of Housing, Reconstruction, and Urban Communities
- Ministry of Local Development
- Ministry of Agriculture and Land Reclamation
- Ministry of Water Resources and Irrigation
- Ministry of Finance
- Luxor City Council and High Council of Luxor

Within the Arab Republic of Egypt, all archaeological sites are owned by the state and administered on its behalf by the SCA, making this organization the major stakeholder and consequently the focus of this chapter.

The successful management of KV requires the coordination of planning and information-sharing procedures. The success or failure of any management plan will lie with its ease of implementation and the successful training of the managers who will have to carry out its mandates. With this in mind, we have studied the existing management framework and suggested an alternative approach below. We have also addressed the issues of site funding, site personnel levels, and training and maintenance levels. Finally, we have investigated how all this information can be managed and successfully utilized.

## The Supreme Council of Antiquities (SCA)

In Egypt, the SCA, under the Ministry of Culture, is the official government agency responsible for the registration, preservation, and management of the nation's cultural heritage. (The SCA became the Ministry of State for Antiquities in 2011.) However, to understand fully how this works in practice we need to look at the structure of the organization and its legal codes. The service began in 1858 during the colonial era. It was originally named the Service des Antiquités, was run by the French, and had control of all archaeological excavations in the country. After Egypt became independent in 1922, the service was increasingly brought under the control of Egyptian government officials and was renamed the Egyptian Antiquities Organization in 1971. After the Revolution of January 2011, the SCA was given enhanced status as a quasi-ministerial agency. What this means in terms of its bureaucratic and financial clout remains to be seen.

The current headquarters of the SCA is in Cairo, in Zamalek and Abbasiya. The organization is headed up by a secretary general and a permanent committee, and has forty-two thousand employees.

The SCA's main role in relation to archaeological sites, in addition to the recording, management, and preservation of these sites, is to:

- Approve all excavation concessions and personnel
- Stipulate conditions under which foreign missions may carry out archaeological work in Egypt

A note should be made here regarding the legislative framework in which the SCA operates. Legislative development regarding antiquities protection in Egypt was meager until Law 215 of 1951 was passed. This was considered the first piece of legislation that covered all aspects of antiquities protection, although it contained many loopholes and was superseded in 1983 by Law 117.

The main points of Law 117 are:
- The SCA was made the legal guardian of antiquities
- An "antiquity" was defined as any object, movable or immovable, over a hundred years old, or objects or sites selected by prime ministerial decree and therefore public property
- The prohibition of the trade in antiquities
- The banning of the exportation of cultural property

## Divisions of the Theban Necropolis

By any standard, the Antiquities Zone on the West Bank is a large area. At a minimum (the 1926 decree definition, for example), it covers about ten square kilometers. By some measures (such as the 1980 decree), it covers twice that. Add to it the 2004 'buffer zone,' and its size again doubles or even trebles. However it is defined, the Theban Necropolis must also be divided into smaller administrative units if it is to be adequately administered and protected.

The West Bank has within its boundaries archaeological sites, agricultural land, touristic facilities, highways and roads, canals and irrigation channels, old villages and new ones. Therefore, officials from such diverse ministries and departments as Agriculture, Irrigation, New Towns, Environment, Culture, Tourism, Interior, Power, Luxor City Council, and others, all have a stake in its administration. Often the goals of these agencies are in conflict.

The West Bank can be divided in several ways into broad zones. These divisions can be based on environmental, ethnographic, sociological, historical, archaeological, or administrative boundaries.
Environmentally, from east to west, they are:
- A. An agricultural zone, also containing modern villages and archaeological remains. This zone can be subdivided into irrigation basins called *hawd*s, which are natural depressions used from ancient times to the 1960s as part of the annual flood irrigation system. *Hawd*s are defined by dikes that today, many decades after basin irrigation was abandoned, serve as the foundations of the roads on the West Bank.
- B. Low-lying desert along the edge of the cultivation. This relatively level area of rolling sand and stone, with occasional small hillocks rising from it, lies only slightly higher than the elevation of the

agricultural zone. It is seriously affected by changing levels of ground water. The water has caused serious damage to the many temples and small tombs that lie here. The area varies from a few hundred meters to a kilometer or more in width, and extends the entire length of the Necropolis.

C. High desert and complex wadi systems, in which lie the East and West Valleys of the Kings, the Valley of the Queens, and many small outlying wadis used as burial sites, work stations, or quarries.

Ethnographically, there are four areas of desert lands, generally called al-Qurna. Each one is associated with founding families who local tradition says came from south Arabia and who settled here in the fifteenth century AD. These are the Hurubat, the Hassasna, the Atiyat, and the Ghabat. They were called Troglodytes by early European travelers and lived in the nobles' tombs at al-Qurna. The agricultural lands of the West Bank have been occupied by an indigenous local agricultural population—some of them Muslim, some Christian—that claims descent from the ancient Egyptians.

Sociologically and bureaucratically, the West Bank can also be divided into a series of about twenty villages, including: al-Gezirat, Qariya Hassan Fathy, Naga Qum Lula (also called al-Kawm), Naga al-Qatr, Naga Medinet Habu, Qurnat Mar'i, al-Bairat, Naga al-Rasayla, Naga al-Ramesseum or al-Sahel al-Sharqi, Izbit al-Ward, Suwalim, al-Qabawi, al-Suyul, al-Genina, al-Tarif, al-Rawagah, Ababda, and Qamula. Nearly all lie within the agricultural zone. These villages and hamlets are recognized by the government as quasi-independent entities, governed by a locally chosen sheikh and a committee of elders who decide on matters of local importance. Some villages lie away from archaeological sites (al-Gezirat, for example); others lie directly atop them (Naga Qum Lula, for example).

Historically, the archaeological zone (mainly desert areas) has been divided into ten parts from north to south. The number of tombs in each counts only those that have been cataloged by the SCA. In fact, at least two or three times this number are known to exist.

A. al-Tarif (meaning 'the limit'), at the northernmost end of the Necropolis, heavily damaged by modern building; site of many Middle Kingdom tombs and shrines, Old Kingdom *mastaba*s, and prehistoric work stations.

B. The Valley of the Kings, actually two valleys, East and West, containing the tombs of Egypt's New Kingdom rulers and others. There are sixty-two tombs in the East Valley, four in the West. This is arguably one of the best-known and most important archaeological sites in the world.
C. Dra Abu al-Naga, between the Hatshepsut causeway and al-Tarif, a hill with tombs of Seventeenth Dynasty rulers, their families, and New Kingdom Priests.
D. Deir al-Bahari, also called Birabi. A natural amphitheater in which the memorial temples of Mentuhetep II, Thutmose III, and Hatshepsut were built.
E. al-Asasif ('interconnected tunnels'), the area north and south of the Hatshepsut causeway, containing about forty New Kingdom tombs.
F. al-Khokha ('hill of vaults'), a small hill north of Sheikh Abd al-Qurna and east of al-Asasif, with five Old Kingdom and fifty-three New Kingdom tombs.
G. Ilwet al-Sheikh Abd al-Qurna, a small hill south of the Hatshepsut causeway and west of the Ramesseum, named for a mythical local Muslim sheikh. A modern wall divides the hill into an upper and lower enclosure. These, plus a third, smaller, area contain about a hundred New Kingdom tombs.
H. Qurnat Mar'i ('the peak of [Sheikh] Mar'i'), southernmost of the private tomb complexes, with about seventeen New Kingdom tombs.
I. Deir al-Medina. Workmen's village and necropolis, home to the New Kingdom craftsmen responsible for carving and decorating royal tombs in the Valley of the Kings and other royal projects.
J. Valley of the Queens. Burial place of various New Kingdom queens and royal family members. About eighty-two tombs are known here.
K. Medinet Habu. The memorial temple of Ramesses III, a townsite occupied until the ninth century AD, and a complex array of other New Kingdom memorial temples.
L. Malqata and Birkat Habu. The palace complex of Amenhotep III and a huge harbor dug by him for celebration of his several jubilees, lying at the southernmost limit of the Theban Necropolis.
M. Outlying areas. A series of small wadis to the north, west, and south of the necropolis proper contain small tombs of royal family

members, Christian hermitages, prehistoric work stations, quarries, graffiti, and Greco-Roman temples.

Archaeologically, the Necropolis contains several types of monuments. These tend to be distributed within the Necropolis in geographic clusters.
   A. Memorial temples, found mostly along the edge of the cultivation. Before the New Kingdom, such temples lay adjacent to their pharaoh's tomb. At Thebes, however, they were separated. This was because, while the king's tomb had to be dug in an isolated, dry, and well-protected place, his temple had to be accessible to religious processions coming by boat from temples across the river.
   B. Nobles' tombs, in the low-lying desert and in some wadis. At least two thousand such tombs, most of them small, many well-decorated, were cut into hillsides along the Nile floodplain.
   C. Royal tombs, in the Valleys of the Kings and Queens. Sixty-two tombs are known in KV, eighty-two in QV. All date to the New Kingdom. They vary considerably in size, preservation, and quality.
   D. Habitation sites, between the memorial temples and in Deir al-Medina.
   E. Prehistoric work stations, surface sites lying largely on top of the *gebel* or to the north of Thebes proper.
   F. Greco-Roman monuments, including temples and tombs, on hillsides and within ancient structures.
   G. Christian monasteries and hermitages, scattered in several different localities. Several dozen such sites are known, and one of them, founded in the seventh century, is still in operation.
   H. Graffiti, stelae, rock-cut chapels, mostly in or on low *gebel* cliffs. Thousands have been recorded.
   I. There is also archaeological material buried beneath agricultural lands, including ancient temple buildings, villages, canals, and landing stages.

Administratively, four different categories of land are recognized on the West Bank:
   A. An archaeological zone under the control of the SCA. Surprisingly, the boundaries of this zone are vague. A line was drawn on the

1925 Survey of Egypt maps purporting to show its eastern extent, but that line in some cases runs through archaeological sites, not around them. The SCA is currently trying to develop legally binding definitions of the West Bank land under its control, but these have not yet been published. It is likely they will result in disputes, court cases, and sequestrations.

B. Non-archaeological areas under the control of the Luxor City Council or other governmental agencies. These lie mainly in undeveloped desert land owned by the state, and on the banks of the Nile.

C. Privately owned lands, mostly agricultural.

D. Illegally occupied lands in both archaeological and non-archaeological areas.

## Current SCA Administration of the Theban Necropolis

Since about 1998, the SCA has divided the Theban Necropolis into three sub-areas for administrative purposes. Each area is under the supervision of an inspector of antiquities who reports to the chief inspector of the West Bank.

A. North Thebes, including the Valleys of the Kings, the Thoth Temple, al-Tarif, Seti Temple, Dra Abu al-Naga, and adjacent archaeological areas.

B. Central Thebes, including everything between North and South Thebes.

C. South Thebes, including Malqata, Medinet Habu, the Valley of the Queens, Deir al-Medina, Qurnat Mar'i, the Colossi of Memnon,

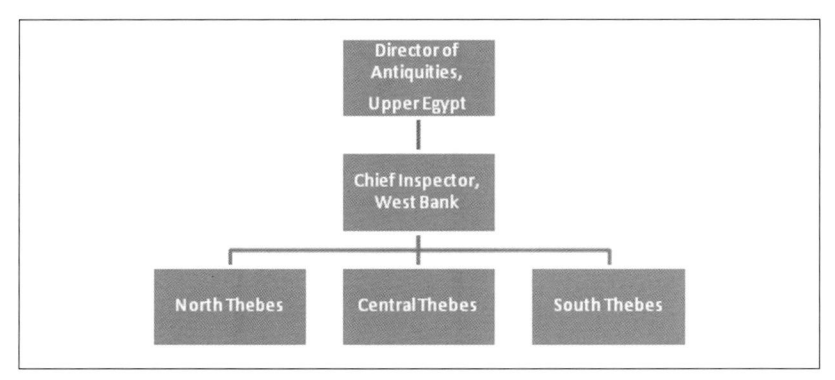

Fig. 87. Current division of the SCA administration.

and adjacent archaeological areas. The rationale for this division is that it divides bureaucratic and archaeological tasks into smaller and more manageable units than the earlier ones.

## Current Valley of the Kings Staffing Levels

The valley is managed on a day-to-day basis by a chief inspector and three inspectors working for him/her. However, the management of KV and its workforce involves many different agencies, and no single individual has overall control of the site. SCA staff includes inspectors, guards, cleaners, restorers, security, ticketing, and engineers. The toilets are managed by a concession and security is covered by the tourist police and the internal security police.

The guards or guardians make up the bulk of the employees. Some 134 guards work in a cycle of three twelve-hour shifts, led by two head guards for each shift. The guardians are the cornerstone of the management of KV. They are in regular contact with the visitors and are the de facto police force of the tombs. They can prohibit entry due to overcrowding and so on; they have to deal with ticketing issues and disputes over camera use, and manage tour leaders and guides.

The inspectors in KV apparently have no responsibilities and their management style is reactive, not proactive. Issues that they can be expected to deal with include crowd control, disputes between visitors and the guides and guardians, emergencies, requests for entry to closed tombs, and inquiries regarding sales kiosks.

## The SCA and Valley of the Kings Funding

As is the situation in most heritage sites worldwide, revenue from ticket sales from KV goes directly to the Egyptian treasury. Funding for the operation of the site is via an annual grant allocation from the Ministry of Finance to the Ministry of Culture, which in turn makes a budget allocation to the SCA. The SCA then grants funds to regional centers for the running of particular sites and activities. Ticket sales at SCA sites throughout Egypt generate a large amount of cash for the Egyptian economy. However, these revenues are not directly linked to the amount of funding the SCA receives. Ticket prices have recently risen substantially; however, these are not excessive when compared with similar attractions in other countries.

Recently the managements of some heritage sites in other countries have questioned this system of funding by central government. For example, at the site of Pompeii in Italy, the management has formed a trust to manage the site, and ticket revenues stay with the site and are used for the site's management and conservation. Calls have been made in Egypt by representatives of the SCA for ticket prices to rise 25 percent across the board to fund ongoing conservation projects. This action would find public backing; many of the responses in our stakeholder surveys indicated a willingness to pay higher ticket prices as long as the funds went into site conservation.

*2012 Update*
In light of the new, quasi-ministry status of the former department of the SCA, the funding model will almost certainly be up for review.

## Site Management and Cultural Resource Management Training

Currently the inspectors working in KV receive little or no site management training. What is available in Egypt is well planned but only provided on an ad hoc basis by outside agencies. Effective management of the site is essential if long-term goals of this masterplan are to be achieved. Many of the site staff are eager to learn more about the work they do and wish to work more effectively.

**TMP Proposals**
A. Development and Implementation of a Training Program in Cultural Resource Management

Cultural Resource Management (CRM) seeks to locate, identify, evaluate, preserve, manage, and interpret qualified cultural resources in such a way that they can be enjoyed and learned from in the present and be handed on to future generations unimpaired. Unfortunately, although Egypt's cultural heritage is among the most extensive in the world, very few of its numerous cultural sites or monuments are "unimpaired" today due to their great age and the various environmental pressures to which they are being subjected. What is worse, only a small percentage of them has ever been adequately documented: deterioration means their total and irretrievable loss. Egypt's cultural heritage is thus becoming increasingly fragile and finite, and the need for CRM training programs has accordingly become vital if this heritage is ever to be preserved in a sustainable and unified manner. Management and documentation must increasingly provide improved interpretation and enhanced experience for those who visit cultural sites.

There is a need for a CRM program that will produce a cadre of trained Egyptian site managers and support staff who can deal with problems of site management and preservation today and in the future. This CRM training program will approach the problems of Egypt's antiquities synergistically, concentrating on the training of young Egyptians who are in, or about to enter, the SCA and other relevant agencies. They will be trained in the planning, management, and monitoring processes that are common to any kind of cultural site, thus allowing them to deal effectively with many kinds of monuments or archaeological materials from many periods. In turn, they will train the future generations of site managers who will inherit the responsibility to preserve Egypt's past.

During the past few years, many agencies in Egypt and America have developed CRM programs at both the national and international levels. These agencies all generally agree as to what CRM is and what it should accomplish. The United States Office of the International Council on Monuments and Sites (US/ICOMOS) states the consensus well in describing one aspect of CRM, Archaeological Resource Management (ARM), as a system to "actively promote the preservation, conservation, and management of the world's archaeological sites and monuments, both excavated and un-excavated, through international cooperation, the sharing of information and technical expertise, and education."[1]

US/ICOMOS, as well as the GCI, the U.S. National Park Service, and numerous other agencies, acknowledge that a host of factors determine the effectiveness of the CRM. However, no factor is thought more likely to determine the success of specific CRM programs than the roles of archaeological site managers, storeroom and database mangers, and their support staff. The duties of these persons are broadly similar:

- To collect all available information on the physical and cultural history of the site or monument in their charge;
- To determine the site's significance and value;
- To document its physical conditions and recognize the implications

of these conditions for conservation and preservation;
- To take into consideration the legal, social, and environmental factors that will affect management responsibilities;
- To preserve and protect the site, also taking into account the needs of tourism, scholarly research, and socioeconomic development.

No CRM program can hope overnight to make major changes in any government's policies or procedures. To realize our goal of maximizing site protection, we propose to initiate a training program consisting of mid-level site management and supervisor-level CRM training for promising young employees in various government agencies, especially the Ministry of Culture, the SCA, and the liaison officers in other agencies who deal directly with them.

The primary reason that CRM problems have not been more effectively dealt with in Egypt is the lack of on-site managers and administrators who are sufficiently trained in CRM that they can allocate funds and staff time wisely, and plan for and supervise their proper use. Thus, in the CRM training program which we propose, each site manager should develop the skills and understanding needed to:

- Identify CRM problems
- Supervise appropriate solutions to small problems of protection, site development, and administration, and work knowledgeably with specialists to treat the larger ones
- Help the local public realize that it is in their own social and economic interest to protect local archaeological sites and historical documents
- Work with tourists and tour guides both to protect the sites and to ensure that visitors gain a sense of learning and satisfaction
- Maintain a database to ensure regular monitoring of a site's changing condition and to improve management decisions
- Understand their country's laws and regulations to help prevent potential problems at a site, and to improve their ability to work with local groups, administrative agencies, and ministerial representatives.

In short, what is needed are managers who have the training to monitor, preserve, and manage this fragile, irreplaceable, and increasingly threatened cultural heritage, and to do so within the constraints of the existing Egyptian bureaucracy. The training program at Luxor established by the American Research Center in Egypt (ARCE) with the SCA has actively pursued many of these goals, with an emphasis on teaching the techniques of archaeological excavation and recording. It remains to be seen whether the program's graduates will have the opportunity to apply what they have learned to the administrative procedures of the SCA on the West Bank. And, of course, there still remains the need for more general CRM-related training programs, which leads us to:

B. A training schedule for all KV site staff should be implemented immediately, not just the ones involved in site management. There is a serious need for training programs in site management at KV, and such programs should be offered and tailored to the needs of inspectors, security personnel, guards, conservators, and maintenance staff.

C. A site management plan should be drawn up by the inspectors in KV, taking account of the suggestions in this masterplan. A suggested template for management activities and goals in KV is also suggested by the UNESCO model below.

---

UNESCO Suggested Site Management Checklist
- Do you have a management plan for the maintenance strategy of your World Heritage site, and is this plan regularly updated?
- Have long-, medium- and short-term objectives been clearly defined?
- Have the values, priorities, and least harmful action been taken into consideration in this plan?
- Is there an inventory, and has the resource been adequately recorded and documented?
- Is the relevant documentation concerning the site accessible?
- Has the site documentation been duplicated in a safe place?
- Is there a fire protection plan, and is it practiced on a regular basis?
- Do you have the disaster hazard plan for your region?
- Have a disaster response officer and alternate been designated?
- Have contacts for effective research programs been established with universities and other institutions?
- Do the laws and regulations that are being applied reflect the latest technical knowledge and attitudes to conservation?
- Is their application effective? If not, where do they fail?
- Is the management infrastructure adequate and effective in fulfilling its role?
- Have lines of communication been established with international organizations concerned with preservation of World Heritage?[2]

D. Finally, one further point to be made regarding site personnel is their visibility to visitors and workers in KV. It is important that inspectors of antiquity assigned to the Valley of the Kings be properly attired. In this way, they can be identified by tourists and guides as the responsible authorities in KV and can be seen to speak with the authority of the SCA behind them. Such uniforms also bestow a sense of pride on the wearer that is reflected in his work attitude and dealings with foreign and local tourists and tour guides. Such a uniform can also be worn by an individual who would operate an inquiry desk in the Visitors Center. Maintenance staff can wear boiler suits like those worn by private maintenance contracting companies. Tram drivers should be attired in uniforms that are of a color or design that cannot be confused with the inspectors' uniforms. Security personnel should be appropriately dressed as well; in particular, those inspecting tourists' bags at the Visitors Center should not wear informal civilian clothes. Medical personnel should be appropriately dressed.

## Emergency and Disaster Planning

Provisions must be made for an adequate response to emergencies such as flash flooding, earthquakes, illness, accidents, theft, vandalism, or

Fig. 88. Emergency response. © Theban Mapping Project

terrorism. A Necropolis-wide Emergency Conservation Response Team should be designated and trained to handle these rare but serious problems, and necessary equipment and supplies should be stored in one of the SCA warehouses for easy access. Debris that has washed into tombs must be removed, small pumps used to remove any accumulated water, and blowers installed to reduce moisture levels. Screwjacks and other engineering devices should be available to shore up fractured or collapsed walls and ceilings until more permanent repairs can be made. Conditions must be carefully monitored.

**TMP Proposals**

A risk assessment plan similar to the one shown below (by UNESCO) should be developed alongside a disaster action plan. All managers and staff should be trained in the procedures to be carried out in the event of such a disaster.

UNESCO Principles of Risk Preparedness
- The key to effective protection of cultural heritage at risk is advance planning and preparation.
- Advance planning for cultural heritage properties should be conceived in terms of the whole property, and provide integrated concern for its buildings, structures, and their associated contents and landscapes.
- Advance planning for the protection of cultural heritage against disasters should integrate relevant heritage considerations within a property's overall disaster prevention strategy.
- Preparedness requirements should be met in heritage buildings by means which will have least impact on heritage values.
- Heritage properties, their significant attributes, and the disaster-response history of the property should be clearly documented as a basis for appropriate disaster planning, response, and recovery.
- Maintenance programs for historic properties should integrate a cultural-heritage-at-risk perspective.
- Property occupants and users should be directly involved in development of emergency-response plans.
- Securing heritage features should be a high priority during emergencies.
- Following a disaster, every effort should be made to ensure the retention and repair of structures or features that have suffered damage or loss.
- Conservation principles should be integrated where appropriate in all phases of disaster planning, response, and recovery.[3]

## Site Maintenance

Maintenance—keeping a site clean, safe, and in proper order—involves tasks that overlap with conservation, clearing, and security efforts. Here, we refer specifically to the cleaning of the site, including rubbish and dirt removal, and to the cleaning of tourist and administrative facilities. A program of maintenance in the Valley of the Kings must be organized as part of a program for the entire Necropolis. Here, we will concentrate on the Valley of the Kings. To ensure the safety of its tombs, the aesthetic appearance of its hillsides, and the quality of the tourist experience, the Valley of the Kings should be subject to regular cleaning.

There are five different staff groups who take part in maintenance programs:
1. General maintenance staff of local-hire employees responsible for cleaning the footpaths, roadways, and hillsides in and around KV
2. General maintenance staff responsible for the paved roadway leading from Carter House to KV, who are part of the Necropolis-wide maintenance staff
3. Toilet attendants
4. Visitors Center employees
5. Conservation staff who are trained conservators responsible for the well-being of KV tomb interiors.

These groups, which may include employees of private contractors, are under the joint supervision of the SCA Inspectorate and the conservation staff.

## TMP Proposals
A. A training program should be required of each employee involved in maintenance programs. It should explain the importance of this work and the care needed for its successful performance. Supervisors should demonstrate proper techniques and emphasize what not to do on site. Employees' work should be regularly evaluated.
B. Maintenance employees should wear an appropriate uniform, designed and provided by the SCA.
C. Rubbish bins should be placed at appropriate locations throughout the Valley of the Kings, parking area, the Visitors Center complex, the

paths and roadways between them, and the rest stops along the road from Carter House. Ashtrays should be provided in each KV shelter.
D. Work schedules. At the outset, before the regular schedules outlined here are implemented, a major cleaning operation must be conducted. Hundreds of piles of construction and excavation debris line the road from Carter House to the Visitors Center, and should be removed to an approved dumping site; raw sewage has for years been dumped here and must be removed; KV tomb entrances are filled with rubbish and human waste; hillsides are littered with plastic bottles and bags.

**On a daily basis:**
- Rubbish—water bottles and soft-drink containers, paper, cigarette butts, and the like—should be collected throughout the working day from the pathways, public facilities, and tomb entrances.
- Rubbish bins should be emptied at least once daily and, when necessary, temporarily removed to be washed and cleaned.
- The SCA should acquire a small truck for rubbish removal as part of its Necropolis-wide maintenance plan.
- Public areas and offices—covered rest stops, the main KV rest area, security checkpoints, the inspector's office, and tram stops—should regularly be swept, wastebaskets emptied, and windows washed.
- Toilets should be cleaned throughout the day by the toilet attendants using water, approved solvents, and other cleaning aids. These, together with toilet paper, are to be provided by the attendants, if the current system of awarding maintenance and operation rights to private contractors is to be continued. At present, individuals are awarded this concession by the SCA in exchange for paying all operating costs plus a fee.
- The cafeteria will be run as a private concession under license to the SCA. The concession contract should stipulate that high standards of hygiene and cleanliness must be maintained, and that items sold should be in containers that are as environmentally friendly as possible. Rubbish removal either should be the responsibility of the concessionaire or, if handled by the SCA rubbish truck, should be charged for.
- The Visitors Center should be thoroughly cleaned each day by its own staff.

- Tomb interiors should be checked for rubbish each morning and at midday by the guards assigned to each tomb. Any other cleaning, however, should be performed by the conservation staff.
- Archaeologists working in KV must remove their excavation debris and cart it from the Valley to an SCA-approved dumping site outside the West Bank archaeological zone. They should ensure that their concession is clean, safe, and orderly throughout their field season. A check of the excavation site should be made by the inspector at the end of the field season and a report filed on its condition.
- The security offices and visitor checkpoints should be cleaned by the staff of the Tourism and Security Police.
- The first-aid station and ambulance should be cleaned by their employees and the highest standards of cleanliness adhered to. Appropriate supplies and equipment should be on hand and in proper condition at all times. This includes wheelchairs, stretchers, oxygen tanks and masks, and bandages.

**On a weekly basis:**
- Wind-blown debris often litters the hills in and around KV, and tourists toss litter along the tram route. The hillsides in KV and between it and the Visitors Center, the road from Carter House, and the footpaths between KV, Deir al-Bahari, and Deir al-Medina should be examined weekly and any rubbish carried away.
- Regular monitoring of the roadway from Carter House to KV should be undertaken to prevent illicit dumping of raw sewage, construction debris, excavation backfill, hospital waste, and other materials that have ruined the landscape in years past. Evidence of such illicit dumping should immediately be reported to the SCA's West Bank office.
- An inspection tour of the KV tombs open to the public should be made by the inspector and a member of the conservation staff each week.

**On a quarterly basis:**
- The interiors of KV tombs in both the East and West Valleys should be regularly inspected by an inspector and a member of the conservation staff at least once every quarter, more often if conditions

warrant. Staff members should check for damage, changes in the structure of the bedrock, changes in paint and plaster, broken electrical or HVAC equipment, and the like. Using a low-power vacuum, the conservation staff member should remove accumulated dust from the wooden walkways and steps. The bedrock floor at the base of walls should be closely examined for traces of fallen plaster or stone before vacuuming. Any problems should be immediately reported to the SCA inspector.

- Until they are permanently removed and replaced by new walkway systems, glass or plastic panels in tombs should be cleaned as necessary by employees under the direct supervision of the conservation staff. Large glass panels should be removed from their mounts before cleaning, and the cleaning should be done outside the tomb. Cleaning should be done with treated rags. Commercial glass-cleaning sprays, which can attract dust and affect walls, should not be used. Containers of water and other liquids should never be brought into the tombs.
- HVAC equipment should be inspected and cleaned according to the manufacturer's instructions. Lamps should be cleaned or replaced as necessary.
- The aluminum signs in KV should be dusted or washed. Signs at the KV entrance and in the rest area should be checked to ensure that "closed" labels are in place adjacent to tombs temporarily closed to the public.

**On an annual basis:**
- A survey of the cleanliness of KV, its tombs, and the surrounding area should be conducted annually by the head of the maintenance staff and a conservation staff member to ensure that work has been properly performed and future needs identified. A report should be made to the office of the chief inspector.

E. When rubbish has been collected, it should be taken by truck to an approved dumpsite outside the archaeological zone. There should be separate sites for rubbish disposal, excavation debris, and garbage.

F. Necessary Equipment and Supplies:
- Storeroom in the Visitors Center area for cleaning supplies
- Rubbish bins of a neutral color
- Industrial brooms
- Two industrial vacuums with speed controls (like that supplied by the TMP)
- Cloth for cleaning of glass panels
- Cleaning solvents for glass panels
- Toilet cleaning equipment (to be supplied by contracted toilet attendants)
- Uniforms for staff, to be designed by the SCA
- Small truck for removal of rubbish. This should be a small, neutral-colored vehicle, identified by an Arabic and English sign and the SCA logo. Like the trams, it should be electric powered so as not to create noise or air pollution.
- Small portable pumps for flood emergencies, to be kept on site and checked every few months to be sure they are in working order. No more than three would be needed, and there should be several hundred meters of hose available. Over long distances, and in some tombs, the pumps would have to be used at intervals along a long uphill line in order to extract water from inside tombs.
- Small, low-power, portable blowers to dehumidify flooded tombs. Flexible tubing should also be available to control the direction of air movement.
- Screwjacks to provide temporary structural support
- Mousetraps to discourage vermin attracted by tourist litter
- Fire extinguishers

G. Maintenance Personnel Requirements:
- Inspectors, appointed by SCA, to supervise the Valley of the Kings
- Conservators, to oversee cleaning of tombs and their condition
- Driver for rubbish truck
- Four or five local-hire men to collect and remove rubbish

It is likely that a part of the maintenance staff will be contracted by the SCA to the private sector, as is already the case at Giza and Karnak. Private-sector employees could perform such tasks as those outlined above in groups 1–4. However, they cannot be expected to perform adequately the tasks of group 5, which requires trained conservators.

## Site Management Information Systems

An effective visitor management system requires full integration with many other key areas of the overall site management plan. The decisions to be made and questions answered about the system include:
1. The infrastructure requirements the system will need, such as electricity consumption
2. Level of integration with the main Valley ticketing system
3. The feasibility of linking visitor number controls to internal environmental conditions, e.g., humidity, temperature, and visitor levels

It will be necessary to decide, at the outset, the level of sophistication and integration of the management information system. Should all management systems be interlinked? How should they be linked to other information and environmental systems? These issues are being explored by the Spanish firm DEFEX.

## Summary of Proposals

- Establish a program for site-management training
- Establish a West Bank site-management office
- Develop plans for emergencies and disasters
- Establish a maintenance program
- Undertake a feasibility study of information-technology needs

# Notes

Notes to Chapter 1
1. Edwin Murphy, *The Antiquities of Egypt: A Translation, with Notes, of Book I of the Library of History of Diodorus Siculus* (New York: Transaction, 1990).
2. Murphy, *The Antiquities of Egypt*.
3. Vivant Denon, *Travels in Upper and Lower Egypt, in Company with Several Divisions of the French Army under Command of General Bonaparte, I*, translated by Francis Blagdon (London: Ridgway, 1802).
4. For references, see Bertha Porter and Rosalind Moss, *Topographical Bibliography of Ancient Egyptian Hieroglyphic Texts, Reliefs, and Painting, 1, 2: Royal Tombs and Smaller Cemeteries*, 2nd ed. (Oxford: Griffith Institute, 1999).
5. Giovanni Belzoni, *Fruits of Enterprise Exhibited in the Travels of Belzoni in Egypt and Nubia* (Boston: Munroe and Francis, 1827).
6. Donald M. Reid, *Whose Pharaohs? Archaeology, Museums, and Egyptian National Identity from Napoleon to World War I* (Cairo: American University in Cairo Press, 2002).
7. Richard Pococke, *A Description of the East and Some Other Countries, 4: Observations on Egypt* (London: Bowyer, 1753).
8. Auguste Mariette, *The Monuments of Upper Egypt: A Translation of the "Itineraire de la Haute Egypte"* (Memphis: General Books, 2009).
9. William M.F. Petrie, *Seventy Years in Archaeology* (London, 1932; repr. New York: Greenwood, 1969).

Notes to Chapter 2
1. M. Maamoun, A. Megahed, and A. Allam, "Seismicity of Egypt," *Helwan Institute of Astronomy and Geophysics* 4, ser. B (1984): 109–62.
2. T.G.H. James, *Howard Carter: The Path to Tutankhamun* (London: Tauris, Parke Paperbacks, 2006).

3   Villiers Stuart, *Funerary Tent of an Egyptian Queen* (Charleston: Rare Books Club, 2012).
4   Abdel Aziz Sadek, *Graffiti de la montagne thébaine*, 4 (Cairo: CEDAE, 1972–74).
5   Kent R. Weeks, "The Work of the Theban Mapping Project and the Protection of the Valley of the Kings," in *Valley of the Sun Kings*, edited by Richard Wilkinson (Tucson: University of Arizona, 1995), 122–24.
6   William Howard Russell, *Travels in Egypt*, 1869.

Notes to Chapter 3
1   *1999 International Cultural Tourism Charter: Managing Tourism at Places of Heritage Significance*. www.ICOMOS.org/tourism/charter.html
2   Bernard M. Feilden and Jukka Jokilehto. *Management Guidelines for World Cultural Heritage Sites* (Rome: ICCROM, 1993).
3   Kees van der Spek, *The Modern Neighbors of Tutankhamun: History, Life, and Work in the Villages of the Theban West Bank* (Cairo: American University in Cairo Press, 2012).

Notes to Chapter 4
1   UNESCO, *Culture, Tourism, Development: Crucial Issues for the 21st Century* (Paris: UNESCO, 1996).

Notes to Chapter 5
1   Kent R. Weeks, *The Lost Tomb* (New York: Morrow; London: Weidenfeld; Cairo: American University in Cairo Press, 1998), 57.
2   UNESCO, *Culture, Tourism, Development*.
3   Frank Preusser, "Scientific and Technical Examination of the Tomb of Queen Nefertari at Thebes," in *The Conservation of Wall Paintings*, ed. Sharon Cather (Santa Monica: Getty Conservation Institute, 1987), 125.

Notes to Chapter 6
1   B. Carter and G. Grimwade, "Balancing Use and Preservation in Cultural Heritage Management," *International Journal of Heritage Studies* 3 (1997).

Notes to Chapter 7
1   Miguel Angel Corzo and Afshar Mahasti, eds., *Art and Eternity: The Nefertari Wall Paintings Conservation Project, 1986–1992* (Santa Monica: Getty Conservation Institute, 1993).

Notes to Chapter 8
1   Feilden and Jokilehto, *Management Guidelines for World Cultural Heritage Sites*.
2   Feilden and Jokilehto, *Management Guidelines for World Cultural Heritage Sites*, 33.
3   Herb Stovel, *Risk Preparedness: A Management Manual for World Cultural Heritage* (Rome: ICCROM, 1998).

# References

Belzoni, Giovanni. *Fruits of Enterprise Exhibited in the Travels of Belzoni in Egypt and Nubia.* Boston: Munroe and Francis, 1827.

Carter, B., and G. Grimwade. "Balancing Use and Preservation in Cultural Heritage Management." *International Journal of Heritage Studies* 3 (1997).

Carter, Howard, and Alan H. Gardiner. "The Tomb of Ramesses IV and the Turin Plan of a Royal Tomb." *JEA* 4 (1917): 130–58.

Corzo, Miguel Angel, and Afshar Mahasti, eds. *Art and Eternity: The Nefertari Wall Paintings Conservation Project, 1986–1992.* Santa Monica: Getty Conservation Institute, 1993.

Denon, Vivant. *Travels in Upper and Lower Egypt, in Company with Several Divisions of the French Army under Command of General Bonaparte, I.* Translated by Francis Blagdon. London: Ridgway, 1802.

Edwards, Amelia. *A Thousand Miles Up the Nile.* New York: Cambridge University Press, 2011.

Feilden, Bernard M., and Jukka Jokilehto. *Management Guidelines for World Cultural Heritage Sites.* Rome: ICCROM, 1993.

Getty Conservation Institute. *Valley of the Queens: Proposals for Conservation, Management, and Presentation,* 2009. http://www.getty.edu/conservation/our_projects/field_projects/egypt

James, T.G.H. *Howard Carter: The Path to Tutankhamun.* London: Tauris Parke Paperbacks, 2006.

Maamoun, M., A. Megahed, and A. Allam. "Seismicity of Egypt." *Helwan Institute of Astronomy and Geophysics* 4, ser. B (1984): 109–62.

Mariette, Auguste. *The Monuments of Upper Egypt: A Translation of the "Itineraire de la Haute Egypte."* Memphis: General Books, 2009.

Murphy, Edwin. *The Antiquities of Egypt: A Translation, with Notes, of Book I of the Library of History of Diodorus Siculus.* New York: Transaction, 1990.

*1999 International Cultural Tourism Charter: Managing Tourism at Places of Heritage Significance*. www.ICOMOS.org/tourism/charter.html

Pedersen, Arthur. *World Heritage Manuals, 1: Managing Tourism at World Heritage Sites*. Paris: UNESCO, 2001.

Petrie, William M.F. *Seventy Years in Archaeology*. London, 1932; repr. New York: Greenwood, 1969.

Pococke, Richard. *A Description of the East and Some Other Countries, 4: Observations on Egypt*. London: Bowyer, 1753.

Porter, Bertha, and Rosalind Moss. *Topographical Bibliography of Ancient Egyptian Hieroglyphic Texts, Reliefs, and Painting, 1, 2: Royal Tombs and Smaller Cemeteries*. 2nd ed. Oxford: Griffith Institute, 1999.

Preusser, Frank. "Scientific and Technical Examination of the Tomb of Queen Nefertari at Thebes." In *The Conservation of Wall Paintings*, edited by Sharon Cather. Santa Monica: Getty Conservation Institute, 1987.

Reid, Donald M. *Whose Pharaohs? Archaeology, Museums, and Egyptian National Identity from Napoleon to World War I*. Cairo: American University in Cairo Press, 2002.

Rosellini, Ippolito. *Treasures of Egypt and Nubia: Drawings from the French–Tuscan Expedition of 1826 Led by Jean-François Champollion and Ippolito Rosellini*. Edited by Christian LeBlanc and Angelo Sesana. London: Grange, 2006.

Russell, William Howard. *Travels in Egypt*. 1869.

Sadek, Abdel Aziz. *Graffiti de la montagne thébaine*, 4. Cairo: CEDAE, 1972–74.

Stovel, Herb. *Risk Preparedness: A Management Manual for World Cultural Heritage*. Rome: ICCROM, 1998.

Stuart, Villiers. *Funerary Tent of an Egyptian Queen*. Charleston: Rare Books Club, 2012.

UNESCO. *Culture, Tourism, Development: Crucial Issues for the 21st Century*. Paris: UNESCO, 1996.

van der Spek, Kees. *The Modern Neighbors of Tutankhamun: History, Life, and Work in the Villages of the Theban West Bank*. Cairo: American University in Cairo Press, 2012.

Weeks, Kent R. *Atlas of the Valley of the Kings*. Theban Mapping Project. Cairo: American University in Cairo Press, 2000, 2003. www.thebanmappingproject.com

———. *KV 5: A Preliminary Report on the Excavation of the Tomb of the Sons of Rameses II in the Valley of the Kings*. Theban Mapping Project. Cairo: American University in Cairo Press, 2000, 2005.

———. *The Lost Tomb*. New York: Morrow; London: Weidenfeld; Cairo: American University in Cairo Press, 1998.

———. "The Work of the Theban Mapping Project and the Protection of the Valley of the Kings." In *Valley of the Sun Kings*, edited by Richard Wilkinson, 122–24. Tucson: University of Arizona, 1995.

Wilkinson, John Gardner. *Manners and Customs of the Ancient Egyptians*. London: Murray, 1837.